Translation goes to the Movies

This highly accessible introduction to translation theory, written by a leading author in the field, uses the genre of film to bring the main themes in translation to life. Through analyzing films as diverse as the Marx Brothers' *A Night at the Opera*, the *Star Wars* trilogies and *Lost in Translation*, Michael Cronin shows how translation issues, far from being a preserve of niche film makers, are in fact at the heart of some of the most widely seen films on the planet.

By tapping into this largely unexplored yet potent intertextual resource, Cronin contextualizes issues of translation and brings alive the enduring engagement of one of the most important cultural media of our time with life on a multilingual and multi-ethnic planet.

Translation goes to the Movies demonstrates how translation has been an abiding concern of film makers dealing with questions of culture, identity, migration, conflict, representation and globalization. The work not only introduces the reader to a number of core concerns in translation theory and practice but it also shows how these issues matter greatly in the wider culture and society as presented on screen.

This is a lively and accessible text and will be of interest to students of translation studies, film studies and cultural studies.

Michael Cronin holds a Personal Chair and is Director of the Centre for Translation and Textual Studies, Dublin City University. He is the author of many works including, *Translating Ireland* (1996), *Translation and Globalisation* (Routledge, 2003) and *Translation and Identity* (Routledge, 2006).

Translation goes to the Movies

Michael Cronin

Routledge
Taylor & Francis Group

LONDON AND NEW YORK

First published 2009
By Routledge
2 Park Square, Milton Park, Abingdon, OX14 4RN

Simultaneously published in the USA and Canada
by Routledge
270 Madison Ave, New York, NY 10016

Routledge is an imprint of the Taylor & Francis Group, an informa business

© 2009 Michael Cronin

Typeset in Times New Roman by
Taylor & Francis Books
Printed and bound in Great Britain by
CPI Antony Rowe, Chippenham, Wiltshire

British Library Cataloguing in Publication Data
A catalogue record for this book is available from the British Library

Library of Congress Cataloging-in-Publication Data
  Cronin, Michael, 1960-
  Translation goes to the Movies / by Michael Cronin.
    p. cm.
  ISBN 978-0-415-42285-7 (hardback : alk. paper) – ISBN 978-0-415-
42286-4 (pbk. : alk. paper) 1. Translating and interpreting in motion
pictures. I. Title.
  Pn1995.9.T685c76 2008
  418'.02 – dc22

                                                        2008011235

ISBN13: 978-0-415-42285-7 (hbk)
ISBN13: 978-0-415-42286-4 (pbk)

ISBN10: 0-415-42285-X (hbk)
ISBN10: 0-415-42286-8 (pbk)

For Emmanuelle

Contents

Film stills

Acknowledgements

As this book argues, watching films is ultimately a social rather than a solitary experience and it has been my good fortune to have worked on *Translation Goes to the Movies* in a context of support, advice and genuine interest. I would particularly like to acknowledge the encouragement and inspiration offered by my colleagues in the Centre for Translation and Textual Studies and in the School for Applied Language and Intercultural Studies, Dublin City University. Special mention must also be made of colleagues from other Schools in the University such as Pat Brereton and Stephanie McBride in the School of Communications, who were timely and challenging interlocutors. Further afield, a debt is owed to former doctoral students such as Gavan Titley, Director of the Centre for Media Studies, National University of Ireland Maynooth and Caoimhghín Ó Croidheáin, a lifelong cinephile and astute commentator on the sorcery of moving images. I would also like to salute the memory of a great translator scholar and dear friend, Daniel Simeoni, with whom I had discussed this book before his untimely death. A special word of thanks to my son, Máirtín, for setting me right about aspects of contemporary popular culture that slipped through the net of age.

I would also like to express my gratitude to the following institutions which afforded me the space to develop a number of the ideas advanced in this book and where students and colleagues were generous with their comments and insights: University of Aarhus, Denmark; University of Limerick, Ireland; Facultat de Traducció i Interpretació, Universitat Pompeu Fabra, Barcelona, Spain; University of Bologna, Forlì, Italy; St. Michael's College, University of Toronto, Canada; Ionian University, Corfu, Greece; University of Barcelona, Spain; University of Warwick, England; National University of Ireland, Galway; Université de Bretagne-Sud, Lorient, Brittany, France.

A special words of thanks also goes to the editorial staff at Routledge, in particular Louisa Semlyen and Samantha Vale Noya, for their kindness and patience in bringing this book to publication.

The book is dedicated to Emmanuelle Marion for her multiple kindnesses and who has been unstinting in her support throughout my work on the manuscript.

Introduction

The full picture

This book is about the visibility of translators. More properly, it is about how translation becomes visible, when we know how to look. And one of the places where we have often neglected to look is a medium primarily concerned with visibility, cinematography. Much recent work in translation studies has been concerned with bringing the translator back into the picture. Whether this has involved the sociological context in which the practice of the translator is grounded or the historical circumstances in which the activities of translators have evolved, the emphasis has been on translators as agents, as active presences in the texts and cultures that they have shaped and by which they are shaped (Gentzler 2001; Gentzler 2007). Less attention, however, has been paid to translators not so much as agents of representation but as objects of representation. That is to say, one way of putting translators back into the picture is to see what happens to translators when they get put into the pictures.

In a special issue of *Linguistica Antverpiensia* devoted to 'fictionalising translation and multilingualism', Dirk Delabastita and Rainer Grutman suggest why in a globalized world, translators might become the focus of narrative interest:

> In stories describing cosmopolitan settings (borderlands, modern cities, the world of international business, politics, diplomacy, espionage ...), or in stories in which changes along the spatial axis play a crucial role (travel, exploration, conquest, migration ...), conflicts are likely to find expression on the linguistic plane as well. Translation – interlinguistic mediation – may then play an instrumental role in their resolution, or, alternatively, the absence or mismanagement of interlinguistic mediation, deliberate or not, may become the main obstacle to a solution.
> (Delabastita and Grutman 2005: 24)

Although the term 'globalization' is of recent vintage, worldwide movements and international axes of influence have been around for much longer. Cinema from its inception at the end of the nineteenth century spread remarkably quickly to many parts of the globe and established itself from very early on as a thoroughly international industry (Chanan 1990: 174–88). In the context of the globalizing mission of cinema, it is hardly surprising that translation should arise as a preoccupation. What is more surprising is that the question of language difference and translation should be largely ignored in the study of cinema itself. There is, of course, an abundant literature on the technical and methodological problems of dubbing and subtitling (de Linde and Kay 1999; Gambier 2003: 171–89) and Mark Abé Nornes's *Cinema Babel: Translating Global Cinema* (2007) is an excellent discussion of the cultural consequences of dubbing and subtitling practices in specific contexts (see also Egoyan and Balfour 2004), but there has been no sustained attempt to examine the thematization of translation in films themselves. In other words, what films have to say about translation and the dilemmas of translation is a largely neglected topic, despite the fact that, as we shall see in the rest of this volume, issues of translation and language difference have been a recurrent concern across a number of very different film genres.

So why should we concern ourselves with how translation is presented on the big screen? One starting point is that to ignore one of the most important intertextual resources of people living in the modern world is a kind of blindness bordering on folly. That is to say, given the continuing popularity of cinema, on both the big and the small screen, and the intensely global nature of its dissemination over a very long period, motion pictures are a potent source of images and representation of what translation might or might not involve. Demonstrating the importance of translation to inter-lingual and intercultural contact and heightening the visibility of translation and translators, demands that we look more closely at a medium where translation has long been a matter of visible thematic and representational concern. The issue is not only, however, one of setting a historical record straight.

An abiding concern of any valid translation pedagogy is that the teaching of translation should matter to those studying it. Not only that students of translation should understand the point of what they are being taught, but also that they understand why the rest of the world should understand the point of being taught translation. Equivalence, fidelity, infidelity, domestica-tion, foreignization, control, invisibility, identity, untranslatability, position-ality, are just some of the themes that recur at different stages in the practice and theorization of translation, but how often does translation teaching make use of the extraordinarily rich intertextual resource that is cinema to illustrate or reflect on these issues? How often is cinema incorporated into the teaching of translation in light of the fact that contemporary students have a strikingly highly developed audio-visual literacy from an early age? In other words, neglecting to use cinema in translation studies is neglecting to use a highly engaging and effective medium for soliciting responses on a wide variety of topics directly related to the business of translation. An explicit purpose of the different case studies in *Translation Goes to the*

Movies is to suggest how the evidence of cinema can be integrated into the teaching and learning of translation through a foregrounding of translational perspectives. Cinema as a resource not only has an immediate resonance for student translators and links directly to their own intertextual competence, but also greatly broadens the range of potential materials at the disposal of the teacher or instructor.

It could be argued, of course, that translation on screen is too important an issue to be left to translators. The globalization of industry, warfare, religion, neo-liberalism, trade and telecommunications in a multilingual world means that no one is immune from the effects of translation, though some may seem to be more susceptible to its effects than others. If translation appears in the narratives of mainstream Hollywood cinema, it is not prompted by altruism but by an acknowledgement that the consequences of language and cultural differences are inescapable whether in the Wild West, downtown Tokyo or in a galaxy, far, far away. Students of modernity and globalization would be well advised to consider how film makers have handled translation issues within their narratives as a further angle to understanding how multilingual and multicultural concerns play out in a globally distributed medium. Though film scholars might be reluctant to dwell on language for fear of relegating image to a secondary position, or only consider translation in the context of the 'technical' concerns of dubbing and subtitling, the issues raised by representations of translation are too important or persistent to be ignored in any attempt to understand the impact of cinema as one of the pre-eminent idioms of the modern age.

The philosopher Charles Taylor has written of the growing distance in the late Renaissance period between elite and popular culture. Christian humanists like Erasmus were more and more critical of what they saw as the idolatrous excesses of popular piety. The Reformation would indeed make the reform of popular religious practices an explicit aim of its evangelical program:

> from the late Renaissance, we find a growing split [between the élite and the populace]. We might say a kind of secession of élites from popular culture; be it devotion to the images in the religious sphere, or Carnival and popular amusements. This secession marks the development of élite ideals of life which are seen as incompatible with much of popular culture, ideals of piety in the religious sphere, and of 'civility' in the secular domain. This secession doesn't remain at that stage, but is the basis for the attempt to remake society, the active re-ordering of mass life, which has had such fateful consequences.
>
> (Taylor 2007: 87)

The relevance of what Taylor has to say about the late Renaissance lies in a lingering suspicion of what popular culture means and has to offer. Not only is popular culture from pilgrimages to holy wells to teenage video games the repeated target of moral panic, but also the consideration of popular culture as an area of legitimate enquiry has been a relatively belated development in the development of cultural analysis. The dismissal of Hollywood blockbusters as mindless pap is another variation on a centuries-old trope in the hermeneutics of learned suspicion.

The films chosen for analysis in *Translation Goes to the Movies* are all drawn from what might be termed the Hollywood mainstream and include some of the most important box-office successes in the history of cinema. There are a number of reasons for the choices, which are related to the overall project of the volume. First, as readily identifiable components of global popular culture, the aim is to show that translation issues are not the recondite concerns of niche film makers but lie at the heart of some of the most widely seen films on the planet. Contesting the invisibility of translation involves making translation visible where it is least thought to be visible. The very prevalence of translation concerns in films that have had such a wide circulation gives lie to the notion that translation is a peripheral concern indulged only in the farther recesses of *auteur* cinema.

Second, accessibility is of paramount importance if the analyses in the volume are to have any widespread pedagogic purchase. By this, we mean whether it is to contest the arguments in this book or to apply translation perspectives to other popular, mainstream films, then it is important that both teachers and students have access to the films discussed. The likelihood of access is much greater in the case of mainstream Hollywood cinema due to the global nature of the distribution of US majors. This is not to condone the nature of this distribution but to maximize the opportunity for students and teachers everywhere to engage with issues raised in the book.

Third, the choice of films is dictated by a desire to complicate the myth, propagated both inside and outside Hollywood, that popular cinema originating in the US is wholly beholden to an unashamedly and blindly monoglot vision of the world. By pointing up the multiple tensions and contradictions in a variety of films from the early twentieth to the early twenty-first century, the objective is to present a more nuanced and differentiated account of Hollywood's engagement with translation and language difference. As Delabastita and Grutman point out, 'in our study of historical concepts and practices of translation, statements *about* translation are no less valid documents worthy of research than the translations themselves' (their emphasis) (Delabastita and Grutman 2005: 29). As some of these statements about translation have been seen by hundreds of millions of spectators the world over, it would seem to be high time that in translation studies we took them more seriously and examined them more closely.

Chapter 1 begins by examining the early aspirations of the cinema to be a universal medium, and the intensely international nature of film production and distribution from a very early period. Although it is commonly assumed that translation and language difference only featured as a preoccupation with the advent of the talkies, the chapter explores the incidence of language on the responses to cinema in the silent era and the implication of the development of new narrative forms in cinema for language diversity. Hollywood cinema is commonly spoken of as one of the oldest and most visible forms of mass popular culture and the chapter explores the spread of US hegemony in the worldwide film industry and the relation to immigration and integrationist pressures in the US. The creation of mass domestic markets internally is seen to have its external correlative in Hollywood's expansion to the rest of the world, assisted by the political tragedies that befell Europe in the last century. The chapter contests the notion, however, that Hollywood influence is unmediated and points to the major significance of language and translation in different cultures of reception throughout the world. Part of the effectiveness of Hollywood as a 'dream factory' lies, in fact, in the distance procured by language and translation. However, it is important in a book on the role of translation in cinema that the many millions of Anglophones who watch major Hollywood films are not left out of the picture and the chapter begins the exploration of what intralingual translation issues might mean for analysis of cinema. One of the countries where English is a major language is India, and the chapter considers how concerns around language plurality have led to the particular development of cinema in India. If different national cinemas tell different stories about the impact of dominant languages, it is equally important to be alert to the global, transnational dimensions to cinema's translation consequences. The chapter concludes by exploring these dimensions through the notions of mobility, circulation and mediation.

Chapter 2 examines the genre most closely associated for mass audiences with Hollywood, the Western. The notion of the frontier is crucial for a nation that would continue to expand territorially throughout the nineteenth century, and the excitement and anxieties around the liminal zone of the frontier provide much of the narrative impetus for the Western genre. The moves westwards and the move southwards had, of course, very real linguistic consequences and part of the anxieties on screen around the idea of frontier is how physical translation will be matched by linguistic and cultural translation. The chapter explores in particular detail three films that were emblematic in different ways of the manner in which language difference and translation express themselves in frontier narratives, namely, *Stagecoach* (1939), *The Alamo* (1960) and *Dances with Wolves* (1990). The greatest danger for the stagecoach on its way to Lordsburg was an attack by the Apaches, but the greatest danger for the linguistic and political survival of the Apaches was the stage-coach and its cargo of white settlers on their way to Lordsburg. The chapter explores how the silencing of the native American languages in the film means the return of the linguistically repressed through other, alternative forms of translation. Crucial to the establishment and operation of communities in the borderlands of the Western are individuals who straddle different languages and cultures, native American and Hispanic. The chapter analyses the pressures on these translating agents in situations of conflict, whether it be Yakima in *Stagecoach*, Graciela in *The Alamo* and Stand With a Fist in *Dances with Wolves* and investigates the importance of gender as an aspect of interlingual and intercultural relations. Another type of translating agent emerges who functions in the intralingual space of the new settler communities with individuals from many different linguistic, ethnic and class backgrounds all aspiring to speak the same language. Doc Boone in *Stagecoach* and Davy Crockett in *The Alamo* are considered in the context of language mediators or brokers who know that a nation under one language is more of a pious fiction than a social reality. If much is taken, mistakenly, for granted in the case of a shared language, then little, if anything, can be taken for granted in the case of a language that is radically other. The extended engagement with a Sioux language, Lakota, in *Dances with Wolves* provides a multitude of examples and situations for exploring the complex and highly charged politics of language and translation in screen treatments of the great move westwards.

Chapter 3 looks at translation as represented in another hugely successful Hollywood genre, comedy. In exploring very different kinds of comedy, from the Marx Brothers' *A Night at the Opera* (1935) to Charlie Chaplin's *The Great Dictator* (1940) to Sacha Baron Cohen's *Borat: Cultural Learnings for Make Benefit Glorious Nation of Kazakhstan* (2006), the chapter seeks to analyze the multiple forms translation takes in comedy on screen. A crucial context for the comic misadventures of translation is the unprecedented migration of populations from the Old to the New World in a period of over a century. Comedy was one way to explore the hope and the heartbreak occasioned by the Atlantic passage. In the clash between cultures old and new in the New World, the opportunities for misunderstanding and mis-translation were many and the Marx Brothers are remorseless in exploiting the hidden pratfalls of language difference. That the comedy of mis-understanding could be mobilized to raise awareness around forces threatening to destroy the Old World is evident in *The Great Dictator*, where the dictator Adenoid Hynkel is translated from Germany to the imaginary state of Tomania. The chapter details the highly effective use of translation and language difference as comic devices to reveal the deeply unsettling pathologies of Hynkel and his associates. The tension between word and image, between representation and expression, is explored in terms of the relentless dehumanization of Hynkel's opponents, evacuated by the closed rhetoric of his supremacism. For the maker of the mockumentary *Borat*, a changing post-war world with the emergence of new, independent states with their own cultures and languages provides an ideal vehicle for the travels of a fictitious language innocent abroad. It is Borat's assumed status as a barely translated being making his way in a new language, English, that provides the controversial film with many of its richly comic moments. However, as the chapter shows, it is the presentation of this translated and translating persona that affords him a license to explore the less attractive sides of the culture that has been powerfully legitimated by the Hollywood screen. Modes of transport may change, but the hapless confusion of cultural disorientation does not.

Chapter 4 concentrates on the drama/thriller genres and on a group of films that, at the beginning of the new century, explicitly acknowledge the fact of translation in their titles, *Lost in Translation* (2003), *The Interpreter* (2005) and *Babel* (2006). The chapter explores reasons for the foregrounding of translation as a concern in major Hollywood productions, particularly the impact of economic globalization and post 9/11 insecurities. The relentless presentation of the world as image, as a commodity to be visually consumed, runs aground on the obdurate local realities of linguistic and cultural difference, which come to the fore again and again in the films analyzed in the chapter. Difficulties around translation of emotion, the false utopias of shared global languages and the vulnerabilities of global communication networks, as the chapter demonstrates, subvert any easy notion of instant or painless translatability. Who controls what is said and how translators and interpreters negotiate the killing fields of divided loyalties are examined through characters like the guide–interpreter Anwar in *Babel* or Silvia Broome in *The Interpreter*. The cinema as a visual medium demonstrates the limits to visualization through the greater visibility of translation. As the characters come to dwell rather than simply pass through different locations, the chapter describes how their perception gradually alters and how translation as a feature of engagement with the world becomes more and more prominent as both a necessity and a way of thinking about difference. If considerable energies are invested to minimize the risks implied by the globalization of activities ranging from tourism and film making to the conduct of war, the chapter outlines how the risks inevitably fail to be contained, thwarted by the irreducible diversity of human languages and local concerns. An argument that runs through the chapter is that translation is not only a form of bearing witness to difference but also that the practice suggests the limits to overly spatialized representations of globalization in which the audio-visual industry itself has been complicit. If there is no time for translation, there may not be time for much else.

Chapter 5 is firmly focused on the future, or rather, on films from the recent past that have tried to talk to us about the future. The *Star Wars* trilogies stretching over a quarter of a century of film making offer crucial insights into the construction and representation of translation and language difference in the science fiction genre. The original trilogy comprised *Star Wars* (1977 aka *A New Hope*), *The Empire Strikes Back* (1980) and the *Return of the Jedi* (1983). The second trilogy begins with *The Phantom Menace* (1999) and continues with *Attack of the Clones* (2002) and *Revenge of the Sith* (2005). The chapter examines the varying fortunes of translation in the different films of the *Star Wars* trilogies and details the importance of translation for the exploration of issues of dependence and autonomy, freedom and coercion in George Lucas's space opera. A prominent figure in the films, particularly in the earlier trilogy is the protocol droid C-3PO who claims to master six million forms of communication. The chapter analyzes the changing representations of C-3PO, and the tension between the framing of translation as a subordinate activity and the crucial role played by C-3PO at key moments in the narrative. Anxieties around clones and doubling and the endless replication of same are considered in the context of C-3PO's creation at the hands of young Anakin Skywalker and his eventual rebellion against his master. If English is the dominant language of the trilogies, this is not say that the language means the same thing to all its speakers and the chapter investigates the role of accent and syntactic variety in intralingual translation, bringing difference back into the empire of the monophone. A marked preoccupation of the second trilogy is the erosion of democracy and the dangerous concentration of power in the hands of one individual. As the chapter demonstrates, the decline of democratic accountability is paralleled by a gradual retreat from translation and from engagement with language difference. The ability of translators to mediate no longer matters when coercion not mediation becomes the overriding concern. As long as the carefully constructed languages in the trilogies are listened to and appropriately translated for interested parties, then dialogue is always possible. When the translation stops, only the deadly fiat of one language remains, amplified by the scale of its speakers' imperial ambitions.

The volume engages with themes that have been abiding concerns of mine over the years, notably, cultural identity, mobility and globalization. The desire in my work has been to seek out practices and effects of translation in domains that had often been overlooked, whether it was national history, travel writing practices, economic globalization or, in this instance, popular cinema. However, an equally important consideration has been a desire to add to the sense of enjoyment produced by the secular miracle of cinematography. Highlighting the often neglected translation aspects of the cinema experience is a way of bringing spectators back to the classics of Hollywood cinema and rediscovering the freshness and immediacy of their concerns. It is also hoped that by giving detailed analyses of more recent films, the spectator will look again at films that were not taken as seriously as they might have been, precisely because of their high-profile, blockbuster status. Indeed, it is arguably part of the success of films that have come to dominate mainstream popular culture that they are not quite as univocal as is often assumed and that they lend themselves to a rich plurality of readings which explains, in part, their appeal. Masses are never undifferentiated and any serious cultural analysis must try to understand how in a plurilingual and pluricultural world specific cultural forms embodying image and sound can be appealing to such a wide range of people. A number of the films discussed in this book have been watched by more spectators than any others in the history of film and they have dealt, in some cases obsessively, with translation and language difference. By making these concerns ours, the aim is to deepen the pleasures of spectatorship and to offer possible frameworks of exploration or analysis for many other films.

Translation Goes to the Movies, therefore, is more in the nature of an invitation than an epitaph. The analysis and case studies proposed here indicate the possibilities for the examination of the many different cinema traditions that have developed across the globe. The language and translation preoccupations detailed in the pages of this book are to be found in a host of cinematographic traditions in a variety of different languages. Part of the excitement of research in this domain is that so much remains to be done in terms of uncovering the representation of translation in world cinema. Exploration of the area not only provides relevant resources for the exploration of translation in individual languages and traditions and their transnational crossover, thus refining interpretations of translation in a global age, but the investigation also points to a more confident vision of where translation stands in the contemporary moment. In other words, paying due attention to the multiple traces of translation in one of the most significant and visible media of the last century is, if nothing else, a way of countering an excessive pessimism about the hapless task of the translator. As an audio-visual medium, cinema has largely represented translation through the oral agency of interpreters, but this understandable bias has not diminished the relevance or importance of the translation issues it has addressed. An awareness of the wealth of attention to the fact of translation contact in cinema and the multiplicity of translation sites challenges the more baleful readings of globalized popular culture as the inevitable prologue to the death of diversity.

1   Translation

The screen test

David Llewelyn Wark Griffith was incensed. The acclaimed director of *The Birth of a Nation* (1915) and *Intolerance* (1916) had heard one of his actresses refer to a film as a 'flicker'. Lillian Gish, another of Griffith's actresses, noted his angry reaction,

> He told her never to use that word. She was working in the universal language that had been predicted in the Bible, which was to make all men brothers because they would understand each other. This could end wars and bring about the millennium. We were all to remember that the next time we faced a camera.
>
> (Gish 1973: 60)

Griffith's belief that the picture that moves is a universal language, a way of undoing the mishap of Babel, was based on his intimate conviction that the picture was a universal symbol (Geduld 1971: 56). The supposed immediacy or accessibility of the image, the universal currency of the symbol, is closely linked to the rise of prestige of the visual and of the importance of visual evidence in the scientific revolutions of the sixteenth and seventeenth century (Rorty 1980). No longer would inquirers after knowledge depend on scholastic antecedent. They would not take previous generations at their word, but would confirm with their own eyes claims about the nature of the natural and material world.

Believing without seeing was a culpable blindness. Where the eyes were defeated by scale, unable to probe the infinitely large or the infinitely small, the new technologies of microscopes and telescopes, could come to the aid of the curious. Visual evidence had a persuasiveness, which appeared to mesh with the universal reach of Newtonian theory. The sanctity of the observable is a central tenet of nineteenth-century positivism but the universality of empirically verifiable truths is also an importance source for the universal ambitions of Enlightenment thought. If seeing was indeed believing, then seeing itself could become the pre-Babelian language of universal progress. The divisive languages of humanity would give way to the unifying spectacle of the moving image.

Integration

The millenarian hopes appeared to be borne out by the immense popularity of the new form of entertainment created in the closing decade of the nineteenth century. Here was a medium that could appeal to young and old, urban and rural, literate and illiterate, native and newcomer, rich and poor. In the country where cinema would enjoy the most spectacular success in the twentieth century and beyond, the United States of America, the cinema was seen to be the site of a bold project of national integration. As Miriam Hansen notes:

> By and large, historiography of early American cinema reiterated the working-class spectator's relation to cinema as a scenario of integration. Besides offering escape from the burdens of sweatshop labor and tenement life – as well as a chance to learn English by way of titles or lectures – the function of the cinema for its spectator was seen as that of an agency of acculturation, introducing newcomers to the social topography of the new melting pot.
>
> (Hansen 1990: 228–29)

The new melting pot was not to be a uniquely national phenomenon. The film industry from its inception was a thoroughly international affair. The film scholar Michael Chanan has observed that 'the film business was international from the very beginning' (Chanan 1990: 187) and Tom Gunning claims that in the early period of the silent movie 'film has an international distribution that is unparalleled in later history' (Gunning 1990b: 89). In the German market, for example, shortly before 1914, the German share of films distributed on the market was around 15 per cent and the rest were sourced from France (30 per cent), the United States (25 per cent), Italy (20 per cent), Denmark and England, either through direct imports or through local subsidiaries such as Pathé Frères and Nordisk (Hansen 1990: 234). In 1907, only a third of the films produced in the United States were from domestic sources, the rest came from Europe and half of these were produced by one company, Pathé (Musser 1990a: 364, 412). George Méliès's *Voyage dans la lune* (1902) was a spectacular hit in the United States and remakes such as Biograph's *Personal* (1904) reappearing as Pathé's *Dix femmes pour un mari* (1905), became increasingly common.

The demand for imports was driven by the phenomenal success of cinematography, which was originally viewed as a largely scientific curiosity. Even when companies realized that audience interest went beyond the technical novelty of their creations, they continued to believe that film was primarily a bait to sell new machines. Companies that dominated the film business up until the outbreak of war in 1914 including Pathé and Gaumont in France, Edison, Biograph and Vitagraph in the United States, and Messter in Germany, all began by manufacturing equipment. It soon became apparent, however, that it was the viewing of the films themselves rather than the exhibition of the technology that would draw in the crowds. Hence, the necessity of imports to feed an apparently insatiable demand for the new art.

Facilitating the international growth of the film business and the acceptability of imports was the fact that the films themselves did not contain dialogue. This was Griffiths' credo, remove the spoken word, and there is no longer the barrier of language. No longer would the curse of translation dog the felicities of human communication. Images would circulate freely, the newly minted coins of a currency of humanitarian exchange. From Boston to Bombay, the same images could be shown to audiences otherwise separated by language, history and creed. This early belief in the messianic properties of the new medium reappears in some of the more exalted rhetoric of latter-day globalization theory (Friedman 2007), but was translation an issue for the silent era and did images before 'talkies' speak for themselves?

The sound of silence

A common misnomer about silent films is that they were silent. From the very first showings the Lumière Cinematograph had films accompanied by piano music. The vast majority of films shown between 1895 and 1927 had some form of accompaniment. This could take the form of live music, sound effects, synchronized dialogue spoken by actors behind the screen or a commentary provided by a lecturer filling out or explaining what was going on in the images (Gaudreault 1985: 25–29). The sounds or words were not recorded so that each event was a live performance, on the spot, with the participatory possibilities implied by such practices. The sound universe of silent cinema was, in part, bound up with the context in which cinema was originally received. The emergence of cinema in the United States, for example, was closely linked to vaudeville and other popular entertainments such as penny arcades, medicine tent shows and Magic Lantern tours (Musser 1990a). In other words, rather than considering cinema in terms of its relation to the high culture genres of the novel and, particularly, the theatre, it is important to situate its moment of emergence in a tradition of screen entertainments. Actors performing behind a screen or lecturers commenting on films already raises the question of language difference. They cannot be expected to hold forth in a language that neither they nor their audience understand. There is, however, another problem at this juncture in the development of cinema that has long-term consequences for how the notion of translation will relate to the moving image.

Part of the tradition from which cinema originates and in which it will be embedded is that of the Magic Lantern entertainments. Niamh McCole notes that,

> Beginning with Christian Huygens 1659 invention of a *lanterne magique*, over a period of more than 200 years the Magic Lantern developed from

basic projectors such as the Sturm Lantern, capable of producing small, dimly lit images, to elaborate trinunial lanterns, capable of simulating changes in time, climate and mood.

(McCole 2007: 248–49)

The projected images would deal with a variety of subjects, geographical, historical or political. The success of the projection would depend, in no small part, on the accomplishments of the speaker who would, in a sense, bring the pictures to life. One provincial newspaper in Ireland commented on the success of a lecturer who compared very favorably with his unfortunate predecessor:

Owing to the miserable failure on the part of a party who advertised himself as a lecturer[…]the people [were] rather wary of trusting another[…]But Mr Lynd as the opposite to the first fraud, for he knew what he was speaking about and could impart his knowledge in a most attractive and receivable form[…]Mr Lynd possesses all the characteristics of a popular lecturer.

(Cited in McCole 2007: 253)

As moving images become more and more sophisticated, the lecturer had not only to provide a running commentary on what the audience are seeing but also to help them make sense of the act of seeing itself.

One of the most popular genres in early cinema were actuality films. However, filming a live event automatically entailed a form of discontinuity. The film maker could not be everywhere at once, the action was non-repeatable and the camera at any one time could only hold a certain amount of film stock. Choices had to be made and these choices forced on the film maker by circumstances will be construed more positively as editing (Elsaesser 1990: 17). In G.A. Smith and James A. Williamson's *Henley Regatta* (1899), for example, shots from the river bank are intercut with shots of waving crowds and the latter shots have been filmed from mid-river. The sequence of images does not reproduce an actual succession of events in real life but sets up a causal relationship that is independent of the reality of the event. In other words, there was no self-evident logic to the succession of images that spectators were viewing if they were not schooled in a new way of understanding images and their relationships in the emerging medium of cinematography. Film itself was a new language that demanded translation. From 1902 onwards, films became longer, their stories became more complex and, most importantly, the number of shots increased. This was hardly surprising as familiarity bred contempt for single-shot films or simplistic story lines. Audiences demanded more of the new medium.

The demands brought with them new problems. If there were several shots in the film, how would audiences follow the story from one shot to the next? If the scene or point of view changed, would they be able to relate one image to the next? For the film historian André Gaudreault, these increasingly sophisticated multishot films demanded that narrative continuity be retained in whatever way possible:

> there were only two ways of ensuring some sort of continuity between the shots and enabling the spectator to grasp the meaning of what lay behind the cuts (camera hiatuses) on the screen: either to turn control of the story over to the *narrative voice of the lecturer*, or to use *intertitles* (which incidentally appeared in 1903). As there was no dialogue to help the spectator grasp what was happening in the diegetic universe, the need for a *narrator* began to be felt when films became longer and more complex. And – until the narrative faculties of *editing* had been further developed – this narrator could carry out the work of narration through the use of words, of articulated language, either in written form (intertitles) or oral form (speaker) [his emphasis].
>
> (Gaudreault 1990: 277 (his emphasis))

Both of the methods employed involve the use of language and, if films were to be viewed in different countries, translation of written intertitles or the production of a commentary in a different language were inevitable. Most production companies offered ready-made prints with intertitles in three or four languages, but some companies were translating intertitles in up to a dozen languages. By the mid-1920s, Sidney Kent, the vice-president of Famous Players-Lasky, claimed that his company was shipping prints to the four corners of the globe with intertitles in 38 different languages (Nornes 2007: 98). The future director, Joseph Mankiewicz, for example, started in the film business translating intertitles for Universal Filmaktiengesellschaft (UFA) in Berlin (96). Externalizing the narrative instance was used mainly for 'serious' subjects, such as Passion films or digests of famous plays or novels, but would not be employed for trick films or burlesques. Not everything had to be explained, of course, as there was an assumption that American and European audiences in the case of Passion films, for example, would be familiar with the broad outlines of Biblical stories, an assumption that breaks down when the films are shown farther afield.

The use of intertitles, however, was a serious obstacle to the narrativization of cinema, either because they could not say enough and therefore left the audience perplexed or they said too much and removed the element of surprise. Similarly, reliance on oral commentary owed much to the individual abilities, stamina and performance of the lecturer. The translational devices, the intertitles and oral commentary used to translate the new medium into a language the audience could understand, were, in a sense, ultimately too cumbersome. The breakthrough of D.W. Griffiths and others of his generation from 1907 onwards was to make a much more sophisticated use of the way in which images were joined together on the screen so that the images could narrate themselves (Gunning 1990a). For example, his use of parallel editing, where sequences or scenes are intercut to suggest that they are taking place at the same time (already anticipated by earlier chase sequences) was just one of the many techniques used to more explicitly link images and allow for the development of a more complex narrative logic.

More adventurous editing leads to the internalization of the translational function, formerly devolved to external narrative instances. The use of naturalistic acting, close-up photography and medium shots, all had the express purpose of situating narrative motivation on the screen itself. In effect, the pictures should tell their own stories. What is striking, in this respect, is that different styles began to emerge on both sides of the Atlantic. Whereas European cinema in the pre-war period tended to emphasize deep staging, the complex arrangement of elements in a particular spatial setting, American cinema favors faster cutting rates, making European cinema appear 'slower' and more akin to theatre than its American counterpart (Brewster 1998). In other words, the internalization of these translation devices leads to emergence of different styles that warrant their own form of translation insofar as they increasingly correspond to the viewing expectations and interpretive grids of different viewing publics. So American cinema begins to appear more action-based and European cinema more 'art-house,' more beholden to competing artistic forms such as the theatre.

Film reception

The shift from external to internal narrative in the early twentieth century and the development of longer, feature-length films is paralleled by an equally momentous shift in the context of film reception. The shift brought with it noticeable consequences for the place of translation and language difference in audience responses to cinema. The opening of the Nickelodeon, a small, storefront theatre in Pittsburgh, Pennsylvania in June 1905 gave a further boost to the popularity of cinematography and ushered in the Nickelodeon boom. A fixed site that showed films continuously for an admission price of five cents, the Nickelodeon was an instant success and was soon copied in many other towns and cities throughout the United States and Europe. The Nickelodeon boom introduced the new cultural form to a wide audience and prompted the more ecstatic pronouncements on cinema as an element uniting people from diverse backgrounds. However, even as the number of Nickelodeons was beginning to burgeon, there was an increasing desire to make the cinema respectable and, more importantly for the film industry, to make the distribution of films more profitable by targeting a more affluent, middle-class audience. To this end, there was gradually a move to situate movie theatres close to city business districts or more upmarket shopping streets (Gomery 1982: 23–29; Merritt 1976: 59–70).

The theatres themselves became grander with the introduction of 'picture palaces,' containing bars, cloakrooms, orchestras and ushers. From 1914 onwards, with the increasing prevalence of feature-length films and an inexorable rise in admission prices, the twin drive towards respectability and profitability became more and more marked. Theatre owners anxious to attract a broader audience:

> were advised to avoid ethnic vaudeville acts as well as nationally slanted programs and to eliminate sing-alongs in foreign languages. On the level of film production, the suppression of ethnic difference was imperative: no actor with distinctive ethnic features was to be cast in a leading role.
> (Hansen 1990: 230; Merritt 1976: 67, 72)

It was not the images themselves that would perform the work of integration or acculturation, but the context in which they were produced and received. That is to say, it was not any quality inhering in cinematographic images that would translate the immigrant masses of the United States into a monoglot community of shared values but a change in the conditions of production and conditions of reception that would favor the promulgation of a particular national and linguistic ideal. Will Hays, President of the Motion Picture Producers and Distributors of America, Inc. (MPPDA), was effusive in proclaiming the assimilationist promise of the movies:

> They [immigrants] are coming to a strange land to live among strange people. Their language in most cases is different from ours. Their customs are different. What is America like?, they ask themselves. The motion picture is able to answer that question, to teach them[…]The picture says to [them]: 'Here is America. See what America, your new home, is like. Look at me and love America.'
> (Cited in Maltby 2004: 6)

Cinema became translation by another means. In order to favor the translation of a multilingual and a multi-ethnic community into a mass body of consumers ready to respond to a product in one language, traces of particularism had to be carefully erased. What the cinema increasingly offered for immigrants was a public glimpse of private lifestyles that were promised by a utopia of unfettered social mobility (Mayne 1982: 32–41). Thus, the films were not silent on social aspiration and the imperative of monolingual acculturation. Mass consumer appeal and the creation of what was ultimately not simply a national but an international world of cultural consumption, meant that language difference could not be ignored. It demanded to be silenced even if, as the subsequent chapters will show, the repressed made many return visits to the fretful consciousness of mainstream Hollywood cinema.

The inclusiveness of this exclusiveness would become a powerful paradigm for the expansion of cinema itself and more particularly, for the decisive global dominance of US cinema from the early twentieth century. Already by 1916, a distribution system was being put in place that would eventually secure 80 per cent of the world's screens for the benefit of American distribution companies (Maltby 2004: 16). By 1917, more than 50 per cent of the films shown in what was generally acknowledged to be a powerhouse of cinema production, France, were American in origin (de Beauregard and Stokes 2004: 26). The political and military fate of Europe was crucial to this evolution. The First World War gravely affected the fortunes of the French, German and British film industries in terms of both production and distribution. On the eve of the introduction of the talkies in 1927, the US Bureau of Foreign and Domestic Commerce estimated that approximately 75 per cent of the films shown on the world's cinema screens were American in origin and 30 per cent of the revenues from all sources for American cinema came from foreign markets (Golden 1928: 41–57). Not only was the US not affected to any great extent materially by the conflict, but the immediate post-war period also saw an exponential growth in American overseas economic activity.

Part of this activity involved the construction of a worldwide communications network involving American radio and cable companies, airlines and wire services (Jarvie 1992; Higson and Maltby 1999; Trumpbour 2002). Owen D. Young, head of the Radio Corporation of America, in July 1930 spoke of the 'economic integration of the world' and in terms not dissimilar from those of D.W. Griffith, saw global communications and altruism as amenable bedfellows, 'The power of communications is greater than that of the combined armies and navies of the world' and 'no international understanding can ever function adequately to preserve the peace of the world unless we can get communication so cheap, so free, that all of the peoples of all of the nations will understand all the questions and problems of the world' (Costigliola 1984: 140, 153). On a less exalted plane, the economist Christine Frederick saw the domestic promise to US immigrants as a powerful rationale for US influence internationally. 'Consumptionism' was the 'greatest idea that America has to give to the world.' This idea was consistent with the idea that 'workmen and the masses be looked upon not simply as workers and producers but as consumers[...]Pay them more, sell them more, prosper more is the equation' (Frederick 1929: 5). The bringing together of migrants from a multitude of 'strange' lands with their different tongues and different customs to form a buoyant market of upwardly mobile consumers would now function as a template for the global spread of cultural 'consumptionism.'

For William Hays, the aim was relatively simple, 'Every film that goes from America abroad, wherever it shall be sent, shall correctly portray to the world the purposes, the ideals, the accomplishments, the opportunities and the life of America.' In short, 'We are going to sell America to the world with American motion pictures' (Gomery 1986: 8). The foreign ambitions of Hays not only articulated the economic interests of American film producers, but also dovetailed neatly with the official anxieties around immigration. A US State Department Official in 1926 noted that the United States would have been submerged by a 'flood of immigrants' if legislation restricting immigration had not been passed in 1921 and 1924 due to the growing influence and prestige of American films. Fortunately, he observed, the 'longing to emigrate is changed into a desire to imitate' (cited in Eckert 1978: 4–5). From this perspective it was more expedient to export films than to import people. If emulation rather than immigration was the desired aim, then trade would inevitably follow the film rather than the flag. Not only were films good for business but films were also a highly lucrative business in their own right. As Jack Valenti, President of the Motion Picture Association, proudly proclaimed in 2001, the motion picture industry was the only sector of the US economy 'in trading surplus with every country in the world' (Valenti 2001).

The descent of Europe into war a second time from 1939 onwards further weakened national film industries, even those such as the French industry which had staged something of a revival in the inter-war period (Ulff-Møller 2001). As Nezih Erdogan pointed out, however, for countries such as Turkey which had modeled itself on European patterns, a ruined, war-torn land-scape did not leave much to be desired. He claims that the United States as 'well as championing the values attached to freedom' was 'more "western" than any European country in terms of its wealth, technological prowess and the scale of its cities' (Erdogan 2004: 121). So, not only were European films not being produced and distributed in any great number in the immediate post-1945 period, but their ability to offer a desirable version of modernity was also overshadowed by the scale and perceived sophistication of the American product. In addition, in a development which had predated the Second World War, Hollywood had evolved a very efficient studio system that allowed for a large number of films to be produced to meet growing domestic and international demand.

The combination of increased production on the supply side and the effectiveness of vertical integration on the demand side in ensuring that distributors and cinemas were closely controlled by the Hollywood majors, resulted in the worldwide penetration of markets by the major US film pro-ducers. War did not only, however, severely limit the capacity of European rivals to engage in cinema production but its aftermath also offered con-venient opportunities for the marriage of commerce and persuasion. In post-war Japan, General Douglas MacArthur's Supreme Command for the Allied Powers (SCAP) and the American film industry were involved in an active campaign to promote democracy and pro-American values through the showing of films. During the period of the US occupation of Japan (1945–52), over 500 Hollywood films were distributed throughout Japan via the Central Motion Picture Exchange, a distribution subsidiary of the major US studios (Kitamura 2004: 99–120). The establishment of the American Movie Culture Association in July 1947, which included prominent Japanese writers and intellectuals, stressed the necessity of learning, 'the finest things that America is spreading across the world through American movies' (110). So successful indeed was the project of cultural diplomacy perceived to be, that eventually foreign enthusiasm for US popular film culture was used as an argument to scale back on the activities of entities such the US Information Agency. During the 1990s, as a further reflection of indifference bred by perceived emulation, US news networks cut back their foreign news content by two-thirds (Maltby 2004: 6). As State Department spokesman Richard Boucher put it early in 2001, 'to know us is to love us' (Dumenco 2001).

Boucher's remarks were somewhat premature as the 9/11 attacks demonstrated that familiarity did not always breed content. However, what is more germane as a preoccupation for students of cultural transmission and the globalization of culture is the extent to which language difference and translation have impacted on the Hollywood hegemony. One approach is to consider how dubbing and subtitling practices have been used in different languages in different parts of the world, and how these practices have responded to linguistic, cultural and ideological constraints (Nornes 2007). The success or the reach of US popular cinema would be inconceivable without the intervention of dubbers and subtitlers, yet in mainstream film studies, even when considering questions of audience reception, their efforts are almost invariably ignored. For this reason, the research carried out by translation studies scholars on the history of subtitling and dubbing practices is vital for a fuller understanding of how cinema has been mediated in different languages and contexts.

There are other ways, however, in which questions of language difference and translation complicate the picture of domination that are not solely to do with the methods used to render films in non-Anglophone environments. Charles Ambler in an analysis of popular films and colonial audiences in Central Africa discusses the reactions of audiences to films in the 1930s, 1940s and 1950s (Ambler 2004: 133–57). The audiences were principally based in the mining cities of colonial Northern Rhodesia (mainly present-day Zambia). Thousands of miners and their families housed in vast company compounds on the Copperbelt proved to be assiduous and enthusiastic spectators of films through the decades, particularly Westerns. At the film showings, audiences were forthright in their expressions of enthusiasm, 'men, women, and children rose to their feet in excitement, bending forward and flexing their muscles with each blow the cowboy gave. The shouting could be heard several miles away' (Powdermaker 1962: 258).

Such accounts confirmed racial stereotypes in the mind of colonial administrators and their metropolitan overlords. When censors banned newsreels for African viewing, which showed Hungarian resistance to the Soviet invasion and the demonstrations that followed in various European cities, a spokesman in the British House of Commons defended the action on the grounds that, 'Africans were more likely to be impressed by moving pictures' (cited in Ambler 2004: 147). Even as late as 1960, Roman Catholic bishops in Northern Rhodesia were still defending racist film censorship on the grounds that the vast majority of Africans have, 'primitive ideas of morality affecting public order and decency'. The widespread nature of this crude imperial folk psychology is reflected in a memorandum from August 1932 entitled 'Pernicious Influence of Pictures on Oriental Peoples', which was prepared for the International Parliamentary Commercial Conference urging greater cooperation between the imperial nations of Great Britain, France, Japan and the Netherlands:

> The simple native has a positive genius for picking up false impressions and is very deficient in the sense of proportion[...]The pictures of amorous passages, many of which, according to his ideas, are very indecent, give him a deplorable impression of the morality of the white man and, worse still, of the white woman. The prolonged and often erotic exhibitions of osculation frequently shown on screen, cannot but arouse in the minds of unsophisticated natives feelings that can better be imagined than described.
>
> (Cited in Jaikumar 2004: 89)

Implicit in all of these comments is the notion of African or 'Oriental' spectators as passive consumers of a highly determined product with a simple causality determining response. In subject peoples, violent films induce violent behavior and prolonged on-screen kissing leads to moral disorder and uncontrollable outbreaks of desire. For this reason, there is a duty on censors to police native gullibility. So not only were scenes of mild passion and women in swimsuits to be cut, but also, by 1951, the list of categories for censorship in Northern Rhodesia included war atrocities, violent battles, arson, masked men, riots, demonstrations and, more generally, any scenes involving violence, in particular, those 'ritual scenes in which American Indians captured and tied up white pioneers' (Ambler 2004: 139).

One of the paradoxical effects of paranoid censorship in imperial settings was that the narrative or storyline was continually disrupted by the anxious cuts of the colonizers. Vulnerable natives were thus unlikely to be affected by the meanings of narratives that the censors' shears had rendered illegible. But there were further contexts to reception such as the fact that the vast majority of showings of films in the Copperbelt were out of doors and the noise levels were such that the soundtrack was not often audible. Even if it had been, this would have made little difference as the miners and their families with limited access to formal education would not have been able to follow extended dialogue in British English or colloquial American English. The African audience appropriated the images they saw in terms of indigenous traditions of plays and other kinds of performance that were not crucially dependent on a linear narrative. More significantly, from the point of view of language, the viewing of a film was a social and a communal event and, of course, the medium of exchange and communication was not the language of the Hollywood screen but the indigenous language or languages of the audiences. In other words, film spectatorship involved not an atomistic individual but a member of a community who through participatory commentary on the film was translating what he or she saw into the language of the receiving culture.

The Iranian film scholar Hamid Naficy explores the concept of reception in a consideration of the film experiences of his early years in Iran. Members of the audience would regularly comment on what was going to happen next and a dialogue would be kept up with the action on the screen. In one instance, when Samson (Victor Mature) in *Samson and Delilah* (1949) stood in the doorway pushing the pillars apart, which would lead to the eventual destruction of the temple, the audience urged him on, applauding wildly (Naficy 2003: 190). In remembering his experiences of film watching as a child, Naficy claims that while the narrative suspense produced an intense and anxious emotional reaction, 'my identification with the diegesis was not total due to the social context of the reception. The moviehouse was a long, narrow tunnel-like hall with high ceiling that was filled with people, smoke and noise' (187).

Screen readers and student translators would frequently be on hand to translate intertitles, subtitles, or foreign dialogue in real time and 'they often resorted to colorful Persian stock expressions, which indigenized and enriched the film experience' (189). Naficy argues that the different strategies 'by which Iranian audiences interrupted, talked back to, translated, dubbed, fetishized, objectified and haggled with the movies and the movie stars, transformed the cinema's 'work' from one of hailing to haggling. By thus engaging with the movies, the spectators were no longer just their *consumers* but were also the *producers* of their meanings' (191). Haggling is pre-eminently an act of speech and the Iranian audiences above all produced their own language in their response to what was happening on the screen. Like the audiences in the Copperbelt, meanings were collectively constructed through socialized translation practices.

For this reason, it is helpful when considering the reception of cinema to situate spectatorship in the broad context of film consumption, understood here to mean all those activities that go beyond the actual act of watching a film (Meers 2004: 158). These activities include reacting verbally to a film, discussing it with friends, buying film magazines, reading articles about films or film stars or seeing trailers or advertisements for new blockbusters. The consumption of film on the Copperbelt is intimately bound up with the integration of film experience into the shared language of the spectators. In other words, the absence of audible dialogue and heavily truncated reels, making any attempt at coherent dubbing or subtitling futile (quite apart from problems of literacy), did not evacuate translation as a valid concern but, on the contrary, translation was the process best used to describe the absorption of Hollywood Westerns into native language and culture. In a wholly different context, the audiences who were enticed to the self-consciously upmarket Marunouchi Subaruza complex in occupied post-war Tokyo were similarly part of a specific context of reception. Programs were produced for showcased films, which, in some instances, were up to 40 pages in length. They contained essays written by film critics, industry professionals and other leading figures in Japanese cultural life,

[t]hese texts conveyed at least three kinds of information: they provided synopses and content description of the films themselves; they also introduced the film's stars, cast and production staff; and they outlined the customs, beliefs and lifestyles of foreign societies (especially the US).

(Kitamura 2004: 105)

The information was largely in Japanese and the patrons of the Subaruza were almost exclusively Japanese as American soldiers mainly frequented cinemas under the direct aegis of the SCAP. So the context in which the Japanese audiences were consuming these American films was primarily a Japanese-language context. The images were being assimilated, commented upon and absorbed in a language that was not their language of production. Similarly, when Philippe Meers investigated the attitudes of young Flemish speakers to Hollywood at the end of the twentieth century, he found film consumption was a collective, socially mediated experience rather than a phenomenon which was discrete and monadic. Peer pressure for the young teenagers meant that having something to talk about meant having to see certain films:

Marie [eighteen-year-old school girl]:[...]thrillers such as *Scream*[...]I don't really like those films, but sometimes you have to because otherwise you're not up to date, what can you talk about if you haven't seen *Scream*?[...]*Hannibal* was the sequel of *Silence of the Lambs* and I hadn't seen it and people said 'Oh no! You haven't seen it.'

(Cited in Meers 2004: 162)

The crucial aspect of the phenomenon Marie is describing is that a practice of watching is embedded in a culture of talking. Going to the pictures is as much about the conversation before and afterwards as it is about what actually goes on in the cinema itself, where the mode of reception is silent in various parts of the world due to internalized norms of what is appropriate behavior in cinema settings. Meers' informant, however, does not talk to her friends in English. If seeing a film gives them something to talk about, then the talking will be done in Flemish. That is, the incentive to watch a Hollywood blockbuster is the occasion of language, the interpretation of the film event within the fold of a specific speech community. For the film to make social sense it must be taken out of its original language context and translated into or recontextualized in the language of the film spectators, whether they be Zambian, Japanese or Belgian.

The translational dimension to cinema spectatorship in a multilingual world does undermine some of the more baleful readings of the globalization of culture. As Ambler notes, there is a curious continuum from colonial censors to critics of cultural imperialism who both share the view that film spectators are essentially passive subjects, on whom meanings can be cunningly and deliberately inscribed (Ambler 2004: 148). Anthony D. Smith, for his part, notes the limits to this particular version of the intentional fallacy:

The meanings of even the most universal of imagery for a particular population derive as much from the historical experience and social status of that group as from the intentions of purveyors[…]images and cultural traditions do not derive from, or descend upon, mute and passive populations on whose *tabula rasa* they now inscribe themselves. Instead, they invariably express the identities which historical circumstances have formed.

(Smith 1990: 179)

The crucial word in Smith's analysis is 'mute.' The 'talkies' have not rendered audiences speechless. Film spectators before and after films are coopted into a network of anticipation and commentary, which has translation into local language as a core element of the filmic experience. The socially mediated activity of language is crucial to the reception of the most all-pervasive of blockbusters, and speakers as the active agents and speakers of language within speech communities make of translation a dynamic process from which effects cannot be anticipated or prescribed in an artful centripetal conspiracy.

This is not to say, however, that the language of production is not without its effects. The same teenagers who eagerly commented on Hollywood blockbusters in Flemish were largely sceptical of the idea that interesting or entertaining films could be produced in their mother-tongue. For Meers, 'language is a crucial factor influencing film appreciation' (Meers 2004: 167). English was judged to be the language of film, it was 'good, spontaneous, cool,' whereas other European languages were considered unattractive or unsuitable. The fact that most of the teenagers surveyed were learning English facilitated their enjoyment of Hollywood films and this provided a further incentive for learning the language. The charmed circle of language acquisition and cultural prestige was thus very much in evidence. As a consequence, however, in the case of other foreign-language films, '[f]ailure to comprehend the dialogue does not merely reduce enjoyment in a particular film, it also promotes a negative attitude in general towards films in that language' (168). In other words, not only is watching film, as we have noted earlier, embedded in a language of reception but also the film itself becomes synonymous with language or rather with the on-screen experience of one particular language, English. For teenagers in Flanders used to listening to English in a local audio-visual culture largely averse to dubbing, the English language and cinematography were one and the same thing.

Giovanni Scognamillo writing about the enthusiasm of Turkish audiences for Hollywood films during and after the Second World War argues that they wanted, 'action, wealth, spectacle and glamour[…]excitement and emotion. They want dreams and they pay to have their dreams' (Scognamillo 1991: 67). What Hollywood offered to audiences was a realm of fantasy, of make-believe, of a life that was more glamorous, more exciting than the humdrum reality of the local. For the Belgian teenagers at the close of the century, the attraction of the Hollywood blockbuster was similar – American cinema offered a world of glamour, money, excitement and power. Part of the prejudice towards films being produced in local languages was that they were too ordinary. They showed a reality that was commonplace. Their very mundaneness meant that films in local languages could not function as a site of fantasy, as an invitation to dream. The tension is between what Ien Ang has described as 'empiricist realism' and 'emotional realism.' Empiricist realism is the attempt to create authentic settings, to put the detailed life of the everyday on screen, whereas emotional realism is primarily concerned not so much with credible settings as with a concentration on characters, modes of action and conflict situations, which are believable or credible within the context of possible life experiences (Ang 1985). The dreams must be real, but not too real.

Erdogan situates this tension between Hollywood and different national cultures in the necessary gap between fantasy and reality:

> Whenever national culture has to articulate a difference and fantasy has to play on this difference, the distance between the object of desire and the subject must be continuously and carefully maintained and disavowed at the same time. America must be neither too close or too remote. Hollywood presents a fantasy screen to Turkish audiences but it is important that the screen is kept at the right distance.
>
> (Erdogan 2004: 126)

Editors of Turkish film magazines were quick to dissuade over-zealous readers from making the trip to America where the film fantasies might not survive an encounter with the prosaic realities of the American everyday. As one potential traveler was warned, among the many difficulties involved in going to the United States was the fact that 'it would oblige you to speak a language' (126). The cautionary note is telling. The language of Hollywood is a language that was actually spoken by real people and going behind the screen, crossing over from celluloid fantasy to local reality, meant an engagement with this linguistic reality in all its complexity. A crucial factor in keeping Hollywood at the right distance is the language of the films themselves. That is to say, whether the original dialogue of the film can be heard through the use of subtitles or whether a film is dubbed thus signaling to the audience that the film was originally in another language, the effect of language difference is to create that distance which keeps the object of desire at the right distance.

The two forms of screen translation, dubbing and subtitling, complement the distancing mechanism of language alterity. It is in a sense because Hollywood cinema needs to be translated that it can continue to function as a site of intense projection and multiple interpretations. For this reason, it is necessary to qualify undue pessimism over the global reach of the Hollywood majors and the creation of a product in a single, dominant language. The necessary multiple translations to which the films are subjected, quite apart from the internal dialogue with translation described in the following chapters, ensures that there are limits to proximity. The scale of Hollywood penetration of global entertainment markets means that familiarity with its products ensures that they are not likely to be 'remote' but they can never get too close either, because of the hiatus of translation and language difference. So although it can be argued that translation does favor centripetal models of globalization through facilitating the spread of Hollywood blockbusters to the four corners of the globe, it can equally be argued that the fact of translation, the fact of language, complicates any narrow cultural causality and opens up a space for multiple viewing and multiple interpretations.

Intralingual translation

But what happens when film audiences share the language of the producers? George Steiner has spoken of the blessings of Babel, the enrichment of humanity by the multiplicity of its tongues. He cautions, however, against restricted understandings of what constitutes translation:

> The blessing of creative variousness obtains not only as between different languages, this is to say 'interlingually.' It is richly operative within any given tongue, intralingually. The most compendious of dictionaries is no more than an abridged shorthand, obsolescent even as it is published. Lexical and grammatical usage inside any spoken or written tongue is in perpetual motion and fission. It hives off into local and regional dialects. The agencies of differentiation are at work as between social classes, explicit or submerged ideologies, faiths, professions.
>
> (Steiner 2008: 61)

Steiner's caveat is crucial for the exploration of translation in cinematographic settings. Language difference is manifold and the varieties of a single language are as likely to excite the interests of film makers as are the complex transactions between one language and another. An example of this preoccupation is to be found in *The Commitments* (1991), a Hollywood-style film directed by the English film maker Alan Parker and based on the novel by the Irish writer Roddy Doyle. In the promotional material for *The Commitments* one of the slogans that was repeatedly used was, '*The Commitments*. At last a film with bollix, tossers, sex, soul, boxes, gooters, the works.' 'Tossers,' 'gooters' and the 'works' are among the words explained in 'A Tosser's Glossary,' which was distributed with the press pack for *The Commitments*.

In a prefatory note to the 'Glossary,' Alan Parker offers his own version of Irish linguistic distinctiveness,

For centuries the Irish were forced to speak English. They got their own
back by using it better. From Wilde to Shaw and Beckett to Behan. But
the truth is, that the Irish haven't been using English for years. They
have their own language. And it isn't Gaelic.

(Parker 1991)

Thus, language becomes central to both the promotion of the film and the
framing of the cultural distinctiveness of the film itself. It is noteworthy
that Parker, a film maker, situates the language in a literary lineage, from
'Wilde to Shaw and Beckett to Behan.' He makes his own, in a sense, the
thesis of the Irish Literary Renaissance that after Douglas Hyde's
vernacular translations of Irish poetry it was possible to create a distinctive
Irish culture in the English language (Cronin 1996: 134–38). He also,
wittingly or unwittingly, articulates the postcolonial reading of language shift
in Ireland as formulated by Declan Kiberd, among others, that what the
Irish did was to turn linguistic subjection to their own advantage (Kiberd
1995). In what might be termed the Caliban moment in Irish history, the
Irish learned the language of the master and then proceeded not simply to
curse him but to undo his rule with the words they had been taught.

The situation in the case of the film versions of Roddy Doyle's novels is,
however, more complicated and even more subversive than Parker's thumb-
nail sketch of Irish history would suggest. In the first instance, Parker cites
literary precedents for the use of a particular kind of language by the Irish,
but the most striking aspect of the film versions of the Doyle novels on the
screen is that it would be the first time ever that a whole array of words and
Dublin working-class colloquial register would be heard in such a sustained
and systematic fashion on the screen. If suburban, working-class Dublin had
rarely been seen in the cinema, then it is true to say that it had never been
heard on screen, literally rendered speechless by the prudishness of producers
who worried about how much 'bad' language their audiences could take.
Therefore, in analyzing the particular soundscape of the film versions of the
Barrytown Trilogy, attention needs to be directed not only to the integration
of popular music into the spectator's experience but also to the manner in
which the language itself, both as words and as accent (operating at lexical,
syntactic and phonetic levels), works to make the films a radical departure in
the filmic representation of social class in Ireland.

Timothy Taylor in an article on *The Commitments* is unpersuaded by
Parker's linguistic radicalism. He objects to what he sees as the air brushing
of language difference out of the film:

The film sanitises the novel in the use of a more international English
language, for like most films, it was made for mass consumption. Words
like 'culchie' from the Irish language wouldn't be understood by non-
Irish audiences. So Dublin slang is virtually absent from the film; the
only slang we do hear is that which is common to both the United

Kingdom and Ireland, words like 'bollix,' 'arse' and 'shite.' But the local
flavour is gone. The pungency of Dublin English, the use of words from the
Irish language, which the English colonizers nearly obliterated, is gone.

(Taylor 1998: 298)

The comment apart from the facile generalizations ('like most films, it was
made for mass consumption') and dubious linguistic knowledge ('culchie' is
generally believed to be a deformed pronunciation of a place name in
County Mayo not a word from Irish), betrays a specific version of linguistic
particularism, which is deeply coercive in its implications. Taylor's objection
that in the end the audiences of Alan Parker's *The Commitments* are left with
a film by an English director about 'semi-exotic musicians who are English –
sort of' (Taylor 1998: 298) is an unnerving echo of the worst excesses of
irredentism with its suspicions about the genuine 'Irishness' of the Irish city
and town.

What is true of the film is also true of the novel, that is, a great deal of the
language is in fact shared between the United Kingdom and Ireland, though
in many instances, words do not have the same frequency of usage nor are
they always used in the same context and there are features which are specific to the syntax of Hiberno–English (Dolan 1998). The implication that
this area of commonality is somehow to be decried, that British directors
making films about Irish novels where there are similarities in forms of linguistic and cultural expression are by definition engaged in an act of cultural
imperialism is poor cultural criticism and worse politics. Parker and Stephen
Frears, the director of *The Snapper* (1993) and *The Van* (1996), in many
respects are a lot more culturally honest and politically courageous in suggesting the similarities with British working-class culture, which have often
been played down because they do not fit into comfortable nationalist narratives about Ireland and its cities. Forever an affront to the standard bearers
of cultural purism, the mixed origins of cities mean that it would indeed be
remarkable in the view of Irish urban history and the story of emigration to
Britain if there were not considerable overlap between cultural practices in urban
Ireland and Britain. A much more insidious form of exoticism would, in
fact, have resulted from a relentless attempt to emphasize cultural distinctness
and 'pungency' with the attendant dangers of cultural stereotyping and
paddywhackery.

What is immediately apparent in the debates around the language used in
the films made by the two British directors is that translation questions are
as pertinent within languages as they are between languages. So just as it is
important not to present foreign-language spectators of English-language
cinema as an undifferentiated, passive, consuming public, unaffected by the
multiple agencies of translation, it is similarly vital to consider translation
issues as they play out for Anglophone spectators of English-language
cinema whether those spectators be American, Canadian, British, Irish,
Australian, South African or whatever. Differences in accent, lexical variety,

non-standard syntax, cultural references, are but some of the resources that make for on-screen linguistic distinctiveness and which create the necessary conditions for the distance of language work.

In thinking then about translation and cinema, it is important to remember that Hollywood films are not just made for non-native speakers of English. Many hundreds of millions of English-speakers have watched and continue to watch films made in English. They, by and large, do not watch these films dubbed or with subtitles, though as we shall see in later chapters, there are some notable exceptions. Does this mean that concerns with translation and language difference can be bracketed when considering films from an Anglophone perspective? Do translation issues only rise in the presence of radical language otherness? There are two reasons why thinking about translation is critical in intralingual as well as interlingual settings. The first relates to the phenomenon of metonymic displacement where difference between languages becomes transposed to differences within languages. That is to say, rather than having a Mexican speaker of Spanish on the screen, the spectator is presented with a character speaking English with a noticeable Hispanic accent. The accent becomes a metonym for the cultural and ethnic origins of the speaker and the marker is often sufficiently robust to allow for the exploration of inter-lingual and intercultural relations through what Robert Moore has called 'accent culture' (Moore 2007: 18–29). Searching for translation questions solely in the dimension of the interlingual means missing a crucial and recurring aspect of language and cultural contact that is internalized within the dominant language of expression of the film. The second reason for paying due attention to intralingual translation is the overwhelming impor-tance of accent and dialectical variety within language to express class, power, regional and national identity and the workings of projects of inte-gration in different times and settings. What we have already seen earlier in the case of the films of Alan Parker and Stephen Frears will emerge in a variety of contexts in the following pages. The films repeatedly complicate any consoling notion of unitary language and show how monoglossia fissures once the cameras start rolling.

Changing places

Translation does not, however, always take place in one direction and with one language, English, as the invariably privileged source. The largest film industry in the world is based not in the United States, but in India. In 2003, for example, the Central Board of Film Certification in India certified a total of 2564 films. Of these films, which included both feature films and short films, 2054 were produced in India and 510 were produced elsewhere (Central Board of Film Certification 2008). The situation was very different in the early decades of the last century when, in 1921, only 64 of a total of 812 films passed by the censor were of Indian origin (Indian Cinematograph Committee 1928: 83). However, by 1935, annual Indian film production was up to 233 films, of which the majority (154) were in the Hindi language (Rajadhyaksha and Willemen 1999: 30). The expansion and growth of the Indian film industry brought further differentiation driven primarily by the linguistic diversity of the Indian subcontinent. As Priya Jaikumar noted, '[b]y the 1940s, the Tamil and Telugu film industries had spawned a large regional fan base, in no small part because the visual aesthetics, narrative themes and musical traditions which informed south Indian films varied from their Northern counterparts' (Jaikumar 2004: 84).

Jaikamur, not unlike many film scholars, does not mention language, but it is language which will most obviously differentiate the different regional film industries and summon them into being. The major regional film industries draw their viability from the importance of the language groups sustaining them, namely, Hindi, Tamil, Telugu, Bengali, Marathi, Kannada, Odiya and Malayam (Barnouw and Krishnaswamy 1981). In arguing that 'the sound era consolidated a national identity for Indian films' (2004: 83), Jaikamur does acknowledge, however, that the presence of Indian languages allows for the desegregation of audiences who had formerly been divided into those European and elite Indian audiences who got to see the first runs of imported films and the non-elite and non-urban audiences who got to see films on their tenth or eleventh run.

In producing films in Indian languages for Indian audiences, it was possible to begin to begin to break down existing hierarchies of access based on class, language and education. The particular genius of directors, particularly those associated with the Hindi-language cinema later to be termed 'Bollywood,' was to translate aspects of Hollywood narrative techniques and production values into films produced in an indigenous language (Bose 2006). In other words, the terms of exchange were reversed, where Indian film makers would translate Hollywood into an idiom that was acceptable and accessible to mass audiences in India and thus strengthen an indigenous film industry. Bollywood would translate Hollywood on its own terms and in its own language. Inevitably, as with all translation, it is not so much the fact as the form of contact that makes the difference. The ability to engage with the dynamics of cultural transmission and appropriate them for a nascent national cinema, subsequently differentiated by regional linguistic identities, points to alternative histories of globalization that are not endlessly beholden to the pessimism of monoglossia and unidirectional translational assimilation.

Part of the success of Indian cinema has been to do not only with large domestic audiences but also with the existence of a significant Indian diaspora in many parts of the world. The top 20 foreign language films released in the UK in 2001 included 11 Indian films (Wood 2007: xv). Implicit in the notion of diaspora is mobility, whether willing or unwilling. If diasporic audiences constitute a potential audience for native film production, it is worth considering in more detail the important link between mobility, translation and cinema. On her first trip to Dublin in 1907, the young Irish writer Kate O'Brien was taken to the Bioscope theatre in Grafton Street.

The seats inside were arranged like those of a tram or a Pullman train and the author declares that:

> in them we travelled by screen, far and high and dangerously, over mountain passes and by rocky shores, through gentle lanes and along busy streets. I remember only all the marvelous travelling. There can have been no story-telling, no human interest.
>
> (O'Brien 1962: 111)

O'Brien's experience was not unique. The travel genre was one of the most popular in early cinema and the fusion of the railway and cinematography in Hale's Tour Car at Kansas City Amusement Park in 1905 was immediately successful. The Tour Cars were simulated railway carriages that functioned as movie-theatres, with the audience seated in passenger seats and the screen replacing the view out of the front or rear window. The Grafton Street Bioscope is a more sober version of the extravagant literalism of Hale's Tours but it does point to a fundamental linking of mobility and cinematography in the early period. Charles Musser, for his part, argues that the railway subgenre in films, for example, Edwin S. Porter's *What Happened in the Tunnel* (1903), *Romance of the Rail* (1903) or *The Great Train Robbery* (1903), was crucial to the development of narrative in early cinema. Musser, drawing on the work of Wolfgang Shivelbusch (1980), stresses the affinities between rail travel and screen journeys:

> The traveller's world is mediated by the railroad, not only the compartment window with its frame but also by the telegraph wires which intercede between the passenger and the landscape. The sensation of separation which the traveller feels on viewing the rapidly passing landscape has much in common with the theatrical experience of the spectator. The allusion of train window with the screen's rectangle was frequent within this travel sub-genre.
>
> (Musser 1990b: 127)

The separation of travelers from the outside world was crucial to educating the gaze of the cinema spectators who had to be schooled into a suspension of visual disbelief. That is to say, spectators had to believe that they were detached observers of scenes that were taking place before their eyes even if, of course, they knew this not to be the case. The early silent cinema with its forms of direct address to the camera gave way to visual norms that eschewed any direct acknowledgement of the spectator's presence. As the cinema moved from a cinema of attractions to a cinema of diegetic absorption, to use Tom Gunning's terms (Gunning 1990a: 57–59), it was necessary to make the film spectators experience differently the evidence of their eyes. They had, in a sense, to stand back from what they were seeing. What new forms of mobility were teaching people was that it was possible to see the world without necessarily dwelling in it.

Erdogan describes Turkish experiences of early cinema as a form of 'visual colonialism' (2004: 122). On the one hand, the audiences could travel around Europe while remaining seated in a cinema in Istanbul and, on the other, they could travel around the cinemas of Western Europe, secure in the belief that the film they were watching was also being watched in cinemas in cities across Europe. Cinema as a form of 'marvelous traveling' made moving pictures, in more than one sense of the word, a moving experience. Part of the marvelous traveling is embarking on what Abé Mark Nornes has called the mystic translation machine of cinema, 'The mystic translation machine of cinema taps into these feelings of fascination, astounding us with its ability to transport us to a foreign world with such vivid, palpable immediacy' (2007: 23). Being transported to a foreign world with such immediacy cannot ignore, however, the problems that translation itself suggests. In other words, the nomadic dimension to the experience of cinema brings to the fore the complex relationship between mobility and translation.

Travel in a world of languages is fraught with difficulty. There are the innumerable pitfalls of translation: the potential for mistranslation; the loss of meaning; the dangers of approximation; the problematic political economy of translation in the Eurocentric appropriation of other peoples and places through former colonial languages; and the seductive myth of transparent translation. The translating agent, like the traveler, straddles the happy or unhappy borderline between cultures and languages (Cronin 2000). By bringing a translation perspective to bear on the study of cinema and a cinematographic perspective to bear on the study of translation, one aim is to investigate the costs and consequences of separation. If the world is viewed through moving pictures, if we picture ourselves as spectators moving through the world, what do we do with the inescapable linguistic opacity of the planet, of the many languages that are spoken and of the many languages which we will never understand and which contribute so powerfully to the shaping of places and identities? These are questions that will be addressed repeatedly by the films considered in the remaining chapters of this volume.

Circulation

One answer to the question of the reach of moving pictures is to ask what form they take. We noted earlier the importance of considering film spectatorship within the broader category of film consumption, and an aspect of this consumption is the reception of publicity materials and their translation for foreign markets. As Sidney Kent, vice-president of Famous Players-Lasky, observed, 'They are to the picture, like the food and ammunition of a soldier, who can't live and fight with only a gun' (cited in Nornes 2007: 98). But the framing of a film by advance publicity is only one aspect of the actual multiplier effect of cinema. There is the further need to consider the global circulation of moving images to situate both the context and the impact of the thematization of translation concerns in mainstream Hollywood cinema.

This circulation can be considered at both an economic and a formal level. One way of assessing circulation at an economic level is to assess the relative size and scale of what was traditionally a competitor for the US majors, the European cinema industry. Mary Woods claims that 'American cinema dominates European cinemas (the traditional exhibition sector), the small screen, the video shop and the racks of DVDs' (Woods 2007: 2). The size of the audio-visual sector in the 25 states of the EU in 2003 was estimated at €104,790 million (European Audiovisual Observatory 2005/1: 31) In 2004, this highly lucrative market was dominated by 449 American films in circulation, released in multiple prints on circuits controlled by the Hollywood majors (Woods 2007: 9–10). The domination does not only extend to the distribution networks but also affects the sums of money available for the production of films.

> In 2002 public funding of the film and audio-visual industry in the 30 countries of Europe amounted to €1,162,230,000, of which €1,084,169,000 was devoted to the 15 older EU countries[…]These sums have to be put into context – 623 films were produced in the 15 countries of the EU in 2004. The majority of European films have small budgets, the average being about $4 million. With the exception of the UK, this average has not increased greatly since 1991, whereas production budgets of the US majors have increased exponentially from $25 million to over $60 million by 2003. (9)

Financing European films often involves complicated financial arrangements across different countries and the existence of initiatives at a supranational level, such as MEDIA and Eurimages, are important to ensure the potential viability of European film production.

Part of the rationale for programs at a European level is to maintain and protect the cultural and linguistic diversity of Europe, languages which are 'minoritized' in terms of the global preponderance of English as the language of Hollywood. National cinemas promote 'the necessity of speaking with one's own voice about the contemporary world' (8), as well as providing employment and eventual tax revenues. The persistence of European cinema in a difficult economic environment would not be countenanced if there was not a sense that not everything can be translated. In other words, the existence of cinema in different languages not only suggests that cinema may not be quite as universal as the more messianic cheerleaders of global communications suggest, but also that the effort to translate it means that there is something to be translated. The fact that something remains to be translated and that cinema exists in different languages, hints at potential differences in tastes, outlooks and desires of different audiences. A tension emerges between the desire for standardization, resulting in industrial economies of scale and increased profitability, and a necessary differentiation to ensure renewal of audience interest. It is arguably, for this reason, among others, that the films discussed in this volume from widely differing genres and periods are so constantly preoccupied with questions of translation and language difference.

The overwhelming dominance of the global market by Hollywood cinema and the use of dubbing and subtitling to deal with international distribution in a multilingual world, does not eradicate the continued presence of language and cultural difference as demonstrated by the productions of European, Indian, Iranian or Japanese cinema. Although Hollywood majors dominate distribution, this does not mean that the issues raised by translation can be adequately dealt with by appropriate subtitling or dubbing strategies. There is a sense in which the inescapable linguistic and cultural diversity of the planet must make its way back into the very structure and narrative of the films themselves. Therefore, it is useful in debates on different national cinemas not only to consider the global context, for example, to European cinema, but also to ask to what extent that same global context for Hollywood cinema does not involve the continuous and historically differentiated exploration in mainstream US cinema of concerns and anxieties around emerging national and transnational communities. The temptation is always to homogenize Hollywood, but what may make temporarily for good business does not in the long run make for effective cultural analysis. Planet Hollywood is just that, a planet inhabited by many different territories of expression, and part of watching cinema is being watchful about the binaries that divide rather than illuminate.

A formal level of circulation relates to the forms in which films circulate. The formal is linked to the economic insofar as a multiplication of forms increases potential sources of revenue. The film appears alongside the book or CD soundtrack recording, and then later, the release of the film as DVD. Potential sites of display for films include not only cinemas or film theatres, but also public and private television companies, pay-TV premium companies, thematic channels and leisure software. One consequence is that the impact of film is not simply felt at the time of its appearance in cinemas but that films enjoy a multiplicity of afterlifes staggered through time. For example, Francesco Rosi's *Carmen* (1984):

> has had a lifespan of over 20 years, first on celluloid, through many video windows (from rental, sell-through, premium satellite, terrestrial broadcasters, low budget cable and satellite companies, budget re-releases), on videodisk, and released on DVD in the early 2000s with 20 language subtitle options (5).

This multiplication of outlets for cinema has crucial consequences not only at economic level in terms of a film's viability, but also, at a cultural level, it means that images are circulating incessantly and are an omnipresent feature of life in communities across the planet. It is this extension of the shelf-life of film made possible by a plethora of new outlets which means that the influence of films is not delimited by the brief summer of box-office release. The images remain on the move and they continue to exert their influence long after they have disappeared from the reviewing pages of broadsheets. The digitization of cinema allowing for multilingual support further amplifies the potential for dissemination of motion pictures. Hence, as part of the contemporary global mediascape, the treatment of translation and language difference in Hollywood narratives is not hostage to the moment of production. Rather, the films in their box-office afterlife on the small screen or in the video store continue to reverberate and, indeed, have the potential to take on new meanings as like texts they move forward in time or move across in space.

Just as it is commonplace to observe that a text is not read or translated in the same way depending on where and in what era one lives, similarly, for film, the shift or translation from one form to the other, in different places, and at different times, demands new responses and new readings. The multiplication of forms has not only increased exponentially the presence of filmic images in the lives of many inhabitants of the planet, making this explosion a salient feature of contemporary globalization, but also the differentiated and staggered nature of the multiple reception of films complicates any simple readings of what it is that films might be doing.

There is general agreement, however, that as the statistics showed above, one of the things that films might be doing is making a lot of money for the media conglomerates that produce them. For Hamid Naficy, there is an important link between the development of cinema in the second half of the twentieth century and the championing by the US government through the United States Information Agency of film as a form of cultural diplomacy:

> It seems to me at the heart of the US policy of technological transfer and development aid for the Third World since the 1950s, was this notion of homogenization and synchronicity of the world within Western consumerist ideology. This is a shift from the earlier policy of diachronicity, promoted by colonists, which tended to keep the developed and the underdeveloped worlds apart. The emerging form of post-industrial capitalism sought synchronicity in the interest of creating global markets.
> (Naficy 2003: 193)

In much the same way that the Marshall Plan was not an act of pure altruism and was designed to guarantee future markets for American produce through the reconstruction of Europe, exporting films was a way of encouraging an ideal of synchronicity. The ideal was, in many respects, an export version of what was earlier a domestic ambition, the integration of US immigrants into the mass market of the Fordist age. The difficulty with synchronicity is that it may not carry with it the amused condescension of earlier forms of colonialism (where the natives would be encouraged to stay quaint and stay put) but it cannot disguise asymmetries of power. Not all languages have the same standing or economic power and therefore it can be difficult to conduct their business on equal terms with the prestigious languages of more financially and politically influential groups.

Albert Branchadell uses the term 'less translated languages' to describe all 'those languages that are less often the source of translation in the international exchange of economic goods, regardless of the numbers of people using those languages' (Branchadell and Lovell West 2005: 1). So as we saw earlier, for young Flemish speakers, English was *the* language of cinema and other languages, including their own, seemed awkward or inappropriate for the big screen. English is overwhelmingly the source language for films in the contemporary world but even among the 'less translated languages,' not all will have the resources to subtitle or dub film titles into their own language as a means of aspiring to a form of synchronicity in the audio-visual field (O'Connell 2003). There is a further problem with the goal of synchronicity, which is to do with the nature of modernity itself. As Shmuel Noah Eisenstadt has pointed out, there has not been in the history of humanity one single civilization, one single institutional pattern, one version of modernity which has spread unimpeded and unaltered to the rest of humanity. There have instead been 'multiple modernities' (Eisenstadt 2000: 38). The notion of unilateral diffusionism is contradicted by the development of modernity in the West, where modernization in Spain followed a markedly different path from modernization in France (Bayly 2004: 49–86). Manuel Castells has demonstrated how the development of business networks in Japan, Korea and China has been deeply inflected by the different, inherited forms of social organization and value systems (Castells 1996: 172–90). Scott Lash and John Urry, for their part, show in great detail, the decisive influence of national histories on the construction of society and the economy in modern Britain and Germany (Lash and Urry 1994: 171–92). Therefore, the emergence of a unitary synchronicity is not only compromised by different historical circumstances and varying routes to modernity but also a shared consumer ideology does not mean that consumers themselves share the same values. The interpretations of film products are as potentially various as the spectators gathered to consume them. They have not followed the same path to get to the cinema so there is no reason why they should all head for the same exit.

The question still remains, however, as to why translation has been for so long neglected as a dimension to the understanding and analysis of film. Film studies do not have a monopoly of exclusion, however, and the history of translation teems with examples of attempts to marginalize or downplay the role of translators in the cultural and political life of many different societies (Venuti 2008). One possible answer to the question lies in the connection between translation, cinema and mediation. Translators are first and foremost mediators. They are the medium by which texts from one culture and language are transmitted to another. Translation is, therefore, a subset of the larger sets of transmission and mediation. In this respect, translation has similarities to other forms of mediation and transmission in our society whether they be radio, television, the railway system or the electricity supply grid. Régis Debray has pointed out that the more immediate or apparently self-evident an experience, the more difficult or indeed undesirable it is to question it. Cinema, for example, appears to offer us unmediated reality, but only through the most complex of artifices. The evening news, which seems to offer an effortless access to the real, is the construction of hundreds of people assembling the program for mass viewing. As Debray observes, '[t]he more constraining the mediation, the more imperious the immediacy. To make apparent on the 'technical' side the mediation which is not or no longer visible on the 'cultural' side, is the first step, occasionally disconcerting or scandalous, in the approach' (Debray 2000: 70).[1]

The principal aim of systems of mediation is to make themselves transparent, and the greater the simplicity of use the more complex the system of delivery. This can be seen in personal computers which become more and more user-friendly as they become harder and harder to repair. What you see is what you get, only if you are not allowed to get at what you cannot see. When we plug in an apparatus or turn the tap, we are connecting ourselves to increasingly complex systems of public utilities. Daniel Bougnoux argues, '[t]he medium is self-cancelling [...] Any progress in a medium conceals the medium-term and shortens the access route, and mediology [the study of mediation] gives the inside story on these short-circuits' (cited in Debray 2000: 159).[2] Translation studies is also about the study of short-circuits. Translation history, translation pedagogy and translation text analysis seek to reveal the complexity of the infrastructure which allows translation to happen in the first place, whether this be at the level of the intrinsic linguistic difficulties of languages and texts, the long and arduous formation of translators, the intricacy of cultural crossover, the state of the publishing industry or the assimilation of technical advances. At times, such is the overwhelming imperative of transparency and immediacy in translation, as in other media of transmission, that translation practitioners and users may not welcome this analysis.

Practitioners may have perfected the short-circuits or short cuts to such an extent that any analysis of their practice will seem unnatural or fastidious. On the other hand, just as film goers are reluctant to be shown that a great moment of cinematographic passion is being shot in a studio full of sound engineers, perchmen, cameramen and vision mixers, the end-users of translation do not always welcome being informed on just how difficult and complex translation can be, particularly if this means paying proper rates for work done. The paradox is obvious. The better the translation, the more successful the medium and the more invisible the mediator. In effect, the medium is self-annulling and in pragmatic translation it is bad rather than good translation which makes the medium transparent. If conference interpreters are like newsreaders – the more visible mediators in our profession – translators generally are inhibited by a widespread taboo against the uncovering of channels of transmission or the detailing of the artifice of media. The suspension of disbelief which is central to the function of much fiction is also at work in the transactions of translation. The study of cinema which is, if nothing else, a detailed exploration, of the 'short-circuits' and the 'short cuts' in film making, an exposure of the artifice of cinematographic transparency and immediacy, has been largely complicit in silencing the operation of that other form of mediation in cinema, translation. In detailing the presence of translation in different Hollywood genres, the following chapters aim to redress the balance and reveal the crucial presence of mediation. We will begin with the place where all borders meet, the frontier.

Notes

1 Plus contraignantes les médiations, plus hautaine l'immédiateté. Faire apparaître des médiations, côté technique, là où n'en voit pas ou plus, côté culture, sera donc le premier moment de la démarche, parfois déconcertant ou scandaleux.
2 Le médium est autoraturant[…]Tout progrès médiatique enfouit le moyen terme et raccourcit le circuit d'accès, et la médiologie fait la petite histoire de ces courts-circuits.

2 The frontiers of translation

Stagecoach to *Dances With Wolves*

In the voiceover that accompanied the original *Star Trek* series, there was no doubt about the tradition to which the men and women of the starship *Enterprise* belonged. 'Space, the final frontier,' clearly situated the intergalactic travelers in a narrative of discovery and territorial expansion, which finds its most quintessential expression in the twentieth-century film genre known as the Western. If the shift from the Old World to the New, as we will see in Chapter 3, provides the Marx Brothers with material for commentary and satire, movement within the New World is another exhaustible source of material for film makers. Central to the promise of migration to the Americas was the promise of opportunities and land for all. As more migrants came, more land was needed to sustain the myth of a promised land of agricultural and mineral plenty for prospective settlers. The relentless push westwards was the precondition of the survival of the frontier myth. By moving ever further forwards, it was possible to make large tracts of land available for the Europeans who were arriving in their millions from a world perceived as restricted in both space and opportunity. The problem, of course, was that Europeans discovered that the New World was not as New as all that, and that for its native American inhabitants the New World was indeed a very Old World. The pioneers and settlers were not so much discovering virgin territory as a highly contested space. The frontier, then, became as much a zone of risk as a place of promise.

Frontiers

The native Americans were not the only complicating presence in the promised land. The Mexican–American war of 1846–48, which followed on from the US annexation of Texas in 1845 (Texas had seceded in 1836 but Mexico did not recognize the rebel province), led to US victory and the signing of the Treaty of Hidalgo Guadalupe. Under the terms of the treaty, Mexico ceded the provinces of Alta California and Santa Fé de Nuevo México to the US government. The result was not only a massive transfer of land to the victors but also the creation of a strong Hispanic presence in these new frontier lands. Part of the justification for the annexation of Texas was to be provided by the notion of 'manifest destiny,' a belief that that United States had a mission to expand, spreading its institutions and concepts of law and democracy (Stephanson 1995). The phrase had originated with journalist John L. O'Sullivan, an advocate for the Democrat Party, who argued in 1845 for the annexation of Texas not only because most Texans, he declared, wanted this but also because it was 'our manifest destiny to overspread the continent allotted by Providence for the free development of our yearly multiplying millions' (Zinn 2005: 151). Pushing the frontier back was not just an opportunity, it was a duty. So the West and the idea of the frontier became a crucial part of the narrative of national identity in the United States and an important ideological underpinning for how the citizens of the American Republic were to present themselves to themselves and to the rest of the world.

In this context, it is hardly surprising that cinema in the United States would not want to tell this story just to American audiences but to anybody else through the marked popularity of the Western genre (Nash Smith 1950; Newman 1990). The Western is not, however, exclusively the tale of collective initiative or the glorification of a higher mission, manifest or otherwise. In fact, what characterizes the cowboy, who becomes a central feature of the Western genre, in print and on the screen, is his problematic relationship with society. As a nomadic figure, he unsettles and is unsettling. As part of the frontier world, he brings out the dangerous, violent and uncertain nature of lives lived in the liminal zone of newly conquered territories. But what carnival was to the life of late medieval Christendom, a world turned upside down, the Wild West was to the life of the expanding US republic, a form of anti-structure which copperfastened the routine structures of civil and religious dispensation. Charles Taylor, analyzing the legacy of medieval carnivals, points out that one of their roles and that of anti-structure generally is to set free people's spontaneity and creativity:

> Seen in this perspective, the power of anti-structure also comes from the sense that all codes limit us, shut us out from something important, prevent us from seeing and feeling things of great moment. We remember that in some rites of passage, the elders take advantage of this liminal condition to instruct the youth in the deepest lore of the society; as if these things can't be learned except by those who have become receptive enough through stepping out of their normal coded roles[...]The general phenomenon here is thus a sense of the necessity of anti-structure. All codes need to be countervailed, sometimes even swamped in their negation, on pain of rigidity, enervation, the atrophy of social cohesion, blindness, perhaps ultimately self-destruction.
>
> (Taylor 2007: 50)

The taglines that were used to advertise John Ford's *Stagecoach* (1939) on its first appearance clearly identify the anti-structural properties of the West, which could not be but Wild,

Danger holds the reins as the devil cracks the whip! Desperate men! Frontier women! Rising above their pasts in a West corrupted by violence and gun-fire! Thrills! Thrills! Thrills! See – The Apache Attack! Charge of the Cavalry! Fight to the Death On the Last Frontier of Wickedness!

(See Cowie 2004)

The hero of the film, the Ringo Kid (John Wayne) has escaped from prison and is being returned to jail while the heroine, Dallas (Claire Trevor), is a prostitute who has been run out of town by members of the Law and Order League and accompanies the rest of the company in the stagecoach to Lordsburg to take up her former trade. When the stagecoach finally makes it to Lordsburg, the town is portrayed as a site of unbridled drinking, gunfighting and sexual promiscuity, not so much the promised land of the puritan imagination, a worthy end to the pilgrim's progress, as 'the last frontier of wickedness.' The liminal condition of the West not only excites the imagination, but also makes manifest elements of society and history that cannot be ignored by the 'free development' of 'yearly multiplying millions.' One of those elements is language difference and the manner in which the contact zone of the West becomes a site of uneasy translation and of the clustering of anxieties around the relationship between possession and expression.

The drama of John Ford's classic Western is partly to do with the often tense relationship between the various occupants of the stagecoach, but the most immediate source of danger for the passengers is the possibility of an attack by the Apaches. The stagecoach loses its army protection at one point on the journey to Arizona and they eventually vote by a majority to continue the journey despite the distinct threat of ambush. Buck (Andy Devine), the driver, is unhappy with the decision and tells his driving companion Marshal Curly Wilcox (George Bancroft) that a 'fellow gets nervous sitting here like a dummy and nothing to think about but the Indians.' The driver's preoccupation is also that of his passengers. Josiah Boone (Thomas Mitchell), a medical doctor, tells his travelling companions that, 'We're all going to be scalped, massacred in one fell swoop. It's that old Apache butcher, Geronimo. Geronimo, nice name for a butcher!' The irony is that 'the nice name' had been conferred on the Chiricahua Apache leader Goyaaé not by the Americans but by Mexican troops who had been the Apache leader's first adversaries (Debo 1976). During his military career, which lasted from the 1850s to 1886, Geronimo regularly clashed with both the US and Mexican armies in attempts to prevent encroachments on tribal lands. If the Mexican sobriquet concealed the true name of Goyaaé, the film conceals his native tongue, Chiricahua.

When the Apaches finally appear, over an hour into the film, Geronimo is shown in a close-up shot but he remains silent. His silence is mirrored by that of the Cheyenne Indian scout (Chief John Big Tree) shown in the opening scenes of the film in the US army camp. The camera gives the spectator a head and shoulders shot of the scout but the scout does not say a word in the extended shot. It is another soldier who reports that the scout's tribe had a brush with the Apaches and that they there were in the area around Lordsburg. He adds that the scout's fellow tribe members 'hate the Apaches worse than we do.' The scout does not give the information directly, it is channeled through the voice and language of a member of the army. If someone else is doing the talking, it is safe to presume that someone else has done the translating but the act or moment of translating does not appear on screen. The native American languages are proscribed from the soundtrack. When Geronimo appears on screen, one of his fellow warriors points to the stagecoach and says something but what he says is inaudible. Prior to the appearance of the Apache warriors the stagecoach travelers are alerted to their presence by the use of smoke signals, which the Ringo Kid translates as 'war signals.'

What is shown on screen is a non-verbal system of communication, but at no point are the 'Indians' to be heard speaking on screen. The only language we hear is the cries of the warriors in pursuit of the stagecoach. As the stagecoach routes spread and settler towns emerge, the territorial encroachment on different tribal territories continues unabated with the assistance of the military. If the native Americans are being removed from the land and either killed or placed in reservations, their language is being removed from the territories they once occupied either through a process of re-naming ('Dry Fork,' 'Lee's Well,' 'Lordsburg') or through the silencing of their articulate speech. We hear cries not sentences. The Apaches become visual ciphers of a menace but not the audible agents of a world view. The only mechanism of translation on hand to allow for their feelings or opinions to be expressed is indirect and off screen and highly instrumentalized, i.e. its sole use is to gather strategic information and enhance the effectiveness of the US military. Translation is exploited in the same way as tension or enmity between different native American communities. One caveat to the interpretation of linguistic silence as cultural obliteration is that the refusal to speak or be translated may constitute in its own way an act of resistance. That is to say, Geronimo is not presented speaking a form of pidgin English, which would either misrepresent him or his people or make him simply a figure of fun or ridicule. The absence of translation can, in fact, be construed as a statement that the Apache language and culture is distinctly other and that there can be no basis for dialogue in a war of mutual destruction, albeit with forces heavily favoring one side in the conflict. The more generous interpretation of native Americans in the film is partly supported by the film's profound ambivalence toward the civilization settlers are allegedly seeking to spread, and the army aiming to protect.

When Dallas finds herself chased out of the town of Tonto by the Ladies Law and Order League, she dismisses the potential danger of Apache attack with the comment that there 'are worse things than Apaches.' The statement is followed by a wide shot of the tight-lipped, unsmiling members of the

League gathered together to make sure she leaves the town. The other object of their ire, the hard-drinking Doc Boone, had previously reminded her that 'we're the victims of a foul disease called social prejudice, my child.' The banker Henry Gatewood (Berton Churchill) and the Southern 'gentleman' Hatfield (John Carradine) who present themselves as the epitome of social respectability throughout the trip turn out to be less than reputable and one of the first scenes when the stagecoach finally reaches Lordsburg is that of Greenwood being arrested for financial embezzlement. When Dallas and the Ringo Kid ride away across the border to a new life in Mexico at the very end of the film, Doc Boone's acerbic comment is 'Well, they're saved from the blessings of civilization.' There is little sense, then, of a triumphant manifest destiny in operation in the film. If anything, the frontier, which in the film is set in Arizona near the border with Mexico, reveals the unseemly edges of a society – financial corruption, class prejudice, sexual hypocrisy – that make the social model an unlikely candidate for moral superiority. In this context, it is possible to see the mute, untranslated presence of Geronimo as a variation on the 'noble savage,' his dignified silence a tacit rebuke to the venal dissembling of the settlers and their claims to civilized virtue.

There is one member of the Apache community who is heard in the film not to speak but to sing and that is Yakima (Elvira Ríos), the Apache wife of Chris (Chris Pin-Martin) who is the Mexican proprietor of the way station. She sings, however, in Spanish. The role of Yakima is eloquent as a demonstration of the manner in which translation in situations of conflict is frequently bound up with sexual and language politics. We are first aware of Yakima's presence through the startled reaction of Samuel Peacock (Donald Meek), 'Savages!,' to which Chris replies, 'That's my wife Yakima, my squaw.' Peacock is not reassured and repeats himself, 'Yes, but she's, she's savage.' Gatewood protests that there is 'something funny about this,' namely the fact that Chris has an Apache for a wife.

Chris's defense is expressed in terms of his own strategic interest, 'Sure, she's one of Geronimo's people. I think, maybe not so bad to have an Apache wife, eh? Apaches don't bother me, I think.' Chris's reasoning is based on both his wife as talisman and as informant in this contested border region of Apache intentions. The Swedish anthropologist Göran Aijmer points out the political and epistemological problems that beset the use of informants although he does not mention the question of language:

> Informants' insights into their own society are interesting, but generally the interest lies in the extent to which the informant grasps his own social environment. There are also other issues, such as the way in which an informant's account forms a conscious strategy for self-presentation and the anthropologist's refutation of indigenous explanations, which have an obvious place in anthropological discourse.
>
> (Aijmer 1992: 296)

A conscious strategy for self-presentation can also be a covert strategy for self-preservation. Neither strategy has endeared linguistic and cultural mediators to their compatriots, and it is possible to argue that the in-between figures of language are fit subjects for a new cultural teratology. Rosa Braidotti in *Nomadic Subjects* (1994) defines monsters as follows:

> Monsters are human beings who are born with congenital malformations of their bodily organism. They also represent the in between, the mixed, the ambivalent as implied in the ancient Greek root of the word *monsters*, *teras*, which means both horrible and wonderful, object of aberration and adoration.
>
> (Braidotti 1994: 77)

An example of ambivalent responses to language and cultural mediators can be seen in the *Lienzo de Tlaxacala*, an Indian picture history dating from around 1550. The history shows Doña Marina, Cortés's interpreter, looming over the other figures in the illustrations including Cortés himself. Doña Marina spoke Mayan because she had lived among the Tabascans and she spoke the language of the Aztecs as she was of Aztec descent. After being captured by the Spaniards, she is said to have learned their language quickly. For some cultural commentators in post-independence Mexico, Doña Marina was monstrous, 'mother of a bastard race of *mestizos* and a traitress to her country' (Mirandé and Enríquez, 1979: 24). For others, her resource-fulness and cultural flexibility have excited admiration and she has been presented as a 'herald of the culturally hybrid societies of the future' (Bowen *et al.* 1995: 262). Mediators thus become recurring objects of ambivalence, in-between figures, loathed and admired, privileged and despised. Like the monstrous, they inspire awe and alienation.

The relationship between language mediation and gender has had many ramifications from the colonial period to the present. Control of the speaking subject in many instances implies control of the body. The control is rendered problematic, however, by the difficulty in controlling/monitoring the translation flow. It was a practice, for example, for certain Crown informers in the period of the Tudor conquest of Ireland to take Irish-speaking wives so as to enhance the intelligence-gathering activities of these Crown agents. The problem was that the women on occasion would change sides and act as double-agents, supplying the Gaelic Irish with valuable information on troop movements (Jackson 1973: 21–28). Hence, there was the repeated conflation of notions of personal fidelity and politico-linguistic fidelity. Fidelity to colonizer becomes infidelity to the colonized, and the colonizer's fidelity, of course, is often purely instrumental. Cortés demands political, emotional and linguistic fidelity from Doña Marina. She must serve the Spanish cause, remain his lover and give him a true account of what the natives are saying. However, Cortés's own fidelity is purely strategic and he abandons Doña Marina on his return to Spain in order to marry a woman of appropriate social rank.

In *Stagecoach*, Yakima's first appearance is not accompanied by her speaking. Dressed in native American dress, the camera lingers on her face and person but she does not reply in any way to what the guests have said. Instead, she hurries off to work when ordered to do so in Spanish by Chris. A marginal figure in settler society, Yakima will assist the socially disgraced Dallas and Doc Boone in delivering a baby girl to Lucy Mallory (Louise Platt). Later that night, Yakima sings in Spanish and is accompanied by Mexican vaqueros playing instruments. Her song is about love and an exile's lament for a native land. She suddenly interrupts her song to tell the vaqueros in Spanish to hurry and get going. It transpires later that they disappeared with all the spare horses. The next morning it is Yakima's turn to disappear. The dual perception of the woman between languages and cultures is revealed in the contrasting reactions to the disappearance of Yakima. Gatewood initially accuses her of stealing his bag and Buck remarks to Chris that, 'that squaw of yours will find some apaches and bring them here.' Chris, for his part, however, is more sanguine, 'My wife people no bother me, I think.' Chris's interest in Yakima like Cortés's in Doña Marina is, of course, highly instrumentalized. He bitterly regrets the loss of his horse taken by Yakima and comments, 'I can find another wife easy, yes, but not another horse.'

The valuing of a horse more highly than his wife and the suggestion that his partners are easily interchangeable shows, if anything, a highly cynical approach to fidelity on the part of Chris but the entire episode, the longest in the film lasting over 24 minutes, is a fascinating condensation of concerns around language difference in the contact zone. For a start, nothing is what it appears to be. Yakima is dressed in Indian dress but she sings in Spanish. She appears to be loyal to Chris and to the interests of the settlers (she helps with the birth of Lucy Mallory's child) but she, in league with the vaqueros, disappears with the spare horses. The staging post at Apache Wells is a place of birth and a potential site of death. The Mallory baby is delivered into the world but the passengers fear that they are being delivered into the hands of their potential executioners. In the staging post, criss-crossed by the different interests of the Mexican, Apache and US settler communities, it is striking that there is a ready conflation of Apache and Mexican interests. These are two groups who will most obviously lose out to the territorial expansion of the US and these are two groups who do not speak the majority language of the new settlers, English. Yakima's singing of a Spanish song and the apparent treachery of the vaqueros with whom she communicates in Spanish, imply a kind of parallelism between language otherness and political unreliability. Chris's own status as both Mexican and married to an Apache makes him suspect to passengers like Peacock and Gatewood. Chris's own interloper status in English is emphasized by the heavily accented nature of the English he speaks and his wayward grammar.

Chris is, in a sense, translating between the different worlds that are coming into contact in Apache Wells. Yakima is part of this translation strategy, but the very indeterminate nature of fidelity in this border region means that the presence of language otherness becomes an immediate object of suspicion. The settlers know they need Chris and Yakima to survive their proximity to border but they are repeatedly anxious over how much control they can exercise over the language/translation/information flow. This anxiety is revealed in a more parodic form in an earlier exchange between Buck and Curley when he claims that he took the job as stagecoach driver over ten years ago so that he could make enough money to marry his 'Mexican girl Julietta.' He goes on to say, 'My wife's got more relatives than anyone you ever did see. I bet I'm feeding half the state of Chihuahua … And what do I get to eat when I get home in Lordsburg. Nothing but frijoles beans. That's all. Nothin' but beans, beans, beans.' Buck, who is the comic fall guy in the film, harbors dark suspicions about what happens to his money, and his monolingual state presumably prevents him from finding out how many relatives his wife does in fact have in the state of Chihuahua. For Buck, alterity begins at home and the lament about bean dishes is a telling metaphor for his own dual status in the border lands of Arizona.

English is the shared language of the passengers in the stagecoach but their common language divides them as much as it unites them. The deep divisions in the society established by European colonists become quickly apparent in the way language is handled differently by the various protagonists. When the Ringo Kid joins the company, Doc Boone claims that he knew his family and tries to remember when he met them, 'Ah, let's see. I'd just been honorably discharged from the Union Army after the War of the Rebellion.' He is interrupted by Hatfield who says, 'You mean the War for the Southern Confederacy sir,' which elicits a sharp response from the generally amiable Boone, 'I mean nothing of the kind sir.' The Southerners Hatfield and Lucy Mallory are notable for a more formal use of language and an accent which is closer to a form of upper middle-class British English. At the Dry Fork way station there is a scene where Lucy Mallory finds herself sitting opposite Dallas and Hatfield very ostensibly shows Lucy Mallory to another seat saying, 'May I find you another place, Mrs Mallory? It's cooler by the window.' Mallory moves and the snub is calculated. But to some extent the social divisions have already been anticipated by the choice of accent and language register, which clearly mark the Southerners as different, a difference further underlined by a different reading of a key event in recent American history.

The banker Henry Gatewood as the neo-liberal apostle *ante verbum* who loudly proclaims at the outset of the film that 'what's good for the banks is good for the country,' speaks the language of pompous self-righteousness. His speech is characterized by the repeated use of a formal language bordering on pseudo-legalese, all the more ironic in the context of his own corrupt practices. He protests to Chris in Apache Wells when told the army had left that 'The army has no right to leave a public place unprotected,' and later when Gatewood gets into an argument with Hatfield, Hatfield threatens to put him out of the stagecoach, to which Gatewood replies, 'You can't put me out of a public conveyance.' As if to further emphasize the alignment between language and class, Gatewood sits at the end of the table with Hatfield and Mallory in the famous scene at the Dry Fork way station. The passengers, the driver and the Marshal are all speakers of a variety of American English, but what characterizes their long journey is not the instances of agreement but the repeated misunderstandings and verbal clashes. In other words, in any examination of language difference and the vagaries of translation in *Stagecoach* it bears repeated emphasis that the dominant language of the dominant community is anything but homogenous. It is as divided as its speakers.

Whereas much has been written about the function of interlingual translators, it is worth considering what the role of an intralingual translator might be on screen. Doc Boone, as we noted earlier, is something of a social pariah in Tonto. An inveterate drinker, he is thrown out of his lodgings for failing to pay his rent. What is troubling about Doc Boone is that he speaks a language which is inappropriate to his lowly status. When he tries to get a last drink from the barman Jerry (Jack Pennick) before leaving town, he begins saying, 'I'll admit as one man to another that economically, I haven't been of much value to you' and later when scolded by Hatfield for smoking a cigar in the presence of a lady, Boone apologizes with the words, 'Being so partial to the weed myself I sometimes forget that it disagrees with others.' He quotes Christopher Marlowe on Helen of Troy to the singularly unimpressed landlady in Tonto and escorts Dallas to the stagecoach with a mock translation from French, 'Take my arm, Madame la Comtesse. The tumbrel awaits. To the guillotine.' He clearly has the cultural capital of his class but his drinking habits have transformed him into a borderland *déclassé*. It is Doc Boone, however, who can talk affectionately to the Ringo Kid, become the confidant of Dallas, deliver Lucy Mallory's baby, earn Hatfield's gratitude and end up at the end of the film having a drink with the irascible Marshal Curly Wilcox. It is the person who finds himself in the space between the social classes, who is in the classic between or interstitial place of the translator who is able to create an, albeit fragile, community of understanding between the different members of the stagecoach party. Only Gatewood remains unmoved, marooned by the force of his multiple prejudices. Doc Boone is an outsider who knows what it is to speak the language of different kinds of insiders from Lucy Mallory to the Ringo Kid, and who also knows that there is a price to pay for the social mobility of the intralingual translator. If *Stagecoach* draws heavily for its cinematographic effects on striking contrasts between light and dark, speech and silence, Ford's contrasts are rarely Manichean, the translatorial presence of a Doc Boone showing that the forms of social and human discrimination are endless, but not beyond redemption.

Re-telling the Alamo

John Wayne's performance as the Ringo Kid in *Stagecoach* established his reputation and he would later as both actor and director return to the theme of borders, territorial and linguistic in *The Alamo* (1960). The film recounts an episode in the Texan war of independence in which a group of ethnic Americans ('Anglos') and ethnic Mexicans ('Tejanos') held out for 13 days in the Alamo Mission in San Antonio de Béxar against forces from the Republic of Mexico. Though the Texans were ultimately defeated, their action stalled the Mexican army and was a contributory factor to the later defeat of the Mexican forces by General Sam Houston at the Battle of San Jacinto. The film is explicitly political in its ringing endorsements of the notion of the Republic, of the need to fight oppression, of the imperative to say that what is right is right and what is wrong is wrong. John Wayne, playing the role of Colonel Davy Crockett, is the principal mouthpiece for a plain-speaking rhetoric of emancipation. It is no accident, of course, that the film echoes the binary logic of the Cold War with 'freedom' on one side and 'tyranny' on the other. Davy Crockett's battle songs of the Republic are not only for Texan or Tennessean ears. However, the film cannot escape the very liminal nature of the territory it is attempting to describe and must struggle to translate the complex realities of place and language into the instrumental language of manifest destiny.

From the outset, the film sets up a tension between unity and diversity. The opening credits sequence is set against the backdrop of paintings of the Alamo mission then fades to a block of text describing Texas in the early nineteenth century, 'Though its inhabitants were made up of settlers from far countries and all parts of the United States, they were Mexican citizens all.' The territory is a place encompassing many peoples, and, one can safely assume, many languages, but what unites them is the fact of Spanish citizenship. The passage, of course, paradoxically prefigures the fate of Texas, which will remain a place 'made up of settlers from far countries and all parts of the United States' but where the unifying factor will be another citizenship, American. So the film is situated firmly in the Western genre through the presence of adventurers like Jim Bowie (Richard Widmark) and Davy Crockett, and it describes a frontier place where the inhabitants are in the process of being translated from one political state to another. The unitary notions of citizenship, the successful political 'translation,' are continuously complicated by facts of language, history and culture which resist the stark contraries (us/them, resistance/oppression, right/wrong) that haunt the public language of the film. *The Alamo* in a sense posits a model of translation with clearly defined polarities and a mechanism for effecting a transition from one to the other (armed rebellion), but what the film, wittingly or unwittingly, reveals is just how problematic translation is, endlessly troubled by the obdurate realities of linguistic and cultural difference.

When Davy Crockett and his Tennesseans first arrive at the mission town of San Antonio de Béxar, one of the group remarks that, 'We're going to have to learn the lingo they use down here, Davy.' The young boy, Smitty (Frankie Avalon) takes a spyglass and spells out the first word that he sees, *cantina*, and asks what it means. The translation of the word takes the form of oblique parody. Smitty's question prompts an exchange between two of the Tennesseans, 'Do it mean what I think it do?,' 'It do,' while Crockett declares that it means the men get out of their deerskins and put on their good clothes for a night out on the town. So rather like the famous arrival or contact scenes in travel narratives, when the Tennesseans come to San Antonio they can see or know they are in a different place. The first thing that attracts Smitty's attention is not landscape or dress or architecture. It is language. He can see through the spyglass from a distance, and the Tennesseans when they arrive are on the brow of a hill overlooking the town, but seeing is not all. When Smitty gets close, visual mastery gives way to linguistic bafflement. San Antonio is not always already there for the Anglophones, it demands translation. Of course, the translations offered vary in their nature and intent.

In an extended sequence Jim Bowie and Davy Crockett discuss their vision of Mexico, and Crockett claims that 'I thought she was a burnover desert most of the time.' Bowie admits that most 'Northerners' view Mexico that way but then speaks of, 'Big valleys between high mountains. Just everything that a man would want by way of country for lookin' at or for growin'.' Bowie, a rancher, sees territory as ready to be taken and turned into a viable asset. In an intriguing linking of tourism and dispossession, scenery becomes a prologue to seizure, land that is good 'for lookin' at' is also good for growing and by extension for taking. Crockett, in an exchange with a Mexican noblewoman Graciela Carmela Maria 'Flaca' de Lopez y Vejar (Linda Cristal), invokes an Adamic precedent. Looking admiringly at a tree, he says to her, 'This tree must have been growed [sic] before man first put his first dirty footprints on this prairie. Kind of tree Adam and Eve must have met under.' So Texas is a new Eden, and Davy and Graciela are a latter day Adam and Eve.

The fiction of a *terra nullius* is crucial to a whole mythology surrounding the birth of the frontier and the enduring appeal of the pioneer narrative, but it is a fiction which presupposes a translation in a physical sense that disavows translation in a linguistic sense. In other words, moving to lands which are presented as a new paradise, a blank slate, a tabular rasa, is to forget Eden's unhappy sequel, the Expulsion from Eden. The expulsion of peoples from their territory to make way for new settlements involves either their permanent removal through displacement or death or the assimilation (translation) of a people to a new language, culture and political dispensation. Spatial translation almost invariably involves other forms of translation, which are less readily acknowledged.

Relationships that do acknowledge the existence of the other forms of translation in *The Alamo* are male–female. Bowie completes his paean to Mexico with a lyrical evocation of the people, particularly the 'womenfolk.' Crockett's laconic response is, 'I figured you favored the Mexican ladies. They tell me you married one.' Indeed, Bowie's marriage to a Mexican makes him an object of suspicion in the eyes of the mission commander

Colonel William Travis (Laurence Harvey) who has doubts about the loyalty of an officer who has married into the 'Mexican aristocracy.' The sense of intermarriage occurring at all levels of the society is hinted at by the telling admission of a drunken Tennessean in the *cantina* in San Antonio, 'I'm going to marry up with Conchita and be the man of this house.' The most extended treatment of a cross-cultural and cross-linguistic relationship is the encounter between Davy Crockett and Graciela. Graciela first appears speaking both Spanish and Spanish-accented English. In a scene soon after where she expresses her anger to the merchant Emil Sande (Wesley Lau) about his efforts to force her into marrying him, the passage is in Spanish without subtitles. Sande makes play of the language difference saying, 'Easy, Graciela, easy! I speak your language but that's too fast for me though I daresay I'm better off not understanding.' Sande is a man of shifting loyalties and his knowledge of the language is strategic. Whatever is necessary to advance his own business interests he will do, whether it be learn a language or marry a native. In his obtuseness, however, he fails to realize that his loyalties are not the only ones that are flexible. Graciela later reveals to Crockett and his companions where Sande has hidden the gunpowder he intends to sell to Santa Anna's forces.

What is striking about the presentation of the main romantic interest in the film is that much of the dalliance is centred around language. When Crockett addresses Graciela by her full name she exclaims, 'My goodness, you remember all that.' He then asks her what the Spanish word is for breakfast and when she tells him, he says, 'Well let's take a *paseardo* [sic] out and get some *desayuno*.' She corrects him saying, '*Paseado*.' Crockett asks, 'That means walk?' to which she replies 'That means have walked but never mind.' If difference for the putative male gaze is a constitutive principle of desire – there is no point in desiring what you already have – then it is hardly surprising that the film will construe the female other as different. Making the language the focus of narrative attention is also a means of staking out the most obvious of differences between Graciela and Crockett. Of course, not all differences are welcome, and part of the authority of Graciela's speech stems from the fact that she comes from an educated and seemingly wealthy background, and is, therefore, empowered to speak her own language. Crockett links her status and eloquence in his parting words to her when he reminds her that, 'Flacca, you have an important name. You know a million words and how they should be used. I'm sending you to fight your war, to talk up a howling mob.' Graciela represents a language reality that cannot be ignored and, even if takes the form of inoffensive banter, Crockett does make an albeit rudimentary effort to translate himself into Spanish.

Crockett's language lessons are not, however, wholly disinterested. Graciela as it turns out is a useful informant in locating the whereabouts of gunpowder and Crockett directly marshals translation to political effect in a crucial scene in the film. Crockett is keen to persuade the somewhat skeptical Tennesseans that the cause of Texas is their cause. To this end, he asks

Graciela to write him a letter in Spanish. He then informs his companions that they have received a letter from the Spanish general, Antonio Miguel Lopez de Santa Anna (Ruben Padilla). Crockett 'can't read it but the young lady will.' Graciela then proceeds to 'translate' the letter purported to be from Santa Anna into English. In this pseudo-translation scene, Graciela's language abilities are instrumentalized by Crockett to excite the wrath of his men against the Mexican general. She forges the original document and Crockett pens the bogus translation. Her knowledge of the source language allows her to produce an authoritative source text and her familiarity with the target language allows her to read out the 'translation,' her accented English a metonymic guarantee of the authenticity of the transaction. Although Crockett later admits that the document is a forgery, the damage to his military adversary is already done.

The film's sympathies lie clearly with the Texan rebels, and in this context the double-dealing of Graciela including her manipulation of translation is clearly perceived in a positive light. Her adroit exploitation of her bilingual status adds to her stature as heroine. However, as we saw in the case of Doña Marina earlier, depending on one's loyalties, loyalty or disloyalty can be interpreted or evaluated in radically different ways. Graciela could equally be seen as a traitor to the cause of Mexican unity, using her skills as a linguist to ensure that her fellow Spanish speakers would ultimately end up as second-class citizens in the new Anglophone world of the United States. From this perspective, her duplicity as translator gives expression to a deeper form of political betrayal. What is important to note is the profound ambiguity of Graciela's position as translator, which, like translation itself, leaves her actions open to a multiplicity of interpretations. A common feature, for example, of her position is that though the men may differ in their

Figure 1 Graciela reads out the pseudo-translation.

The Alamo (1960) Directed by John Wayne, USA: Batjac Productions nationality and character they, rather than she, remain ultimately in control. Her marriage to her first husband, now dead, was arranged by her family. Sande wants to possess and control her for his own interests and Crockett, for all his linguistic gallantry, is equally aware of the strategic military and political importance of a well-connected Mexican speaker of Spanish. Therefore, questions of translation remain inextricably bound up with issues of power and control and nowhere more explicitly than on the edges of competing polities.

In the opening scene of *The Alamo* we find General Sam Houston (Richard Boone) entrusting the defense of the Mission to Colonel William Travis. The difficulty for Travis is that part of the mission of the Mission is to bring a semblance of unity to a highly disparate group of people. When the Mexican army finally appears, it is not only their uniforms and organization that distinguish them from the defenders of the Mission but they also are speaking on screen and giving orders in a different language. What becomes immediately apparent is that within the Mission community itself, there is no sense of a group united by language, and, if anything, it is language which proves to be the most sharply divisive issue among the guardians of the outpost.

When Houston wants to establish the whereabouts of Jim Bowie, an officer present tells him that Bowie is 'indisposed.' Houston is scathing in his response, 'Indisposed. By God, if you mean drunk, sir, you say drunk sir!' Houston's plain-speaking is not, however, to the liking of the Mission commander Travis who is quick to establish differences between himself and more irregular elements of the army in the persons of Davy Crockett and Jim Bowie. Travis's diction throughout is marked by a highly formal register ('Colonel, I'd be pleased if you could join me in my quarters for some refreshment') and an accent reminiscent of British Received Pronunciation. His language, not unsurprisingly, excites the hostility of those around him, Jim Bowie describing him as a 'long-winded jackanapes' and Blind Nell Robertson claiming derisively that she 'was not fancy educated like you Will Travis.' The most telling scene in terms of language difference comes when Travis meets Crockett and seeks to enlist his support and that of his fellow Tennesseans in the conflict opposing the Texans to Santa Anna. When Crockett offers his eloquent defense of the notion of a Republic, Travis reacts not so much to the ideas as to the language. He remarks to Crockett, 'You're not the illiterate country bumpkin you would have people believe. You speak an excellent and concise English when you please. The bad grammar is a pose.' Crockett is not slow to acknowledge the performative aspect of language when he informs Travis, 'a fella's got to do a lot of things to get elected to Congress.' But Travis is not all that different from Crockett.

Good grammar is as much of a pose as bad grammar in that it signals status and cultural capital. Travis seeks to impose order and unity on his Mission defenders through both the observations of the niceties of military regulations and a discipline which is articulated in a prestigious variety of the language he speaks. In doing so, however, he runs the risk of appearing to undermine the Republican egalitarianism that he so warmly applauds in the speech of the former Congressman from Tennessee. In translating the informal arrangements of comradeship into the formal language of military hierarchy, Travis attracts considerable ire. Crockett translates Travis's elaborate diction into a language that the rancher Jim Bowie can understand, aware of the continual danger of mistranslation for the unity of the garrison. To this end, indeed, Crockett's language continually oscillates between the unmarked language of dialogue with Travis and the dialect he uses in exchanges with his fellow Tennesseans. The phrase 'it do' is repeated throughout the film, the ungrammatical, dialectical usage a signature tune for regional and class differences. Crockett's role is not unlike that of Doc Boone in *Stagecoach* in that he must act as the translator between the different varieties of language competing for attention in the emerging polity. Without his language mediation, the garrison would have collapsed long before the final assault.

If intralingual tensions make for translation difficulties, the difficulties are exacerbated when information is dependent on the conduit from another language. As noted above, the centrality of information to the exercise of power gives informants a particular status in multilingual situations, especially in times of conflict. The Mayor of San Antonio, Juan Seguin (Joseph Calleia), goes to the mission to inform Travis that 'Indians' have sent infor- mation to his 'vaqueros' that they observed a large force of Mexican troops heading in their direction. Travis is immediately dismissive saying, 'I'm sorry, señor Seguin, but as a civilian you cannot realize how worthless this sort of information is' and parodies the process through paraphrase, 'some Indian told some vaquero.' Bowie is furious at Travis's public rebuke to a highly valued informant and an already poor relationship deteriorates further. Travis later explains his action claiming that he could not demoralize his men further by revealing the extent to which they were outnumbered by the Mexican forces.

Whatever Travis's motives, the public humiliation of Seguin shows both the vulnerability of both the informant and the informed. To operate in the multilingual space that is the frontier, information is crucial and only those competent in more than one language can perform the function. However, the translator/informants also have to believe it is in their own interest to provide the service, whether this be under coercion (to escape torture, repri- sals) or as a result of an economic or political choice. Thus, the translators possess a highly valued good and their role is essential to the operation of an army in a conflicted territory. Nonetheless, their status is relative not absolute. If the translation process is not deemed valuable or important, for whatever reason, then the translator is quickly relegated to the position of worthless subordinate. Juan Seguin, as village mayor, is a person of some prestige in the area. The Texans value his sympathy for the Republican cause and he is personally greeted by General Houston in the opening scenes of the film. In the scene with Travis, he is, however, ultimately an informant/translator, a local who is quickly reminded of his inferior position in the larger military scheme of things.

Status is also bound up with or dependent on the autonomous or heteronomous position of the translator. For example, Bowie says goodbye to Seguin in Spanish after his public dressing down by Travis. The use of Spanish at a moment of marked intercultural tension is not innocent. Bowie is declaring his own understanding of or sympathy with Seguin's loss of face. That Bowie is familiar with the Spanish language is further indicated in a passage where Bowie, Crockett and their men find the barrels of gunpowder belonging to Sande. The camera provides a close-up of the Spanish inscription on the barrels, 'Polvora Peligro' and when Crockett asks the question, 'Polvora?' Bowie provides an instant translation 'That's gunpowder,' and they proceed to move the barrels from their hiding place. Bowie is in the position of the autonomous translator, an American who has learned Spanish, unlike Seguin, a Mexican who has learned English and is therefore a heteronomous translator in an Anglophone context. Travis is without doubt suspicious of Bowie's relationship to the local language and his marriage to a Mexican but their repeated standoffs do not suggest a difference in status despite Travis's position as overall commander of the Mission.

Bowie has decided to 'learn the lingo they use down here' and this enhances his importance as an ally for Travis and Crockett, but he is of course also a substantial landowner and, in Travis's words, 'married into the Mexican aristocracy.' As an autonomous translator, he has a standing that is markedly different from that of his friend and ally, Juan Seguin. In this respect, translation relationships are not only freighted with the weight of earlier histories of engagement but they also point to possible futures. Spanish signs are everywhere in the film, but the dominant voices are English. Bowie and Graciela still have to translate, but the question is for how much longer? Will the Tennesseans ultimately have to 'learn the lingo' or, on the contrary, will the relationship be reversed and it is the Spanish speakers who will have to translate themselves into a new language? In Crockett's emotional tribute to the Republic there is no mention of language rights and, given the inevitable connection between language and power, the power of Anglophones in the new Republic does not offer much hope for a language which will no longer correspond to the dominant political reality.

Spanish is a vital presence in *The Alamo* but there are no traces of native American languages. The film is a Western where there are recognizable cowboys but where the 'Indians' are strangely absent. They are mentioned as a source of information for the Seguin's cowhands but they are not a presence on screen. Yet, we learn that one of the film's main protagonists, Davy Crockett, got the title of Colonel during the 'Indian War' and when Graciela lists the epithets that speak of his legend, she includes 'Crockett the bear-killer' and 'Crockett the Indian fighter.' Later, in an exchange with Travis, Crockett claims, 'I'm not a real soldier. I've never fought anybody but Injuns, unless you count the British.' The 'Indian' parallels are crucial in that the composition of the Mission garrison implies a continuity between the Indian wars and the military campaign against the Mexican army. After clearing lands of native Americans, the settlers as pioneers move to the new frontier which is Mexico. The 'cantina' in San Antonio becomes an ersatz saloon and Spanish dancing is intermingled with Tennessean song in English. The Alamo is the new West.

However, the absence of native Americans is an uneasy reminder of what happens to cultures and languages in periods of conflict and dispossession. They are not part of the Mission forces. English and Spanish are the languages of Travis's and Santa Anna's troops that we hear on screen, but neither on the Texan nor on the Mexican side do we hear the languages of indigenous peoples. They are off screen, silenced by defeat. In his long, reflective exchange with Graciela before she leaves the Mission, Crockett expresses a sentiment which he argues applies to 'all people, everywhere.' He claims that an individual's most important duty is to, 'say a word for what's right though you get walloped for sayin' that word.' The difficulty is the universalism of the truth (applying to 'all people, everywhere') is undermined by the positionality of the speaker. Crockett as a veteran of the Indian Wars must know, among other things, that saying a word for what's right is unlikely to get you far if no one can be bothered to listen to what you are saying or is interested in finding out what it is you are saying. Similarly, in imperial or colonial encounters, it is eminently possible to get 'walloped for sayin' that word,' but the punishment is not on the basis of what the word means but what it represents, unacceptable otherness.

Crockett is unwittingly expressing an important truth about particular forms of language contact and the role of translation. Justice is inseparable from the conditions of utterance and the politics of language reception. In other words, saying a word for what's right can only be effective if speakers are free to use the words and languages of their own choosing and if their listeners, coming from a different language group, are prepared to extend the courtesy of translation. There can be none of the ethical universalism envisaged by Crockett if there is no awareness of the context and forms of expression. Getting walloped for using the wrong words is a metonym for forms of dispossession, both material and cultural, which mean that the politics of language in the Western can never be an idle or innocent affair.

One way of circumventing the challenge of language difference is to present 'wordless' versions of the other language community. The motion picture with soundtrack is a powerful vehicle for the portrayal of cultures as an identifiable sequence of sights and sounds. The scene in the *cantina* is one of music and dance, and distinctive music and dance routines become ready signifiers for Mexican culture. It is striking that in a much later film such as *Babel*, which we will discuss in Chapter 4, Mexico is again depicted largely through the images of dance and the sound of music in the extended wedding scene. When Crockett, Bowie and their companions go to rustle cattle from Mexican army, as they wade through water, passing under the noses of

Spanish officers, what holds the attention of the officers is the performance of a flamenco dancer. Already Bowie suggests a possible frame for the representation of Mexicans when he claims that, 'today's important to them, not the dollar that tomorrow might bring.' Playing the card of cultural relativism he admits the 'Yankee says that's lazy' but 'for me I say it's a way of living.' The Mexican army may represent a genuine military threat but the Mexicans are more often than not associated with playtime, leisure, the carnivalesque.

The images of distinctive dress and recognizable steps and the sounds of specific music reinforce a particular form of exoticization of the other. What is important to note is these representations rely almost exclusively on visual and aural messages. The only Mexican who speaks at any length is Graciela, a privilege granted by her class and political sympathies, but most of her spoken dialogue on the screen is in English. The Mexican Spanish speakers are observable on screen, we hear orders and brief utterances in Spanish, but there is little sense in which they act as hermeneutic subjects. They are there to play their allotted roles as local sympathizers or as professional soldiers but there is no sense in which the audience are afforded the glimpses of an inner life which is so evident in the case of a Crockett, Bowie or even Travis. In the absence of extended speech in Spanish and without an extensive use of translators, the Mexican citizens are largely silenced by the predominantly monolingual soundtrack. Or rather it is their speech that goes largely uncomprehended. The music can still be heard, but whether the music can do anything more than titillate the jaded palates of weary horsemen is an open question. The frontier may be an unstable, unpredictable place but even at the heart of anti-structure the future structures of power and language hegemony are clearly discernible.

When Major Famborough (Maury Chaykin) asks Lieutenant Dunbar (Kevin Costner) in *Dances with Wolves* (1990) why a decorated officer wants to be sent to a remote posting, he replies that 'he always wanted to see the frontier' and, in particular, he wanted to see it 'before it's gone.' Before the credits roll at the end of the film, a short text informs the audience of the eventual fate of the Sioux people and 'how the American frontier was soon to pass into history.' The American frontier was, of course, the creation of history in the first place and one could say that the frontier passed not so much into history as into myth. Part of the myth was that the 'Indians' were bogeymen, either menacingly silent or vociferously violent. The most successful Western ever in box-office terms and winner of seven Oscars, *Dances with Wolves*, however, presents a direct challenge to this myth. In Kevin Costner's film it is the native Americans not the white settlers who do most of the talking. Not only do they do most of the talking, but the Sioux in the film do it in their own language, Lakota. The film is a striking illustration of the thesis that translation issues are at the heart of any serious interrogation of stereotype and that a sensitivity to questions of translation and language difference is fundamental to any investigation of cultural realities distorted by reductive falsehoods.

Talking the talk

When he finally reaches Fort Sedgewick, Lieutenant Dunbar finds that there is no one there. The previous garrison had abandoned their posts for want of supplies and Dunbar begins a Robinson Crusoe-like existence, building, repairing, organizing and, the literate addendum to the activities of the busy settler, keeping a diary. The diary provides a counterpoint to, or reflexive commentary on, the images of Dunbar's gradual transformation. The illusion of solitude is just that, an illusion. There are the animals, his horse, Cisco, and the wolf he names 'Two Socks.' Even more importantly for his future development there are the Sioux inhabitants of the Great Plains. As he soon realizes, this is no *terra nullius* waiting to be made legible by the descriptive ordinances of the white settler but a land that is already occupied by a people who have a profound and intimate sense of place. But to reach that awareness, Dunbar has to be able to communicate with the community he comes to refer to as his 'neighbors.' The film dwells on the process of communication, not evacuating it or taking it for granted but foregrounding the means as much as the ends of communication.

When Dunbar arrives at the Sioux camp for the first time bearing the injured Stand With a Fist (Mary McDonnell) his comment that 'She's hurt' causes consternation. Nobody has any idea what he is saying and the young warrior Wind in his Hair (Rodney A. Grant) advances threateningly and shouts at Dunbar to go away. Dunbar does not understand what Wind in His Hair has said and repeats, 'No, she's hurt' and the warrior shouts at him again saying that Dunbar is not wanted. The contact scene is one of mutual misunderstanding. There is no common language and no translation and, in the absence of both, hostility and suspicion are to the fore. Before Dunbar arrives at the camp, there is a classic master-of-all-he-surveys moment where he arrives at the brow of the hill and looks down over the Sioux camp. The visual mastery is soon undone, however, by his linguistic vulnerability. The limits to his understanding become apparent when he receives his first visit from the medicine man Kicking Bird (Graham Greene) and Wind in the Hair. His greeting 'Hi' and hand wave cause puzzlement not only to the two Sioux delegated to speak with him but to the warriors waiting in the distance. When he makes gestures imitating a buffalo, Wind in the Hair concludes that the army officer has taken leave of his senses. Kicking Bird eventually concludes that Dunbar must be referring to buffalos and he uses the Lakota word, *tatanka*. The word is mispronounced by Dunbar whose pronunciation is then corrected by Kicking Bird. Dunbar, in turn, uses the word buffalo which Kicking Bird tries to pronounce saying 'buff.' So what we have is an initial translation scene where the army officer and the Sioux medicine man try to find some form of rough equivalence.

The scene shows that in translation nothing can be taken for granted. The hand wave is meaningless to the Sioux and in a second scene where Dunbar hams it up as he operates a coffee grinder, he finds that humor is no more universal than gesture as the Sioux stare back at him in solemn incomprehension. The language of the Sioux proves to be as difficult to pronounce as English and Kicking Bird is careful to correct Dunbar's pronunciation and obviously does not hold with his language being spoken carelessly. Wind in the Hair and Kicking Bird are not speaking in the pidgin English of the comic book 'Indian' but in Lakota, and in the contact scene both Lakota and English have equal status. The fact that the Sioux are not always already translated into the broken English of the conventional villains but are accorded the dignity of subtitles has an effect that is at once alienating and alluring. Alienating because non-Lakota-speaking spectators are presented with a language that is wholly other, utterly different from English, and which is a constant reminder of the very distinct cultural and linguistic identity of the Sioux. Dunbar's great difficulty in pronouncing a simple word in Lakota shows the full complexity of the language spoken by his 'neighbors.' For this reason, any attempt to translate between the two languages will be anything but easy.

The alluring presence of subtitles lies in their according to the Sioux the status of hermeneutic subjects where the members of the community can express a full range of sentiments, even if the actors in the film speak a somewhat simplified version of Lakota. There is a sense then for the audience that they have a greater awareness of the richness and depth of Sioux culture because members of the community are going about their business in their native language. Spectators are accorded the courtesy of professional subtitles rather than the caricature of defective self-translation of the 'me see iron horse' genre.

Dunbar becomes increasingly aware of the necessity of translation in his relationship with the Sioux community. He notes in his diary that, 'real communication is slow[…]and the quiet one [Kicking Bird] is as frustrated as I am.' He wants to ask about the young woman he found injured on the prairie but admits that it seemed, 'far too complicated a subject given our limitations.' Dunbar, as he himself observes, is not the only person frustrated by translation difficulties. Kicking Bird is equally preoccupied, but his concerns are more strategic. It is not simply a question of getting to know the neighbors better, he is worried about the future of his people. To this end, he asks Stand With a Fist to act as an interpreter. Stand With a Fist was born the daughter of white settlers and was originally called Christine, but she lost her parents as the result of a dispute with Pawnee warriors and the orphan came to live among the Sioux. Kicking Bird pleads with a reluctant Stand With a Fist to take on the translation task and tells her that he is asking her 'on behalf of all our people.'

The reason for the request is that Dunbar will be able to provide information on the white man. Here there is a reversal of the usual terms of exchange where it is the white settler rather than the native who becomes the informant. Dunbar is seen as a potential source of information, which is deemed to be vital to the survival of the Sioux community and translation is duly recruited to the cause of self-preservation. The army lieutenant becomes aware of his role in the economy of information and confesses on more than one occasion that he was holding himself back, reluctant to answer all the questions put to him by Kicking Bird. He even notes the complicity of the interpreter in this retention of information claiming that 'Stand With a Fist knows I'm holding back but to her credit, she says nothing.' The interpreter, for her part, is not untypically between two cultures and two languages. When Dunbar does come to speak with Kicking Bird for the first session where an interpreter is present, Stand With a Fist speaks in hesitant and broken English. Partly through lack of practice and partly through repression of childhood trauma, the words in her first language do not come easily.

Stand With a Fist has been fully translated into Sioux language and culture but what her job as bilateral interpreter reminds her is that translation is a bi-directional process. Stand with the Fist is, like many other interpreters discussed in this volume, female. The gender dimension is crucial to the working out of the film's narrative in that a relationship develops between Dunbar and Stand with the Fist, which ultimately culminates in marriage. So the language lessons become a form of extended courtship and sexual attraction is intermixed with cultural curiosity in a blend that is a familiar trope in the literature of the exotic (Forsdick 2005). Furthermore, Lakota is a language which is morphologically marked for gender and particularly with regard to the use of enclitics, forms change depending on the gender of the speaker. All of the actors in *Dances with Wolves* use the female form of the language throughout the film despite the obvious incongruity for native speakers of Lakota (Mithun 1999).

Stand with a Fist must work in both English and Lakota, and for that reason she must re-acquaint herself with her native language. However, though her fluency greatly improves, she retains throughout the film an accent that would tend to place her as a non-native speaker of her mother tongue. So as she interprets for Dunbar and Kicking Bird, the audience are constantly made aware of the interpreter herself as a translated being and of the effort that it costs her to constantly move between Lakota and English. The extent of the effort is revealed in Dunbar's initial efforts to learn Lakota. When he says what he thinks is the sentence 'That man is a warrior,' his tutor, Stand With a Fist, bursts out laughing because what Dunbar has, in effect, said is, 'That man is a bone.' Here it is the white settler not the native American who appears linguistically inept as he struggles with the rudiments of one of the Sioux languages. What is apparent is that the acquisition of Lakota is a major challenge, and that, by extension, trying to mediate between languages which are not in any way cognate is a significant task. It is that distance which shadows the accented English of Stand With a Fist and demands time and effort from Dunbar as he initiates himself into Sioux culture and language. It is time and effort that reveals the true complexity of Sioux culture and undermines the stereotypes of 'beggars and thieves,' which Dunbar repeatedly refers to, stereotypes that are powerfully reinforced by linguistic incomprehension.

The perils of challenging the stereotypes are brought home to Dunbar at the end of the film when he returns to retrieve his diary from Fort Sedgewick only to find that the army have finally arrived at the outpost. He is wearing Sioux dress and is mistaken by the soldiers for an 'Indian' and they proceed to start shooting at him, killing his horse. If the metaphor of dress was repeatedly used in earlier centuries to describe the process of translation, translation from one language to another analogous to a change of dress (Hermans 1985: 105), the film picks up this visual metaphor to present Dunbar in his altered or translated state. The army officers ask him repeatedly why he is out of uniform and the taunt by one of the more brutal officers is that he 'turned Injun.' The attractiveness of dress as metaphor is that, like metaphor itself, dress both conceals and reveals. Dunbar's dress conceals his identity as the army officer, Lieutenant John J. Dunbar, but reveals his new identity as the Sioux Dances with Wolves. Going native is not perceived, however, as wholly disadvantageous. He is made an offer, 'Now if you will guide us to these camps and serve as an interpreter, your conduct will be re-evaluated.' When Dunbar fails to respond to the offer his own position is made clearer, 'Your status as a traitor might improve if you choose to cooperate with the United State Army.' Dunbar's choices are framed in terms of competing loyalties. If he is loyal to the United States army, he will betray his Sioux companions, giving information on their whereabouts. If he remains loyal, on the other hand, to his adopted community, then he will be considered a 'traitor' by the Army and duly tried for dereliction of duty.

What is striking is that the question of loyalty is presented as a choice concerning translation. If Dunbar consents to work as an interpreter for the army, if he agrees, in other words, to practice what we have described earlier as an autonomous form of translation, then his loyalty will be no longer in doubt and his conduct can be 're-evaluated.' The return of the native, however, is rarely comforting. Return offers the promise of closure, the synthesis of retrospection, the gathering in after the voyage out. But in the biblical account, the Prodigal Son is a figure of disquiet and Ulysses' arrival in Ithaca is marked by a bloodbath. The Bible and Homer intimate that return usually unsettles, disturbing the settled community. The dilemma for inter-preters in colonial contexts is whether they can remain unaffected by contact. The risk for their masters is that they not only go native but also that they stay native. Dunbar's return to what he had earlier described as his 'home,' the army post of Fort Sedgewick, is deeply unsettling for his army colleagues, who wonder whether they should 'salute him or shoot him.' Any questions about his loyalties are answered by Dunbar through the medium of language, but the language now is Lakota not English.

He begins by giving his Sioux name, *Shu-mani-tu-tonka Ob' Wa-chi*, Dances with Wolves, and continues in Lakota, 'I have nothing to say to you. You are not worth speaking to.' Of course, Dunbar's statement is something of a performative contradiction. By speaking in a native American language, far from saying 'nothing,' he is saying a great deal and particularly in view of the offer of an interpreting assignment, translation as a form of redemption, he is signaling not only his new linguistic loyalty but also his identification with his new community. It is his ability to speak English that saves him from immediate execution, he is able to tell his story to, albeit skeptical, army officers, a shared language making him available as a subject of enquiry. When Dunbar refuses to speak that language, and by extension to work as an interpreter into that language, the message to his fellow army officers is clear, Dunbar has 'turned Injun' and betrayed the interests of white settlers. The opacity of his new language reveals the limits of comprehension and tolerance of the colonists, who believe as did the Elizabethan poet Edmund Spenser speaking of Ireland that, 'the speech being Irish, the heart must needs be Irish for out of the abundance of the heart the tongue speaketh' (Spenser 1970: 68).

Dunbar's gesture of defiance is articulated through naming, he gives his name in Lakota to the army officers. It is, of course, a translation of Dunbar's name in Lakota that gives the film its title. In the first scene at which Stand With a Fist is present as an interpreter, much of the sequence is given over to the identification of names. Stand With a Fist makes liberal use of gestures to communicate the names to Dunbar, as if names were not readily translatable and did not admit easy equivalence. Stand With a Fist is well placed to understand the importance or significance of naming as we learn from an earlier episode in the film that she was formerly called 'Christine' when she lived with her settler parents. She later explains the story to Dunbar of how she got her new name, which involved standing up to bullying by an older woman in the community. When she first hears Dunbar's name, she thinks he is saying 'Dunbear,' trying to translate his name in an image that might make some sense for the Sioux. Names as a class of proper nouns pose particular difficulties for translators (Tymoczko 1999). Should the names be left unchanged or transliterated, or the meaning of the name be translated into another language? If the meaning of the name is to be translated into another language, the question is raised as to whether the name has any meaning in the other language as it is taken out of its context of origin in the source language. Stand With a Fist makes little sense as a translated name in English if there no is understanding of how the name came to be. Maria Tymoczko has described how cultures with names that had clear referents in terms of the relationship between the name and the person named, gradually came to be dominated by cultures of naming where the a person's name or names did not bear any necessary or explicit relationship to the person named. As a result, previous cultures of naming were deemed primitive or simply comic as is almost invariably the case in stereotypical presentations of 'wild Indians,' their names further evidence of their hopelessly fallen state.

Naming is inextricably bound up with power and the demand that names be either suppressed or be translated is a recognizable consequence of conquest. When Lieutenant Dunbar arrives at Fort Sedgewick he is taken aback by the state of disrepair of the abandoned outpost. As he settles into his new home, he declares that the 'country's everything I dreamed it would be' and that 'there can be no place like this on earth.' Dunbar's initial isolation and the repeated wide-angle shots of the surrounding countryside suggest not only Crusoe but Adam. Dunbar inhabits a new Eden, and one of the traditional Adamic attributes is the authority to name. So it is that he decides to name the wolf who comes regularly to the fort, 'Two Socks.' In a sense, his own fantasy of frontier, of wide, open spaces, appears to becomes a reality out on the Great Plains. Having survived near-death and amputation, he experiences rebirth in his prairie posting. But his earthly paradise is threatened by the traces of the fallen.

He finds animals rotting in a lake and, on closer inspection, notes that the animals have been shot not poisoned. He wonders what kind of people did this and notes in his diary, 'I can make no sense of the clues left me here.' But there is one clue that takes Dunbar most of the film to try to work out and that is the very name of his outpost, Fort Sedgewick. This European name, which is an alien presence in the native topography of place, shows that in advance of settlement the explorers and the cartographers and the military are beginning to translate the Great Plains into a language that the white settlers can understand. Naming, then, is an act of appropriation, a form of possession, which prefigures the translation – in the sense of physical displacement – of large numbers of white settlers to the area. Kicking Bird, like Dunbar, is equally preoccupied by the need to understand what is happening to him and his people and admits to the Chief, Ten Bears (Floyd Red Crow Westerman) that there are good and bad 'signs' and that some signs are 'strange' and 'difficult to understand.' Alone among the Sioux, Kicking Bird makes an effort to learn some English as if he were trying to decipher the foreign signs and arrive at a better understanding of the long-term intentions of the speakers of 'white words.' Both Dunbar and Kicking Bird are trying to translate the cultures they are confronted with into a language that they can grasp and in the hope that they may be able to avert cultural meltdown and ecological catastrophe.

It is easy to accuse Costner of sentimentalizing native Americans and offering a recycled version of the Noble Savage of the Enlightenment. However, such a critique ignores the internal evidence of the film which points to the inherent difficulty in any attempt to translate into or out of another language and culture. In a scene in the film where Wind in His Hair and his fellow warriors celebrate a successful expedition that involved the killing of a number of white settlers, Dunbar confesses that as he looked at familiar faces he felt that the 'gap between us was much greater than I ever could have imagined.' As the celebrations continue into the night, he felt that 'it was hard to know where to be.' Like his acquisition of the language, Dunbar's progress in getting to know his Sioux companions takes time and, crucially, what this involves is his dwelling among the people. Initially sustained by a notion of universality (implied in the language of gesture), by a sense of being a citizen of the world, he gradually comes to realize the significance of being a denizen, of being a person who knowingly inhabits and moves through a particular place.

An illusion of ready understanding is undermined by the cultural and linguistic distance that the film repeatedly brings to the fore, as if to emphasize that careful translation of a culture requires not only the requisite attention to language but also an acknowledgement of an otherness that cannot be wished away in the multicultural bonhomie of feasting. Indeed, in the celebrations that follow on from the successful buffalo hunt, tension emerges when one of the Sioux takes Dunbar's military hat and refuses to hand it back on the grounds that because he found it, the hat was his. Wind in the Hair brokers a deal that avoids further argument but the existence of very different notions of what constitutes private property and ownership are some of the many intercultural faultlines which compromise any facile version of understanding. Similarly, Dunbar has difficulty in understanding the precise reasons for the Sioux going into battle because there was no 'dark political objective' nor were the battles 'a fight for territory or riches or to make men free.' What he understands as he becomes more and more skilful in Lakota is how much remains to be understood. The extent of the 'gap between us' also reveals how problematic translation is as a process and how much time must be properly invested if translation is to be based on genuine understanding. When Kicking Bird tells Dunbar in English at the end of the film, 'we come far, you and me,' he is pointing to the distance that must be travelled if translation is to be a meaningful exercise.

In a scene that occurs shortly before Dunbar returns to Fort Sedgewick to retrieve his diary, Ten Bears slowly removes a cloth covering the helmet of a Spanish conquistador. He then talks of their successors, the Mexicans and later, in his time, of the Texans who 'take without asking.' The scene offers an abbreviated history of colonization in the Americas which proved so dramatic in their consequences for the indigenous peoples of the continent. But 'asking' implies an act of communication, an acknowledgement that the other has a language and is worth talking to and is not to be coerced into silence. When Dunbar finally leaves the Sioux camp in the company of Stand With a Fist, he tells Ten Bears that 'I must find people who will listen to me.' His desire to translate what he has heard and experienced into an alternative account of the 'wild Indian' represents the final frontier, the most arduous of all, the frontier of understanding. But understanding is not all, misunderstanding too is part of the experience of translation and what is more, rich in comic not only tragic possibility. In the next chapter, the question will be asked as to why translation should make us laugh as well as cry.

3   Translation howlers

A Night at the Opera to *Borat*

Before 1800, Europe had sent between two and three million people to her transatlantic colonies. However, between 1800 and 1961 a staggering 61 million Europeans moved across the Atlantic (de Landa 2000: 151). The majority of these migrants left Europe in a 70-year period. The historian Alfred Crosby stressed the singularity of the phenomenon:

> And so the Europeans came between the 1840's and World War I, the greatest wave of humanity ever to cross oceans and probably the greatest that ever will cross oceans. This Caucasian tsunami began with the starving Irish and the ambitious Germans and with the British, who never reached the peaks of emigration as high as some other nationalities, but who have an inextinguishable yearning to leave home. The Scandinavians joined the exodus next, and then towards the end of the century, the southern and eastern European peasantry. Italians, Poles, Spaniards, Portuguese, Hungarians, Greeks, Serbs, Czechs, Slovaks, Ashkenazic Jews – for the first time in the possession of knowledge of the opportunities overseas and, via railroad and steamship, of the means to live a life of ancient poverty behind – poured through the ports of Europe and across the seams of Pangaea.
>
> (Crosby 1989: 300)

These migrants brought with them different cultures, but above all, different languages. Linguistic diversity was an inescapable fact of the Old World, and part of the challenge for the New was what to do with this diversity. Cinema as a medium both produced by and watched by the migrants that poured across the Atlantic was inevitably going to become a site for the challenges and concerns which clustered around language difference. How were the many languages of the migrants to be 'translated' into the new linguistic and cultural reality of the United States, the country which emerges after the First World War as the leading producer of motion pictures? One way of exploring the tensions implicit in language encounter was through parody or satire, laughter both a guide and a caution to the hybrid polity coming into being.

In *A Night at the Opera* (1935), Sam Wood directs a film that uses comedy to examine the manifold consequences of translation for a society which had come through one of the most profound shifts in population in modern history. The screenplay by George S. Kaufman and Morrie Ryskind is continually alive to the nuances of language difference as they foreground the tangled politics of language in the New World on screen. The film begins not surprisingly in the Old World in Rome, where arts patron Mrs Claypool (Margaret Dumont), her business manager Otis B. Driftwood (Groucho Marx) and Herbert Gottlieb (Siegfried Rumann), Director of the New York Opera Company, are involved in a deal to bring the tenor Rodolfo Lassparri (Walter King) to New York to sing. But this is an Old World which is already in a sense the New. All the characters speak English and only signs and forms of address such as *signore* and *signora*, and signs such as '*Entrata alla Platea*,' alert the spectator to the fact that this is not New York but Rome. A further metonymic reminder of the foreignness of the location is accent. This is most notably the case in the person of Fiorello (Chico Marx) who becomes involved in a plot to bring Ricardo Baroni (Allan Jones) to America to sing with his sweetheart Rosa (Kitty Carlisle). Fiorello is given a stereotypical Italian accent ('The Manager he a fix everything') and this accent is retained throughout the film.

It is notable, however, that while Fiorello has a strongly marked accent and distinctive non-native syntax, his putative compatriots Rosa and Ricardo do not. The Old World has been translated linguistically into the New but, in order to sustain an illusion of the Old, the translation remainder is a random concoction of signage, foreign accent and foreign food (the first shot of Gottlieb is of the Director of the New York Opera Company struggling with a plate of spaghetti). Italian-speaking migrants were no doubt sensitive to the anomaly of a predominantly Anglophone Italy, but, of course, Italian migrants were only one of the many migrant communities in the United States. For other non-Italian-speaking spectators the remainder was a reminder. That is to say, the gestures toward language difference established a sense of otherness without compromising a myth of transparency, that what translation on screen showed was that the culture of the Old World could be accessible in the language of the New.

Migrations

This is not to say that there are not lingering anxieties about the relationship between language and culture of origin. Part of the *raison d'être* of the film is to bring an Italian tenor to New York to sing an Italian opera *Il Trovatore* in his native language. Mrs Claypool in an accent close to English Received Pronunciation haughtily declares to a skeptical Driftwood that even in the arena of lovemaking, 'I think the Europeans do it better.' There may indeed be a prestige associated with the earlier cultural production of Europe rooted in native languages and championed by Europhiles like Mrs Claypool, the

German-speaker Gottlieb and the affluent opera-going public in New York, but the medium in which Mrs Claypool appears begins to tell a different story. When Ricardo pours out his affections to the departing Rosa from an Italian quayside, he sings in English not Italian. This is the language of the Hollywood musical rather than the Italian opera. Ricardo bursts into song further on in the film in an extended song and dance sequence set in the steerage section of the ship on its voyage to the United States. The sequence is crucial not only because versions will be played out in later films like *Titanic* (1997) but also because it clearly signals migrant diversity which melds into the dominant idiom of Hollywood, the new homeland of the new medium.

The scene on the lower deck when the trio of Fiorello, Tomasso and Ricardo arrive is already reminiscent of a parody of light opera with mountains of spaghetti piled up on plates to which are added fruit, vegetables, bread and wine while the other travelers cheerily sing *Santa Lucia*. Spurred on by generous helpings of pasta, Ricardo then breaks into the second major song of the film 'Così Cosà.' As he sings and moves through the crowd on the deck, it becomes apparent that the migrants are dressed in a variety of regional peasant costumes and the dances are an eclectic mixture of different national styles including the French *cancan*. The song itself is about the Italian phrase 'così cosà' and the humorous intent of the song in English is that the phrase itself is, in fact, untranslatable. Ned Washington's lyrics tell us that it means neither yes nor no, but means both yes and no, and it is a phrase which in effect can mean everything and nothing. The phrase then becomes a general marker of 'Italianness' or rather a generalized Italian *bonhomie* rather than anything in particular. As it does not have a precise meaning, it can be invested with many meanings. The difficulty in translation makes paradoxically for its ease of translatability, a kind of catch-all phrase which can be used indifferently by non-native speakers of the language.

The song's significance stems from its setting. The migrants on the lower deck have already begun to merge in the dance routines where the different costumes and dance styles combine to produce the hybrid song and dance routine of the film musical. The voyage to the United States is above all a journey into translation. Traditions of dress and dance will be subsumed or more properly translated into new forms of popular culture. What is to going happen to food, costume and movement is also a fate that awaits language as the speakers of different languages find themselves on their way to being translated into an emerging form of English, US English, which is heavily marked by borrowings from various migrant languages (Bryson 1994). The untranslatable remainders of other languages (*così cosà*) go to expand the word stock of the language that will be the dominant host language for the migrants on their journey to a new world.

A Night at the Opera extracts much comic capital from the fact that translation might be seen to be inevitable but it is certainly not unproblematic. Part of the comedy derives from the fact that ambiguity is constantly

marshaled to show the humorous potential of mistranslation. When Fiorello
and Driftwood conclude an agreement to bring the Italian tenor to New
York (though they both have a different tenor in mind), Driftwood produces
a contract. The contract scene is partly a play on the sublanguages of
English and how misunderstanding can result from terms inappropriately
applied. Driftwood starts reading the contract for the illiterate Fiorello
saying, 'The party in the first part shall be known as the party in the first
part' and then goes on to say, 'the party in the second part shall be known as
the party in the second part.' When Fiorello intimates that he does not like
the second party, Driftwood replies, 'Well you should have gone to the first
party, we didn't get home till four in the morning.' The scene is partly a
parody of legal sublanguage in English but it is also a reminder that translation
is as much an intralingual as an interlingual phenomenon.

The language of contract is in a sense as impenetrable to native speakers
of the language as it is to foreign learners. Tearing off parts of the contract
as Driftwood reads through it is as much an admission of internal defeat
(impossible to translate the contract into intelligible, standard English) as it
is of external incomprehension (impossible to translate the contract into
anything that makes sense in any other language). In the pun on 'party'
Driftwood is, of course, exploiting his superior knowledge of the English
language, and it is the polysemic nature of language which is an obvious trap
for learners attempting to make sense of what they hear. What makes languages
difficult to translate, the presence of ambiguity, is also what makes them
difficult to learn. The pun, the verbal game, exposes the vulnerability of
language acquisition and the peculiar trials of translation. When Driftwood
at the end of his reading of the contract refers to the clause that the contract
is null and void if any of the parties to the contract are found to be mentally
unsound, he refers to the provision as the 'sanity clause.' Fiorello's response
is immediate, 'You aint foolin' me. There aint no Sanity Clause.' What the
scene draws on for comic effect is Fiorello's imperfect knowledge of the
English language revealed in the unwitting pun of 'sanity clause' and 'Santa
Claus.' He translates what he hears into what he knows, but knowledge and
understanding are not always co-terminous.

The migrant speaker translates what he hears into a known cultural
referent but his imperfect knowledge of the language leaves him open to the
pratfall of misunderstanding. On the other hand, his misconstrual of what he
hears reveals a creative dimension to migrant translation in that he brings
out a possible meaning to 'sanity clause,' which might have otherwise
remained opaque to native speakers of the language. The contract is the
basis of Fiorello and Driftwood's relationship and the reason for their journey to
the United States. The contract is a written document and part of Fiorello's
difficulty is, of course, that he cannot read or write. But the difficulty is further
compounded by the fact that although the scene takes place in English it is
not supposed to be his native language. His contractual relationship as a
migrant is not only with a new business partner but also with a new language,

and part of the difficulty is trying to understand the full implications of the language contract for his own sense of self and ability to communicate with others.

If contracts are as much about laws as language, a constant concern for Fiorello and his companions is their relationship as migrants to the law. They are, in fact, illegal, and part of the intrigue of the film revolves around trying to get them onto the ship in Italy and off the ship in New York. The device used to get them ashore in the United States is the object of a prolonged narrative development in the film and is centrally concerned with questions of language and translation. When Fiorello, Tomasso and Ricardo are rumbled as stowaways at the end of the musical meal on the lower deck, they are brought to a detention cabin. Tomasso manages to escape to another cabin occupied by three famous aviators, the Santopoulos brothers (Rolfe Sedan, Leo White, Jay Eaton), on their way to a triumphal reception in New York. They are bound and gagged and the three stowaways assume the identities of the hapless trio. It is at this stage that Driftwood assumes a new identity. When the delegation from City Hall arrives, Driftwood introduces himself saying, 'Gentlemen, our distinguished guests have asked me to represent them and act as their interpreter.' He is no ordinary interpreter, of course, and when the head of the City Hall delegation begins to read a prepared speech he is immediately interrupted by Driftwood who tears up the speech and declares, 'Let's cut this short. The whole thing's very simple. They want you to go to City Hall and the Mayor is going to make another speech and we can tear up the Mayor's speech when we get there.'

This comic and startling abuse of the power of the interpreter makes visible a mediator who is assumed to occupy a peripheral rather than a central role. By not doing his job, Driftwood shows just how important his job is. The point will be further stressed in the farcical episode of the aviators' public address in the presence of the Mayor. Fiorello recounts their famous aviation exploits but his account is so burlesque and improbable that some members of the audience began to have their doubts as to the identity of the visiting airmen. These doubts grow stronger as a mute Harpo is asked to speak and drinks glass after glass of water to stall the impossible. Sergeant Henderson (Robert Emmett O'Connor) from the Police Department eventually accuses the three of being 'phoneys.' Driftwood then goes over to the 'aviators' and an animated conversation takes place in what is apparent gibberish but is supposed to pass for a foreign language. Driftwood then turns to the Mayor saying, 'You hear what they say? They say they've never been so insulted in their life and they absolutely refuse to stay here.' The Mayor is aghast and pleads with Driftwood to tell the foreign guests that the police officer 'didn't mean' what he said. Driftwood starts speaking gobbledygook to two of the aviators and then they storm off. Driftwood leaves with them and his parting shot is, 'Of course, you know that this means war!'

The scene is entirely founded on the fundamental ambiguity of translation. The presence of the interpreter is based on an ideal of understanding, what

Figure 2 Otis B. Driftwood (Groucho Marx) interpreting for foreign aviators and official delegation.

A Night at the Opera (1935) Directed by Sam Wood, USA: Metro-Goldwyn-Mayer (MGM)

translation is supposed to do, among other things, is to allow people to understand each other. What happens in the scene, through the manipulative agency of Driftwood and the power conferred on him by his putative language ability, is that people misunderstand each other, a misunderstanding that is given a further comic edge by the bellicose declaration, 'Of course, you know that this means war!' Behind the humorous conceits of Driftwood is genuine unease about language difference. The foreign aviators come to New York to be feted, but the difficulty is can they be trusted? Are foreigners not all the same (the aviators have identical beards and identical uniforms), and, more importantly, do they not all sound the same in their linguistic otherness? Fiorello gives his false account of aviation prowess in heavily accented Italian English and then speaks gibberish to Driftwood and both are accorded the same status of being a 'foreign' language. Henderson, the police officer, senses they are phoneys not because Fiorello speaks a relatively fluent variety of English but because Tomasso's beard comes unstuck. If one cannot be sure what the other is saying, is there not ample opportunity for deception and manipulation? And even if translators are brought into the picture, what is to stop those translators becoming a party to the deceit as happens in the case of Driftwood? It is worth remembering that the scene is taking place at a liminal moment in the film, the point of entry into United States. The reception is taking place in the contact zone between the Old World and the New. This is the zone of language contact, Fiorello makes an effort to speak in English, and of language difference, Driftwood must 'interpret' for the foreign aviators. But translation emerges as much of a problem as a solution.

The real aviators are there to visit the United States but the false aviators want to stay. They are migrants rather than visitors. Part of the drama for migrants is that they must acquire an identity which is not only legally founded, but that can also be made to cohere in language as well. When Fiorello in an aside to Driftwood asks him what he should say, Driftwood replies, 'Tell them you're not here.' Fiorello then wonders, 'What if they don't believe me,' to which Driftwood retorts, 'They'll believe you when you start talking.' Later on, when Fiorello affirms, 'I know what I'm talking about,' Driftwood interjects, 'That's a novelty.' Implicit in Driftwood's witty rejoinders is the sense that because it is a foreigner speaking to the crowd in a language not his own that the language somehow counts for less, that in a certain sense, he might as well be 'not here.' Fiorello is loudly applauded at the end of his speech although it is manifest nonsense. Earlier in the film when Driftwood first meets Fiorello, he wants to know the name of the tenor he represents and Fiorello's reply is merciless, 'Who cares? I can't pronounce it.' His remark points to the particular drama of naming for the migrant moving to a new culture and language. It is the drama highlighted by Eva Hoffman in her memoir *Lost in Translation*. Hoffman and her sister are taken by their guardian, Mr Rosenberg, to a school in Vancouver where they are to learn English. They have arrived as immigrants from Poland and Ewa is not too keen on speaking the harsh-sounding language of the children in the schoolyard. One morning, she and her sister are renamed. 'Ewa' becomes 'Eva' and her sister 'Alina' is rechristened 'Elaine':

> My sister and I hang our heads wordlessly under this careless baptism ...
> We make our way back to a bench at the back of the room; nothing
> much has happened, except a small, seismic mental shift. The twist in
> our names takes them a tiny distance from us – but it's a gap which the
> infinite hobgoblin of abstraction enters. Our Polish names didn't refer to
> us; they were as surely us as our eyes or our hands. These new appela-
> tions, which we can't yet pronounce, are not us. They are identification
> tags, disembodied signs pointing to objects that happen to be my sister
> and myself. We walk to our seats, into a roomful of unknown faces, with
> names that make us strangers to ourselves.
>
> (Hoffman 1989: 105)

The change from Ewa to Eva is the beginning of a long odyssey of translation for Hoffman, reconstructed as a new North American referent to match
her new name. The gap persists, however imperceptible, and Hoffman
struggles as she grows into adulthood with the trauma of a translated self. So
there is an appropriateness in the calling upon Tomasso to speak as he, of

course, cannot. His congenital silence articulates at a different level the potential muting of the voice of the migrant, silenced by the indifference of the more powerful host language. Driftwood is literally rendered speechless by Tomasso. There is nothing for him to do if there is nothing to translate. So translation always implies that there is something to be articulated, a message to be communicated, and a context that facilitates the communication. Tomasso's immediate difficulty is that he is mute but the more general problem for his companions is that their status as illegal migrants could also extend to language, that they are somehow there under false linguistic pretences and that what the whole rocombolesque episode depicts is the enormous potential for misunderstanding in language shift.

Popular culture

A Night at the Opera remains, however, a cautionary tale against any facile binary division of people, languages or their cultures, or of easy essentialist distinctions between natives and newcomers. Translating between language A and language B involves, of necessity, a highly differentiated picture of what constitutes culture A and culture B. Gottlieb, a migrant who utters the German expletive *Schweinhund* when he is particularly irritated, retains the accent of his origins but he is fully integrated into US society and occupies an eminent position in the New York arts scene. He travels first-class with the other privileged passengers on the S.S. *Americus*. His prestige, indeed, could be said to rely on his association with the musical culture of the Old World, the European continent that Mrs Claypool describes as producing superior lovers. Mrs Claypool as a socially ambitious member of society in the New World is eager to seize on the cultural capital offered by aligning herself with the artistic projects of Gottlieb. The host society in the United States is not one undifferentiated bloc with all class distinctions dissolved in the comforting crucible of representative democracy.

The opening scene with the imperious Mrs Claypool shouting in an upper-class accent to the foreign waiter (on the principle that speaking a foreign language interferes with your hearing) is centrally concerned with class in the new as much as the old society. Otis B. Driftwood's express mission is to introduce Mrs Claypool into 'society.' As if to indicate the scope of his ambition, Driftwood keeps referring to his patron as 'my good woman.' The phrase self-consciously repeated to enhance the parodic inappropriateness of Mrs Claypool's social climbing, nonetheless indicates that if distinctions are about anything in a society, they crucially involve language. If Mrs Claypool is to be elevated among her peers, she must not only bankroll the artistic ambitions of Gottlieb, but she must also be translated into a different register, a new kind of language that will make her socially as new. The significance of this intralingual translation is borne out in reverse in the extended scene that gives its name to the film, the opening night of the opera *Il Trovatore* in New York. The scene itself plays heavily on opposition between elite culture and popular culture. Fiorello and Tomasso turn up as conductors and then improvise a baseball game. Driftwood walks through the aisles throwing packets of peanuts to members of the audience as he if were in a sports stadium rather than an opera house. The score for *Il Trovatore* is surreptitiously replaced by music for the waltz, 'Take Me Out to the Ball Game.' When Driftwood makes a speech in place of the missing Gottlieb, the genre is more appropriate to vaudeville comedy than the gala opening night of a prestigious Italian opera.

Driftwood causes further consternation when he accidentally drops his top hat from his box and shouts down to an audience member in formal dress, 'Hey Jordie, will you toss up that Kelly.' When the member obliges he causes further offence by throwing down a tip saying, 'Atta boy, here, give yourself a stogie.' The language register is clearly from the wrong side of the tracks and Driftwood's colloquialisms are a calculated affront to the social standing of the opera goers. Although opera ironically had its own origins in Italian popular culture, successive translations of the art form through time and place have led to the genre being closely associated with class privilege. It is, of course, no accident that it is one of most of the spectacularly successful forms of popular culture, cinema, which acts as the instrument for the presentation of class tensions in US society. By mobilizing music (the waltz), sport (baseball), performance (stand-up comedy) and language (Driftwood's colloquial register), the director brings together the most potent manifestations of popular culture to suggest that culture is always plural and that no cultural form enjoys uncontested hegemony. When translators as part of their education are expected to acquire an in-depth knowledge of the different cultures associated with their working languages, this education is as much an exercise in cultural humility as it is a precondition for effective performance. The need to know (you never know when knowledge of a particular form will come in useful when translating) is also the need to be aware of how linguistically diverse and culturally variegated societies are, no matter how often they are fingered as culturally or linguistically homogenous.

If cinema as a form of popular culture is firmly rooted, as we saw in the first chapter, in various forms of popular entertainment, it is noteworthy that *A Night at the Opera* continually poses the question of cinema as a form of entertainment, which may or may not be beholden to language difference. Harpo Marx as Tomasso does not, of course, speak in the film and his on-screen presence is a reminder of the silent origins of cinema itself. Many of the gags for which he is responsible, such as the making of sandwiches with cigars and tie ends in the hotel room after they have been unmasked at the welcome reception, are primarily visual. They would have worked as effectively in the silent era as in the period of the talking pictures. What characterizes these gags, of course, is that they do not involve language. They may be specific to particular cultures and to what particular cultures are likely to find funny, but they do not of themselves depend on words or language to achieve comic effect. In that respect, they point to an important dimension of comedy – its non-verbal components, components that do not require the explicit translation of the subtitle even though translation takes place at another level, as it is by no means the case that all cultures find everything equally funny (Antoine and Wood 1999).

Where Tomasso does break his silence is when he takes up his instrument. What happens, in fact, is that it is his audience not he who is silenced. The children who react hysterically to his clowning on the lower deck lapse into reverential attention once Tomasso's fingers bring the harp to life. Music, as the title of the film suggests, figures prominently in *A Night at the Opera* and again gestures to the world of popular entertainment from which film emerged and against which it, in a sense, competed. The music played by Tomasso and Fiorello is purely instrumental and it is, of course, possible to appreciate the two major songs in the film, 'Alone' and 'Così Cosà,' without understanding the lyrics. Thus, music, like the visual gags and Tomasso's clowning, point to forms of communication beyond language, forms that would appear to eschew the necessity of translation and bring the spectator back to the putative, universal filmic language of the silent era. However, their effect in the context of talking pictures is to show through their very difference that once language enters the picture, nothing is ever quite the same again.

Pseudo-language

Not all of the migrants to the New World were economic. As the political situation worsened in Europe in the inter-war years, many refugees tried desperately to escape to America in flight from the totalitarian dictatorships that were asphyxiating democratic life on the continent. Charlie Chaplin, who had become world famous in the silent era, wanted to make audiences aware of how the threat to democracy from demagogues like Adolf Hitler was very real. In *The Great Dictator* (1940), which he wrote and directed himself, and in which he starred, Chaplin uses comedy as a way of exposing the ludicrousness of Hitler's ambitions and the utterly sinister consequences of his pathological anti-semitism. The project implied from the outset a very real translation problem in that Hitler spoke only in German and the effects of his political actions were being felt primarily in non-Anglophone countries. How would Adenoid Hynkel, the dictator of Tomania, appear credible as a caricature of Hitler in a film that was to appear in English? How would verisimilitude be obtained if the cast was to be exclusively English-speaking?

Chaplin's solution was to have the dictator in the film, Adenoid Hynkel, partially speak a language which was a form of pseudo-German where actual German words such as 'Sauerkraut' and 'Wienerschnitzel' were randomly associated with fictitious German words such as 'shtunk.' This invented language was to give the appearance of sense and audible language difference. For German-speakers it is immediately obvious that Hynkel's 'German' is utterly meaningless, but this, in a sense, is part of the point. For all the emphatic gesticulation and verbal furore, the language comes across as empty bombast. For the English-language spectator who speaks no German, the language can sound like German but it is a 'German' which is so utterly different and strange in its rhetorical and phonological exaggeration that it becomes a parody of itself. In this play with language difference, Chaplin mobilizes translation as a means of further discrediting the dangerous ambitions of Hynkel's real-life model.

One of the earliest scenes in the film where we have Hynkel speak his native language is his address to the Sons and Daughters of the Double Cross. His speech is the first example of the ersatz German that will be used throughout the film. Adenoid Hynkel takes particular care to exaggerate the more guttural sounds in his language, which has the inevitable effect of provoking coughing fits. At the end of the extended opening sequence, a 'translation' is provided in the form of a voiceover which simply says, 'The Führer has just said that yesterday Tomania was down but today she has risen.' The voice of the interpreter is calm and matter of fact, and is in marked contrast to the histrionic delivery of Hynkel. The translation voice-over involving a highly condensed form of consecutive interpreting has a dual effect in the film. On the one hand, the very succinctness of the summary involves ironic deflation. For all the theatrical passion and explosive rhetoric, Hynkel's message is banal in the extreme. Translation by going to heart of the matter exposes the essential hollowness of what Hynkel has to say. On the other hand, the gap between the amount of time Hynkel spends saying what he has to say and the striking brevity of the interpretation can signal doubts as to the reliability and ultimate function of the translation process in the broadcast of Hynkel's speech.

These doubts increase toward the end of Hynkel's address where he launches into what appears to be a fierce and prolonged diatribe where the words 'France,' 'Finland,' 'Russia' and 'Blitzkrieg' among others can be made out. The consecutive interpretation in the voiceover is again disturbingly succinct, 'In conclusion, the Führer remarks that for the rest of the world he has nothing but peace in his heart.' It is apparent that the translation is less than adequate as the content is so obviously at variance with the vehemence of Hynkel's language. The comic ineptitude of the translation could be seen as evidence of the enrolment of translation in the propaganda process itself. Not only is Hynkel lying to his people but also through translation he lies to the world at large. That this might be the case is signaled by what is described as 'a pause for station identification.' Another voice is heard, which gives the occasion for Hynkel's address and then adds, 'The English interpreter is Herr Shtick, Adenoid Hynkel's personal translator who is apparently reading from a prepared script.' The information that the interpreter is 'apparently' reading from a prepared script does little to reassure the spectator that what they are getting is an accurate version of what Hynkel is actually saying. The suspicion is that the translation itself is part of the propaganda of appeasement, language difference being exploited to make it appear that Hynkel does not, in fact, mean what he appears to say. What generates the comedy of the translation moment, however, and what undermines its credibility even before the reference to the 'prepared script' is the starkness of the contrast between Hynkel's violent demeanor and the words that can be made out in English, and the apparent innocuousness of what the translation supposes him to say.

Crucial to the hybrid language Chaplin invents for Hynkel is that not everything needs to be translated. So in his address, Hynkel says 'Liberty shtunk' interpreted as 'Liberty is odious' and 'Free sprachen shtunk' is rendered as 'Free speech is objectionable.' There is a further reference to 'tighten die Belten' in a call to the people of Tomania to make sacrifices and tighten their belts. The insertion of obviously English words into Hynkel's language serves to further ridiculize him by making the foreign language seem somehow absurd in its putative difference. The fact that not everything Hynkel says is incomprehensible to his Anglophone audience does provide clues to what is at stake in his public orations. They are thus given some clues as to whether the official translation can be trusted or not.

As noted earlier, one of the repeated elements of bathos in *The Great Dictator* is the coughing fits brought on by the markedly guttural nature of Hynkel's speech. Another motif which is frequently employed is the

Figure 3 Adenoid Hynkel (Charlie Chaplin) addressing the rally of the Sons and Daughters of the Double Cross.

The Great Dictator (1940) Directed by Charles Chaplin, UK: Charles Chaplin Productions

exaggerated pronunciation of certain vowels corresponding to the use of the umlaut in German. What both these elements emphasize is the materiality of language, its particular phonic properties, so that what Hynkel's pseudo-German repeatedly emphasizes is the force of the signifier, the impact of the material form of words. This reaches its most extreme form in the tendency of Hynkel at certain points in the film to make snarling sounds. In his amorous advances toward his secretary he makes the same sounds which are to be heard in the more apoplectic moments of his public speechmaking, as when, for example, he orders the assaults on the Jewish ghettoes. His speech is broadcast over the public address system in the ghetto and, though no translation is offered and the language is incomprehensible in its ersatz form, the effects are all too obvious in the speed with which everyone clears the streets and seeks refuge inside. The transformation of Hynkel's speech into pure sound, the snarling and baring of teeth, suggests a non-human or animal-like dimension to his speech as if the fading of the possibility of translation was also the fading of the potential for humanity.

If the root of the word 'barbarian' is the Greek belief that non-Greek speakers were not capable of producing human language, they expressed this by pointing up the odd, formal property of foreign language-speakers, who appeared to the Greeks to 'stutter' as they spoke. The portrayal of another language as utterly foreign with the implication that it is inhuman and, therefore, the language of 'barbarians' has a long history in interhuman relationships. The implications of this portrayal for translation in society and culture are many and it is no accident that it comes to play such a central role in *The Great Dictator*.

In her discussion of Mungo Park's *Travels in the Interior of Africa* (1860), Mary Louise Pratt describes 'arrival scenes' as 'particularly potent sites for framing relations of contact and setting the terms of its representation' (Pratt 1992: 78–80). Park's desire for communication with native Africans is consistently frustrated, and he becomes mainly an object of curious scrutiny for the indigenous peoples in these arrival scenes. However, Pratt at no point mentions language, though it would appear obvious that in the absence of a common language the Europeans and Africans could do little else but stare at each other. Moreover, Pratt misses the link between visual apprehension of reality and the collapse of language-based systems of communication. In the absence of language, the arrival scene is a tableau, a spectacle where the native other becomes an object of consumption. It is in this context that the full significance of the interpreting transaction must be understood.

Descartes in his *Discours de la méthode* (1637), F. Max Müller in *Lectures on the Science of Language* (1861), Claude Hagège in *L'homme de paroles* (1985) and Chomsky in his discussion of discontinuity theory, all see language as defining *homo sapiens*. If language differentiates the animal from the human, then denying the utterances of others the status of language-that-can-be-translated is to reduce them to the condition of animals. Charles Darwin made the following observation on the language of the Fuegians:

The language of these people, according to our notions, scarcely deserves to be called articulate. Captain Cook has compared it to a man clearing his throat, but certainly no European ever cleared his throat with so many hoarse, guttural, and clicking sounds.

(Darwin 1986: 17)

Edward Tylor in *Primitive Culture: Researches into the Development of Mythology, Philosophy, Religion, Language, Art and Custom* (1871) noted that the hunting down and killing of indigenous peoples of Tasmania was possible because colonists heard the languages of the aboriginal peoples as grunts and squeals. Deprived of language, and therefore of culture, the Tasmanians were dehumanized and treated as prey for imperial hunters.

If a central problem of nineteenth-century anthropology is whether human beings are the positivistic objects of a natural science or the human subjects of a hermeneutic inquiry, then it is arguable that the presence of the interpreter, the emergence of language mediation, is a crucial moment in the shift from the positivistic object to the human subject. The surgeon Wilson on the H.M.S. *Beagle* uses the classic language of positivist objectification to describe the Fuegians, 'The Fuegian, like a Cetaceous animal which circulates red blood in a cold medium, has in his covering an admirable non-conductor of heat' (Beer 1996: 60). Alongside this observation, however, is a rudimentary vocabulary of Fuegian languages. This juxtaposition is significant as pointing to the borderline of translation, the paradigm-shift that results from access to language through interpreting. One could argue that the moment of translation is a shift from an encounter scene as a site of consumption to an encounter scene as site of interaction. The traveler through translation is no longer an observer but part of what is observed.

The shift from non-human to human status that is implicit in accession to language and, by association, to culture, does not mean, of course, that there are no other means of exclusion. The other language can be described as inferior, the speakers as lazy, malevolent, treacherous. Nonetheless, once understanding is admitted through the possibility of translation, then the way of dealing with or describing the other must be fundamentally reorganized, if only because liberal elements in the imperial centres will accord full, hermeneutic status to the subjectivity of the colonial other on the basis of the evidence of translated language. It is precisely because Montaigne wants to challenge the pseudo-objectivity of Eurocentrism that he is intensely frustrated when the interpreting proves inadequate, as he relates in his famous essay on 'Des Cannibales':

Je parlay à l'un d'eux fort long temps; mais j'avois un truchement qui me suyvoit si mal, et qui estoit si empesché à recevoir mes imaginations par sa bestise, que je n'en peus tirer guiere de plaisir [I talked to one of them for some time; but I had an interpreter who followed my meaning so badly, and was so hindered by stupidity from grasping my ideas, that

I could hardly get any satisfaction from him (translation by J.M. Cohen)].

(de Montaigne 1988: 214)

There are echoes of Darwin in the construction of Hynkel's language, which has indeed many 'hoarse, guttural and clicking sounds.' One unfortunate consequence was a plethora of stereotypical representations of the German language in the post-war period in comic strips and on screen, in which the speakers of the language were presented indiscriminately as inarticulate, unthinking oafs (Fiebig-von Hase and Lehmkuhl 1997). What is worthy of our attention, however, in Chaplin's film is the manner in which a language that borders on the animalistic deprives the speaker of any human compassion and removes hermeneutic agency from the objects of his hatred. Mr Jaeckel (Maurice Moscovich), Mrs Jaeckel (Emma Dunn) and Hannah (Paulette Godard) share a language with Hynkel as is apparent particularly in Jaeckel's German-accented English. But what Hynkel does to language is not only to make a nonsense of the language he allegedly speaks (his German is not German but German-sounding gibberish), but also to undermine that fundamental translational condition of language, that is, the ability to understand and empathize with others. He changes fellow speakers of his language from hermeneutic subjects into the positivistic objects of his genocidal hostility, to be disposed of in the murder machine of his concentration camps. His language becomes a wall of sound, an impenetrable barrier of pure materiality, that renounces any attempt to make language a medium for exchange and instead makes the refusal of translation, the refusal to entertain the human claims of fellow others, the basis of his hectoring monologues.

If Hynkel's monologues are in ersatz German, the dialogues in the film, including Hynkel's are in English. The film presents the spectator with an obvious contradiction, which runs right through the history of Hollywood cinema once human speech enters the frame, how to present audiences with a foreign reality in a language they can understand. Hynkel speaks to his Minister of War, Herring (Billy Gilbert), and Minister of the Interior, Garbitsch (Henry Daniell), in English. In the ghetto, English is the language spoken by Hannah, the Jaeckels and their friends and neighbors. When Benzino Napaloni (Jack Oakie) turns up to meet his fellow dictator on an official visit, he speaks English, although with an accent and slight syntactic modification ('Hey, whatsa this mix-up,' 'You signa treaty first') that, as we saw with Fiorello, becomes the screen trademark of the native Italian-speaker. What is striking in the construction of the set for the ghetto is that it becomes a kind of generic ghetto representing the fate of both German and Central and Eastern European Jewry. Thus, there are signs for 'Wartz: Pickle Factory,' 'Heinrich,' 'Restoricz,' 'Papervendissn,' 'Barber,' 'Harü Tondadoz,' 'Ambroj,' 'Takab,' 'Cigaroj' and a sign in the window of Hannah's house, 'Laundry Done Here. Inquire With In.' There is no attempt to create any kind of coherent or credible linguistic reality in the ghetto. The effect is a general one of linguistic otherness with Slavic affixes in many instances generating a sense that the ghetto is elsewhere but with enough linguistic clues for Anglophones ('Papervendissn,' 'Cigaroj,' 'Restoraciz') to make translation possible.

It is, of course, possible to see the cavalier treatment of other languages as more evidence of a general Anglophone disregard in cinema for a world that does not speak the language of the Hollywood majors. Translating the world into English makes it a safe and a recognizable place with nothing to disrupt the monoglot fiction apart from the occasional untranslated residue of language shift. But Chaplin's decision to make Tomania and the victims of its policies predominantly English-speaking is infinitely more disturbing than comforting. The fact that their language, presumably the one spoken by Hynkel in his tirades, is, in a sense, translated into English allows the film to have a resonance which goes beyond the immediate historical context of the fascist politics of Hitler and Mussolini. An example of the effectiveness of Chaplin's move is in the portrayal of Garbitsch, Hynkel's Minister for Interior and Propaganda. In a film where the other major protagonists Napaloni and Herring (modeled on Benito Mussolini and Hermann Goering respectively) are depicted as buffoons and are regularly the object of comic satire, Garbitsch is a creature apart, immune to and from humor. He speaks throughout the film in an English which is obviously that of an educated speaker of the language. When he consents to give Hynkel lessons in 'applied psychology' and describes how to humiliate his fellow dictator, Napaloni, the outcomes may be funny, the scene with the seats in the barber shop, but the tone of instruction is not.

It is Garbitsch who tells Hitler after his initial address that 'I thought your reference to the Jews might have been a little more violent.' The tone of educated disdain is all the more disconcerting in that there is no foreign language to distance the Anglophone spectator from the content and implications of what Garbitsch is saying and proposes to do. His lessons in 'applied psychology' may be an ironic reference to the manipulative politics of presentation in the propaganda work of Leni Riefenstahl, but the tendentious use of psychology and imagery did not cease with Hitler and his acolytes – this is a standard part of the toolkit of spin in contemporary electoral politics. In other words, by having Garbitsch speak untranslated (or translated, depending on what one imagines to be the default language of the film), Chaplin raises questions about the nature of spectacle and representation in modern political life which cannot be easily avoided. Unlike Hynkel, Garbitsch does not rant or vituperate in a language which is essentially meaningless, but speaks in the measured and readily understandable tones of one who is utterly convinced of the rightness of what he and his master are doing. If he has a distinct role, it is in effect to translate the rationale and implications of Hynkel's rhetoric into a language clearly understood by all. For this reason, in the famous final scene of the film where the Jewish barber is mistaken for Hynkel and goes on to make a speech, he is preceded and introduced by Garbitsch who spells out exactly what Hynkel's policies mean in terms of the repression of fundamental freedoms. As Hynkel's 'translator,' Garbitsch is committed to communicating his message, making sure that the film audience are left in no doubt about what Hynkel means as opposed to what he says.

Charlie Chaplin shared more than a moustache with Hitler. They were both born in the same month of the same year, April 1889, and both became known throughout the world, for very different reasons. If the iconic image of Hitler is of an orator vociferating at mass political rallies, the iconic image of Chaplin was of someone who did not speak at all, the silent tramp an image that circled the globe in the era before talking pictures. Chaplin playing the role of both Hynkel and the Jewish barber is almost playing the two sides of his own cinematographic personality, one which is heavily dependent on speech and on the mechanism of translation and the other which appears to dispense with translation in its appeal to the universality of hapless victimhood and the visual gag. The Jewish barber does speak but not much. In his dress, behavior and indulgence in non-verbal humor (such as when he shaves a customer in time to Brahms' *Hungarian Rhapsody no. 5*), he is remarkably, and no doubt deliberately, similar to the tramp of Chaplin's silent films. Hynkel talks a great deal but the summary nature of the translation implies that he does not say very much, even if what he has to say is alarming in the extreme.

The Jewish barber, on the other hand, says very little but what he communicates by his on-screen presence is immense in terms of the manner in which he silently translates the plight of an entire community. There is one extended scene in the film which is an exception to the division of spoken labor and this is the scene when Hynkel indulges in a grotesque ballet with a globe. The globe in the form of a balloon is a dance partner in a scene that is a parody of Greta Garbo's famous declaration that she wanted to be alone. When Hynkel is left alone, the global ambition that has been so clearly articulated for him by Garbitsch turns into the puerile fantasy of megalomania, the globe a plaything in the dangerous dreaming of the autocrat. There is music but no speech. The scale of his demented ambition has left him, for once, speechless. When the balloon finally bursts, his balletic routine comes to an abrupt end but there is no Garbitsch on hand to let the audience know whether the dictator's manic overreaching will destroy the world or whether the Führer's ambitions will finally and dramatically implode.

Images

If *The Great Dictator* is a film about language and about the need to translate what is happening in a foreign language to alert the democratic world to the perils of fascism, it is also inevitably about pictures. What Leni Riefenstahl had offered the Nazis with *The Triumph of the Will* (1935) was the aestheticization of power, a way of portraying politics which would use the camera to persuade and seduce. The final sequence of *The Great Dictator* is a clear parody of the type of theatrical showmanship indulged by organizers of the Nazi mass rallies and celebrated by Riefenstahl. What the radio did for Hitler's voice, Riefenstahl's documentaries would do for Hitler's image. Hitler himself was an avid fan of the cinema and, in fact, is reputed to have tried unsuccessfully to get a copy of *The Great Dictator* for a private viewing (Brownlow and Kloft 2002). However, the nature of images and their power to distort but also reveal is an issue which recurs throughout the film. Just before Napaloni arrives in the Tomanian capital, Garbitsch gives strict instructions to the official photographer that Hynkel be shot facing the camera and not from the back. When Napaloni finally alights his train both dictators jostle with each other for the best photo opportunities and both Hynkel and Napaloni are comically self-conscious in their efforts to appear photogenic. Hynkel's voice is clearly distinctive, in particular his histrionic rhetoric, but what is equally important is that his image be instantly recognizable.

In his extended conversation with Garbitsch in his palace about his vision of a pure, Aryan world, Hynkel goes over to a wardrobe and opens the doors to study himself in the mirrors. What Hynkel's posturing suggests is not only the incurable narcissism of the megalomaniac but also the manner in which images themselves must be assembled or translated into a pictorial language that will present power in the best possible light. The *mise en scène* of Hynkel's person is a bleak parallel to the transformation of Hannah at the hands of her Jewish barber, where her beauty is revealed through a simple shampoo and cut. She, too, looks in the mirror to see a person who is no longer soiled by the misery of her condition. She even goes as far to say to her admirer, 'If you were fixed up, you would look handsome.' The tragedy for Hannah and others in the ghetto is that the 'fixing up' of language and image, the deliberate assembly of words and images, will give their persecutors an unprecedented power to wreak misery and destruction. For Might to become Right, Will must be seen not just heard to Triumph. Part of Chaplin's task in *The Great Dictator* is to use what he knows best, comedy, to try to translate the images of might and power into a language which makes the meaning of autocracy painfully clear.

There are two extended speeches in the film, the first is Hynkel addressing the Sons and Daughters of the Double Cross and the second is the Jewish barber who has been mistaken for Hynkel making a speech to the crowds gathered to celebrate the successful Tomanian invasion of Osterlich. The first speech as we saw earlier is in pseudo-German with occasional translation in the form of a voiceover. The second speech is delivered entirely in English and there is no translation. Like Tomasso in *A Night at the Opera*, the barber is initially reluctant to speak, but unlike Tomasso, of course, he can and does speak. The Jewish barber is disguised as Hynkel but in the speech there is no attempt to disguise the sentiments of the barber whose speech articulates Chaplin's own humanitarian vision. A core argument in his speech is that the science and technology of communication and mobility are a potential force for the good. The airplane and the radio have brought humanity closer together, he claims, and the 'very nature of these inventions cries out for the goodness in men.' As proof of this, the barber states that 'even now, my voice is reaching millions throughout the world,' millions of despairing men, women and children. The barriers that are broken down by new forms of communication will, in time, remove the barriers of hatred and distrust between human beings and prefigure a humane future for all. The barber in his speech does not mention cinema, but this, of course, is a medium which reaches millions. Nor does he mention translation, but without translation his voice will never reach many millions of men, women and children throughout the world, no matter how relevant his message or how desperate their plight. As the power of the media of communication increases, so does the necessity for translation to become manifest in all its forms. It is by ignoring translation, by failing to acknowledge that local circumstances can subvert global designs, that the pathological universalism of autocracy is gradually undermined. The surest hope for the fraternal vision predicted by the barber from the ghetto is not so much to talk but to listen to the voices of the millions. There is no democracy without the reciprocity of dialogue and the fundamental courtesy of translation.

Found in translation

Adam Philips has claimed that, 'Not finding the same things funny that you or anyone else finds funny is, of course, a common immigrant experience' (Phillips 2000: 354). He might have added that part of finding the same things funny often involves speaking the same language. That this is the case explains the particular difficulties encountered by literary translators in trying to render humor in one language in another (Delabastita 1993) or the obstacles faced by interpreters when trying to capture the comic thrust of an anecdote that leaves an audience helpless with laughter in one language and rigid with indifference in another. To paraphrase Frost, humor is potentially what gets lost in translation. But there is another form of humor associated with translation, which is connected to the process of translation itself. In this form, it is the very attempt to cross over from one language and culture to another which becomes the focus of comic attention. Humor, here, is what gets found in translation.

Borat: Cultural Learnings for Make Benefit Glorious Nation of Kazakhstan (2006) indicates from the very title that the film will draw heavily on the transaction costs of translation in the presentation of the journey by the eponymous TV journalist and presenter Borat Sagdiyev (Sacha Baron Cohen). The unidiomatic and ungrammatical English signals what might be termed a translation effect, namely, the sense of a text which is clearly translated by virtue of the fact that is clearly beholden to the syntax or lexicon of the source language. These translation effects are redoubled in the DVD format where standard phrases are 'translated' into translatorese, 'Prerecord Moviedisc for purpose domestic viewing of moviefilm' and 'Selling pirating of moviedisc will result in punishment by crushing.' These translations are, of course, all pseudo-translations in that it is not a question of interference from a genuine source language but of the creation of fictional translation effects in the target language. What then is the function of translation in such a context? What can *Borat* tell us about translation and the comic genre in cinema and what can the comic genre on screen tell us in turn about translation?

Borat presents himself as on a journey of exploration. The Kazakhstan Ministry of Information, he claims, is prepared to bankroll the road movie so that the people of Kazakhstan can learn lessons from the 'greatest country in the world,' the 'US and A.' The opening scenes of the film are set in Borat's fictional home village of Kuzcek (they were actually shot in the village of Glod, Romania). Images of pigs, donkeys, horses, primitive forms of transport, and scenes of obvious poverty situate Borat in a world clearly signaled as pre-modern. The purpose of the journey is to bring the *ingénu* to one of the heavily mediated sites of Western modernity, the United States. If imperial travelers travelled to other parts of the world to judge their distance from the superior form of modernity they embodied (Fabian 1983), Borat is a post-imperial traveler who travels toward forms of modernity he deems prestigious or worthy of emulation. In a sense, Borat is depicted as a some-what less than noble savage who feigns innocence to foreground aspects of cultural behavior or belief that are unseemly, or in some instances potentially, dangerous. Crucial to the persona constructed in the mockumentary is that Borat is an individual operating in the translation zone and his interactions with others are routinely framed by issues around translation and meaning.

When Borat first appears on camera, it is clear that the incongruous English of the film's subtitle is echoed in the speech of Borat himself. Referring to his neighbor's envy he claims 'I get a window from a glass, he get a window from a glass,' later when he appears on a news broadcast in the United States, he says to the presenter, 'Before I start I want to make a urines and then I come back here,' and when the item starts he begins shouting, 'I'm excite. I'm very excite.' The solecisms are used repeatedly throughout the film both in dialogue and in voiceovers and a distinctive feature of the character of Borat is the fiction of his translated speech. This language difference provides Borat with a particular license. When he goes to meet members of the Veteran Feminists of America he makes comments that one of the member describes as 'very demeaning' and he is then asked, 'Do you know the word demeaning?' Pat Haggerty, a 'humor coach,' tries with limited success to teach Borat how humor works in the US and the impor-tance of dramatic pause. He quizzes his new pupil saying, 'Do you know what a pause is?' The difficulty for Borat's interlocutors is that they are uncertain how much is in fact getting lost in translation, whether this is in what they have to explain to him or what he has to say to them. This uncertainty means that often what remains implicit or tacit knowledge in a culture has to be made explicit, whether it is being told that certain misogynistic views are unscientific and unacceptable or that it is considered inappropriate to make fun at the expense of particular groups in the society.

The belief on the part of others that Borat is a genuine non-native speaker of English allows him to draw out beliefs, ideas, values, that would not normally possess that degree of explicitness in the native language community. At one point, Borat decides to take tuition from an etiquette coach. He asks her 'what I should say if I need to go the shit hole.' The coach rephrases the query in a more polite register, 'You mean, to the restroom.' Borat repeats his question in a slightly different form but ignores the cue about register and says, 'To the place, to make the shit.' The coach tells him to say that he needs to go 'upstairs.' When Borat ends up at a gathering of the Magnolia Mansion Dining Society a whole series of comic consequences ensue from his faked ignorance of toilet etiquette. What the exchange with the coach and the subsequent debacle at the dinner reveal is that the move toward translation, the desire to translate and be translated, can function as an extremely powerful way of both exposing the most intimate rituals of daily life and uncovering deeply held beliefs in a community. Borat can ask the questions he asks and use highly inappropriate registers because his interlocutors believe that he is not fully or properly aware of what he is saying in English. The innocent abroad can trade on linguistic naiveté to violate taboos. It is not so much because he is an accomplished linguist that Borat is afforded insights into particular aspects of American society but because he appears to be such a poor one, obviously and publicly laboring under the burden of translation.

When Borat appears at a rodeo in Salem, Virginia he is ostensibly there as a foreign guest to sing the US national anthem. Before he sings, however, he makes a short speech which begins 'My name a Borat. I come from Kazakhstan' and then declares 'We support your war of terror' to loud applause. The sentiments expressed become more extreme as he gives voice to the wish, 'May George Bush drink the blood of every man, woman and child of Iraq.' In a sense, the audience would not have applauded if they had listened more carefully to what Borat was saying as the deliberately bungled preposition ('of' rather than 'on') dramatically alters the meaning of his declaration and the logical outcome of killing the entire population of Iraq would be to undermine the rationale for any form of military intervention. It is more than likely that the audience while no doubt aware at some level of the oddness of the speech concurred with what they felt to be the patriotic tenor of Borat's sentiments. If what came out in his speech was a mangled translation of what he intended, then allowance had to be made for the perils of language crossing.

But transgression has limits. When Borat begins to sign the US anthem off-key and with words purportedly from the Kazakh national anthem, the crowd begins to boo and Borat has to be removed from the ring. The words of the pseudo-anthem, which proclaim Kazakhstan to be greatest country in the world and the 'number one exporter of potassium,' are a clear parody of the national hubris of many anthems. Borat, in fact, mainly sings in Hebrew and the subtitles bear no actual relationship to the words that he uses. It is the point at which the translation ceases, when Borat begins to sing in an incomprehensible language and therefore is no longer translating that the hostility to his presence becomes manifest. For spectators of the film, subtitles provide a translation but in a sense these subtitles are as spurious a 'translation' as Borat's own pseudo-translation of the *Stars and Stripes* into what is assumed to be Kazakh. The scene in the rodeo through the orchestrated disingenuousness of language difference brings to the fore less palatable aspects of gung-ho militarism. The translation 'mistakes' may be articulating a truth, a war on terror mutating into a war of terror, which is more than enthusiastically embraced in certain quarters. Translation functions at two levels in the Imperial Rodeo. At one level, the subtitles through parodic exaggeration (the celebration of potassium) mock the coercive self-congratulation of national anthems as a genre. At another, generation of translation effects in Borat's speech provides the narrative with something of a verbal Trojan horse where attitudes can be revealed from within the community by careful cultivation of linguistic faultlines.

One such faultline is of course within the target language itself and the varieties which exist within the language. On his journey to meet and wed the actress Pamela Anderson in California, Borat meets a group of African American youths. He professes an interest in their dress and in particular in their speech habits. Later, he arrives in the reception of a fashionable hotel where emulating the style of urban African American culture he has his pants lowered so that his underwear is visible. This initial transgression is

Figure 4 Borat (Sacha Baron Cohen) singing the US national anthem at a rodeo.
Borat (2006) Directed by Larry Charles, USA: Dune Entertainment

compounded by the language he uses in addressing the white receptionist, 'What's up with you, vanilla face? Me and my homey ass just parked our slab outside.' It is not long before Borat is escorted off the premises by security staff. Here he is using a variety of the target language that is deemed wholly inappropriate in the context, and, apart from the somewhat ludicrous effect of Borat attempting to mimic urban cool, there is a clear underlying tension to do with language and race. What Borat as foreigner is allowed is access to different groups in American society, he is allowed a mobility that would be arguably much more problematic for a native. However, the mobility is not only social, it is also linguistic. He can translate his thoughts into the language variety of his choosing. What he soon realizes, however, is that translation like language is a social event. People react in particular ways to specific varieties of language. The conditions of utterance reveal themselves to be as important as the contents of utterance. Language produces effects and what those effects are is determined by who can speak in what way and in what context. The translation zone is a way of exploring what those effects might be and what attitudes they might express.

The character of Borat appears to cheerfully embrace misogyny, homophobia, xenophobia and just about any other prejudice calculated to shock liberal opinion. Implicit in the film, however, is that these are not simply personal opinions but ones widely shared by his Kazakh compatriots. In this respect, *Borat* could be construed as a crude caricature of a developing nation with parody masquerading as sociological truth. The very clumsiness of Borat's expression could equally be seen as evidence of Anglophone condescension toward language difference (Foreigners speaking Funny) and the relentless normative drive of its domesticating strategies in translation. However, it is worth remembering that Borat is embarking on a voyage of discovery and what he discovers is not a progressive utopia that compares favorably with a deeply reactionary homeland. The foreignizing strategy of his heavily accented and grammatically wayward speech gives a license to those he encounters on his US journey to express a variety of anti-semitic, homophobic and misogynist opinions. When Borat, for example, is given a lift by a group of young men from a University of Southern California Fraternity, they are keen to know whether women are slaves in Russia (sic). After regretting the disappearance of slavery, one of the group complains loudly that in the US, 'anyone who is a minority has the upper hand.'

In this mockumentary, it could be argued that the depiction of the United States is as crude as the characterization of Kazakhstan, that there is no desire for well-documented truth but a relentless search for comic opportunity in the form of anomalous behavior or opinion. But this in a sense is to miss an important point about the film, namely that any initial sense of cultural or linguistic superiority is undermined as the journey progresses. Borat's encounter with the young Californian students is followed by his arrival at a Christian Evangelical meeting. Among those addressing the meeting are a Member of Congress and a US Chief Justice. Another speaker satirizes the findings of Darwinism. Borat (introduced as Bolok) tells the meeting, 'I have no friends. I am alone in this country. Nobody like me.' He is then inducted to a kind of baptismal ritual where he appears to lose consciousness. At two moments in the sequence, the camera gives us a close-up of men who appear to be 'speaking in tongues,' producing an exalted, inchoate babbling sound. The irony is that Sacha Baron Cohen as Borat is an Anglophone assuming the 'gift of tongues' (pretending to be a Kazakh speaker) to explore what it might mean to convert to the lifestyle and beliefs of an economically advanced Western society. There is no sense, on the evidence, of what he encounters, that he has encountered a manifestly superior society or value system.

Crucial to the persona of Borat and the effectiveness of the film is the parallel soundtrack of language difference. Sacha Baron Cohen is a British Anglophone and speaks neither Russian nor Kazakh. For the purposes of the film he speaks mainly in Hebrew interpolating phrases, which bear some similarity to Polish and other Slavic languages. The producer, Azamat Bagatov (Ken Davitian), who accompanies Borat on his trip, speaks in Armenian. The initial sequence as noted earlier is shot in Romania and the villagers including Borat's alleged wife, Oxana, speak in Romanian. Therefore, what passes for exchanges in Kazakh, are in fact nothing of the sort. What the film presents is a simulacrum of language otherness. When Borat and Azmat appear to be engaged in heated exchanges with each other, they are in fact communicating in mutually unintelligible languages. Similarly, Borat and the villagers do not have a language in common. The subtitles, therefore, are systematically inaccurate. Their function is not so much to translate as to sustain the illusion of translation. They are a target text without a source text. The cavalier approach to authentic language detail could be seen as a piece with the rest of the film, the portrait of Kazakh culture as spurious as the depiction of the language. However, at another level, the linguistic inauthenticity could be seen as making a point about the limits to intercultural understanding in an era which makes much of the possibilities of global travel and the planetary spread of communications media.

In a convenience store Borat and Azamat engage in a prolonged and heated exchange about their future travel plans watched by amused onlookers. Later, when Borat meets up again with Azamat after a brief separation, they have a further robust exchange watched by puzzled bystanders. The bystanders and the onlookers are intra-diegetic representations of the majority of cinema goers, who not having access to Hebrew, Armenian, Russian or Kazakh would not be any wiser to the languages Borat and Azamat are speaking or what they are actually saying. Even the subtitles provide the illusion rather than the substance of understanding. What the fallibility of the subtitles point up is the larger fallibility of communication in a global age, particularly with respect to the Anglophone world. The growing dominance of English, which among other things favors the growth of a global tourism industry heavily mediated through the English language, means that other languages potentially lose their distinctive histories and identities and begin to merge into an undifferentiated language other. What matters is not that they are a specific language from a specific place but that they are not-English. If that is the case, then reliance on translation becomes more, not less, important, as the only way of accessing the totality of the world's languages is through the offices of translation. But for this to be effective, there must be an assumption that the translation is faithful, valid or accurate.

Borat exploits the vulnerability of Anglophone audiences by offering translations which are, in effect, nothing of the sort. Borat's feigned ignorance of US culture and language is an uneasy mirror image of the ignorance of foreign languages, which bedevils the Anglophone world evident in everything from the significantly low levels of translated literature to a sharp decline in interest in modern languages (Lea 2007). The 'cultural learnings of America' like much of the rest of the Anglophone world are unlikely to be significant if they do not involve a genuine engagement with linguistic multiplicity. In a sense, the license allowed to Borat as a result of his being deemed to be a non-Anglophone and therefore functioning through translation is revealing not only of prejudices or beliefs but of the perils of monolingualism in a globalized society. Strength without understanding is a poor recipe for dialogue. It is not so much Borat who has to do the learning as his Anglophone interlocutors who remain ignorant of the linguistic complexity which informs the world that is the object of their political, cultural and economic influence.

An effective mnemonic for unsettling monolingual assumptions in *Borat* is the use of a map to track the progress of the picaresque pair as they make their way to California. The map of the United States uses the Cyrillic alphabet and transliterations of American placenames to defamiliarize the familiar. Borat and Azamat, the Don Quixote and Sancho Panza of intercultural contact, are proceeding through a territory that is ostensibly mapped in their language. We learn in the film that the map they are using dates from 1917. The cartographic trace of the cultural pilgrims' progress is a parodic imitation of the standard colonial procedure whereby new territories were renamed using points of reference from the colonial culture (Pratt 1992). These are travelers arriving from the periphery but they boldly appropriate the new country in their old language. The sense of entitlement extends to the carelessness with place and location. When Borat tries to persuade Azamat that they should head west and go to California, he lists off Texas and Pearl Harbor as two sites of attraction to be found in the American state. The sense of confusion may strike the Anglophone spectator as comic but the cavalier disregard for geography and history is not any more surprising than a routine indifference to the niceties of place and situatedness that are embedded in foreign placenames and languages. Translating the United States cartographically is a way of re-framing on screen perspectives which are all too often Anglocentric in the extreme.

One of the characteristic ways of reframing a foreign reality for Borat is to translate cultural realities into a language with which he is putatively familiar. So when Borat goes to Washington he arranges a meeting with a Republican congressman Bob Barr. Borat describes Washington DC as 'home of mighty US warlord, Premier Bush' and describes Barr as a 'party official from ruling regime.' As Cohen is not in fact translating from any existing language, the foreignizing cast of his descriptions are deliberate. To describe someone as a 'warlord' in English is usually to suggest a military chief who is not always constrained by the principles of liberal democracy and for whom warmongering is a way of life. The translation 'error' is calculated to hint at a less than sympathetic interpretation of the direction of the US president's foreign policy. In a similar vein, to describe an elected representative in the same language as that normally reserved for the apparatchiks of totalitarian regimes is a double-edged translation. On the one hand, Borat is ostensibly translating American political realities into the undemocratic polities with which he is allegedly familiar. On the other, presenting an elected member of the Republican Party as a simple servant of the presidential regime is signaling a relationship between the legislature and the executive which might not be as democratic as expected or desirable. The ambiguity of the translation effects in Borat's speech leave open a space for interpretation, which means that the spectator is ultimately never quite sure who the joke is on.

Translation in *Borat* is not, however, only a matter of words. It also about contexts, when it is appropriate to act in particular ways in different situations in different cultures. From his first journey on the subway in New York, Borat is immediately singled out for aggressive attention as he attempts to greet the men he meets by kissing them on the cheeks. The fact that he presents himself as a foreigner, 'Hello my name Borat. I'm not American. I new in town' does not lessen the hostility. When he gets to Texas the manager of the Imperial Rodeo supplies a context for the adverse reactions telling Borat that, 'People who do the kissin' over here are the ones who float around like this.' He then imitates an exaggeratedly effeminate man and he and Borat indulge briefly in a bout of homophobia. Borat's actions are, of course, calculated to create unease as he tests the willingness of those he meets to accept behavior which they in their own culture interpret in a particular way. Thus, kissing men and what is perceived as an unacceptable violation of private space produce reactions of fear, anger and loathing. A gesture that is wholly anodyne in one culture is connoted radically differently in another. What we see happening on camera is response in a target culture to the literal translation of a custom or mode of greeting ('you kiss me and I'll pop you in the fuckin' balls, OK?'). In other words, *Borat* teases out the consequences of a failure to read cultural cues and to appreciate the power of context in a target culture. Implicit, of course, in the knowing transgression by Sacha Baron Cohen of cultural norms of behavior is a potential critique of homophobic stereotypes and a particular relationship to the body and personal space. Even if being approached by a total stranger in a public space who wants to embrace you is likely to excite suspicion in a great many cultures, Cohen constantly uses exaggerated cultural distinctiveness to probe the very distinctiveness of the cultures he explores. If Borat's mission is to translate what he has seen in the 'US and A' for 'make benefit of Glorious Nation of Kazakhstan' he demonstrates in his own inimitable way the perils of cultural mediation and the endless potential for tragi-comic mistranslation. In parodying the format of the documentary with its implicit truth claims, Borat nonetheless reveal truths about people and attitudes which he encounters. In the end, he is not so much translating the centre for the periphery as exploiting his self-engineered status on the periphery to translate the centre back to itself in a language it might not always recognize or like. If peripheries are sensitive to the goings on in the centre, the next chapter will explore how translation makes spectators think again about the place of the local in the global sweep of the camera.

4   The long journey home

Lost in Translation to *Babel*

Bob Harris (Bill Murray) is in Tokyo to shoot an advertizing commercial for a well-known brand of Japanese whiskey. On the phone back to his wife in Los Angeles, he tells her about places he has been going to and the people he has been meeting. She offers the comment, 'I'm glad you're having fun' and his self-defensive reply is, 'It's not fun. It's just very, very different.' Harris's rejoinder in Sofia Coppola's *Lost in Translation* (2003) sums up what the main characters find most perplexing about this new environment in which they find themselves, namely, that it is, 'very, very different.' In this chapter, we will examine a number of films which consider what happens when translation becomes a way of examining the contemporary consequences of living in a globalized world. The films, *Lost in Translation*, *The Interpreter* (2005) and *Babel* (2006) are all major productions featuring well-known cinema actors, appearing within a relatively short time of each other and all involving explicit references to the problem of translation.

Globals and locals

Translation as a named concern in contemporary Hollywood cinema is in a sense to be expected if the late modern world is working through the implications of current processes of globalization. Anthony Giddens defined globalization as, 'the intensification of worldwide social relations which link distant localities in a such a way that local happenings are shaped by events occurring many miles away and vice versa' (1990: 64). One way of linking distant localities is of course to put them on our screens and the sociologist Zygmunt Bauman has written about how the vast numbers of 'locals' across the globe watch a privileged number of 'globals' perform in the area of sport, popular music and cinema:

> In the Panopticon, some selected locals watched other locals … In the Synopticon, locals watch the globals. The authority of the latter is secured by their very remoteness; the globals are literally 'out of this world,' but their hovering above the worlds of the local is much more,

daily and obtrusively, visible than that of the angels who once hovered over the Christian world.

(Bauman 1998: 53–54)

What these globals have to tell us about different locals and locales on a multilingual planet must inevitably engage translators as agents and translation as practice. If 'worldwide social relations are intensified,' then one consequence is that linguistic, faraway languages, like faraway events, are much closer and all of these new realities must be understood, both on the screen and off the screen. For local happenings to be shaped by events occurring many miles away, some sense must be of these events and translation, or indeed its failure, is an integral part of the sense-making process.

Bob Harris is a former 'global,' a successful movie star from the 1970s who still has a sufficient aura of globality for a Japanese advertizing firm to want to use his services. He has worked in the motion pictures industry and his work in Japan involves a less ambitious form of film making supplemented by photo shoots. *Lost in Translation* is saturated in the processes and products of image-making, whether it is the extended sequences involving the making of the short advertisement or the session with the Japanese photographer, the zapping through late night television programs or the repeated snapping at the party held by Charlotte's (Scarlett Johansson) Japanese friends. As the taxi carries a jetlagged Bob into Tokyo city, he rubs his eyes at one point not only to emphasize fatigue but to express his surprise at seeing his image on a large billboard advertising a drink, a global offered up for visual consumption by locals. The fundamental preoccupation with image has a clear parallel with the construction of Japanese reality on the screen. The long opening sequence taking Bob Harris from the airport to his hotel in downtown Tokyo is mirrored by an equally extended sequence at the end of the film bringing Harris from his hotel to the airport. In both sequences, the camera pans not only the buildings of the metropolis but also dwells in particular on the neon signs and advertisements in the Japanese language.

Tokyo is a strikingly visual experience and therefore appropriate to cinematographic treatment but part of the visual experience is the writing system of the language itself, the characters of a non-Latin alphabet. For the Western traveler, the disorientation is complete. If Bob and Charlotte are partly adrift in their sense of personal crisis – Charlotte with her young husband, John (Giovanni Ribisi), and Bob with his wife of 25 years standing – the sense of dislocation is compounded by their being in a culture and language not their own. What becomes quickly apparent is that though Bob, Charlotte's husband, John, and many other characters in the film work with images, there is a reality beyond (and a context for) images which immediately brings questions of language and translation to the fore. Martin Heidegger's claim that the 'fundamental act of the modern age is the conquest of the world as picture' (Heidegger 1977: 134) is hardly surprising given the centrality of seeing to the rise of Western science. As we noted in Chapter 1, relying on the testimony of the eyes rather than the authority of texts became the touchstone of the new scientific method championed by Francis Bacon and others (Rorty 1980). The importance of ocularcentrism was relayed by the development and enhancement of optical instruments such as the microscope and telescope. Literacy and the advent of printing gave further impetus to visualized and spatialized perceptions of experience (Ong 1989). In more recent times, the process of commodification itself has a strong visual correlate as noted by Eamonn Slater:

> As the process of commodification penetrates deeper into the cultural realms of society, commodity production takes on a more visual char-acter: this corresponds to a process of *visualization*. Images and visual symbols become the universal language of commodity production across national boundaries. Television, movies and the advertizing industry can replicate images endlessly and beam them virtually anywhere (his emphasis).
>
> (Slater 1998: 4)

Bob Harris is integral part of this process of visualization, his image enjoy-ing a global currency whether it appears in the film on a billboard or on the side of an articulated truck.

The limits to this process, however, are underlined in two major scenes in *Lost in Translation* which are primarily concerned with visual construction. In the first scene Harris is being directed in an advertisement for *Santory* whiskey. The scene opens with whispered voices in Japanese saying that an interpreter is needed. When an interpreter is found, the director talks directly to Bob in Japanese explaining to him where he is, to look at the whiskey bottle, to express emotion in a slow, gentle fashion as if the whiskey was an old friend he was meeting again and then he suggests an analogy with Humphrey Bogart. He emphasizes the importance of the product and slogan by making an emphatic gesture and saying 'Santory time.' Only after this extended passage in Japanese does the interpreter, Ms Kawasaki (Akiko Takeshita) begin to translate. Her translation is extremely summary and she simply says, 'He wants you to turn, looking at camera.' Harris's bemused comment is, 'That's all he said?,' to which the interpreter not wholly truthfully replies, 'Yes, turn to camera.' Harris then wants to know whether he should turn from the right or from the left. The interpreter is voluble in making the request to the director, again to Harris's surprise, particularly as he does not then understand why the director who has told the interpreter in Japanese that he does not care from which direction Harris turns, and that they are under time pressure, should once again launch into a long explanation in Japanese about the nature of the emotion he wants Harris to experience as he savors Santory whiskey before the camera. The interpreter once more radically abbreviates the extended passage by saying to Harris, 'Right side and with intensity.' The puzzled American actor protests, 'Is that everything? It seems like he said a lot more than that' but his protests are to no avail as two further explanations by the director are interpreted as 'like an old friend and into the camera' and 'could you do it slower' and 'more intensity.'

A notable feature of the scene is that the director is intent on communicating directly with Harris and pays scant attention to the presence of the interpreter. When she does directly address the director, he shows signs of barely concealed impatience. The direct address suggests at one level the making invisible of the all-too visible translator or a gendered relation of power with male director and female interpreter (the male director only feels comfortable speaking to the male actor) but at another level, such behavior is perfectly normal as it is commonplace in bilateral situations for participants to try to construe some form of direct communication with each other (Wadensjö 1998). The effect on screen, however, is to project the non-Japanese speaking spectator into the position of the actor who is not so much lost in translation as lost for the want of translation. Harris may understand the technical language of his trade (where to look, camera angles and so on) but he is utterly at a loss to understand what is going on in the language of the studio. The extended passages of speech before the consecutive interpretation and the clear incompetence of the interpreter make manifest not only Harris's dependency on the skills and the good offices of the interpreter but also the reliance of the successful outcome of the advertisement on the effectiveness of the translation. The director is extremely unhappy with

Figure 5 Bob Harris (Bill Murray) with Japanese interpreter bending down toward him giving instructions in studio.

Lost in Translation (2003) Directed by Sofia Coppola, USA: Focus Features

Harris's performance on screen because he is not expressing the specific emotion he wants associated with Hibiki whiskey in the Santory range, an emotion that the interpreter is unable to successfully translate into English. The images fail to convince because the words are found wanting. The global is lost in the language of the locals.

It is possible, of course, to treat the scene as simply another example of a well-established Anglophone comic routine of decent chaps encountering Funny Foreigners. Language opacity heightens the importance of gesture and gesticulating foreigners speaking barbarous tongues are, of course, seen to be irresistibly comic. There is, however, a dimension to the translation performance in the scene which has implications not only for how translation is portrayed but for what its significance might be in a globalized world. As we noted earlier the main stumbling block for the interpreter is that she fails to communicate to Bob Harris the precise nature of the emotion he should portray drinking Hibiki whiskey. As the director tirelessly points out, a sense of prestige, of sharing exclusive company, of seasoned familiarity are crucial to the brand image of the whiskey. Branding is of course a salient feature of globalization and what brands trade on is less the intrinsic material value of the product than the associated cultural image or emotional value (Lash and Urry 1994). So brands are associated with emotions of psychological or physical or social wellbeing. The difficulty, of course, is that for emotional resonance to be effective it must first be understood and emotions are conventionally assumed to be what it is most difficult to express in language ('words failed me'). In a sense, though the interpreter can be faulted for bringing the profession into disrepute by her poor performance on camera, the dilemma highlighted in the scene is an important one. Not only the American actor but also the Japanese interpreter has great difficulty in communicating a precise quality of emotion. The fate of the image (the advertisement, the brand) is inextricably bound up with the fortunes of the word. The inexorable logic of visualization and the irresistible rise of the brand image can suggest a centripetal version of globalization as a gallery of images, freed from the nets of language by the universal currency of the gaze. *Lost in Translation* suggests otherwise by reminding spectators of the intractable, local realities of translation on a multilingual planet. Indeed, it is one of the many ironies of the scene that it demonstrates so clearly that the only way a 'global' icon (Bob Harris) can function in 'local' settings is through a firm embedding through language of the experiences and expectations of locals. What the studio scene makes obvious is what is less obvious in the visual sleight-of-hand of the brand, the mark of translation.

The advertisement scene is in essence a film within a film. It functions as a commentary on the making of the film *Lost in Translation* itself in that it foregrounds what happens when the business of film making encounters the irreducible realities of language and culture. In this reflexive moment, not only do we see cameramen, sound operators, and the other members of the production crew but we also observe the work of translation negotiating a linguistic and cultural divide. That this should be so is hardly surprising as Bill Murray commented in an interview that the 'bilingual challenge of working in Tokyo was significant' and he in fact compares the making of the film to a 'war' where he claimed that it 'seemed like you could never make yourself understood' (Coppola and Murray 2003). Even if the military analogy is illuminating but unfortunate, Murray's comments on the challenges faced by a relatively small crew working on a tight budget points to the omnipresence of translation as a concern not just for what the film talks about but how films come to be made. As the film is shot primarily on location, the politics of location are inescapable. In other words, if in Murray's words, the crew often felt like 'a fish out of water' and knew themselves to be 'a long way from home,' this was an explicit admission that film making cannot massage context out of the picture. The plethora of misunderstandings in the failed advertisement episode bring context into the text. Translation is not a peripheral concern for local operatives but a central issue that confounds any easy optimism on the universality of the language of image.

The second major scene in *Lost in Translation* involving the process of visualization is an extended photo shoot where the dialogue centres on exchanges between Bob Harris and the Japanese stills photographer (Tetsuro Naka). The scene opens again with the exposure of the artifice of image as Harris is shown being prepared and made up for the photo shoot. The studio is crowded with the people and equipment necessary to make the shoot possible. However, in this scene, a notable absence is the interpreter. There is no one on hand to interpret as Harris and the photographer communicate in English. Dispensing with the services of the translator does not mean, however, that translation is no longer an issue, on the contrary. The photographer initially asks Harris, 'Can you put your hand, close your face?' The omission of the preposition momentarily throws Harris who does not appear to fully understand the request and then he replies 'I don't get that close to the glass until I'm on the floor.' Harris's absurdist literal rendition of the request is intentionally ironic but this irony is clearly directed to an external audience and not to the photographer who is left nonplussed by the remark. Similarly, when by way of cue for a shot, the photographer says to Harris, 'You wanna whiskey,' Harris's literalist rejoinder is, 'This is not whiskey, this is iced tea.' When the photographer urges 'I need more mysterious,' Harris comments, 'more mysterious, I'll just to try to think where is the whiskey.'

The exchange is taking place in one of the global lingua francas of the fashion and entertainment business, English, but what is brought into sharp relief is the very different levels at which parties engage in the exchange. Each request from the photographer produces a moment of temporary bewilderment on the part of Harris as he is not quite sure that the words mean what he thinks they should mean. English may be the shared language but do they both know what they are saying when they use it? The requests are then followed by a metalinguistic rephrasing of the statement where

Harris plays with the ironic possibilities of the language. This level of language play presupposes an easy familiarity with English and it is clearly indulged at the expense of the photographer whose more limited knowledge of the language presumably obliges him toward a more restricted and non-self-reflexive form of dialogue. Features of Japanese use of English such as r/l phonemic inversion ('Lat Pack,' 'Loger Moore') and syllabic insertion between consonants ('Sinatora') are then introduced to the exchange where each time, Harris's initial bafflement gives way to his correcting the mis-pronunciation. If the photographer is in charge of the pictures in the scene, it is his subject who is clearly attempting to control the words.

There is no interpreter in sight but the effort of translation is audible. On the one hand, Harris is repeatedly unclear about what he is being asked to do and who he is being asked to imitate. He needs constant clarification as if the process of translation was being mimicked in the action of repetition, rephrasing, reformulation. On the other, the photographer is clearly experiencing difficulty in trying to communicate in English emotional expressions or cultural referents that he believes necessary to the success of the photo shoot. He, too, produces a translation effect through repetition of words or phrases ('mysterious' is repeated three times) and only the resultant poses of Harris can produce a confirmation that the message has been properly understood. There is, however, not just a dialogue going on between Harris and the photographer but between Harris and two audiences, the immediate audience in the photographer's studio and the assumed audience of an English-language film called *Lost in Translation* who possess native speaker competence.

Harris's linguistic knowingness as a mother tongue speaker is set against the more restricted use of the code by the photographer and this dis-symmetry in mastery is then used as a comic subtext for the scene. When Bob is asked by Charlotte in a later scene in the film why 'they switch the r's and the l's here?,' Bob's response is, 'you know, just to mix it up, they have to amuse themselves because we're not making them laugh.' But laughter is rarely innocent and as Adam Phillips has noted, 'the philosopher on jokes, and indeed the jokey philosopher, has to be mindful of the fact that the joke is always on someone' (Phillips 2000: 348). Here English is performing its habitual role as a language of global communication but the repeated translation difficulties are foregrounded not so much as tragedy as farce. So if there are elements of farce who is the joke on in this film theatre of international communication?

The photographer is clearly set up for a fall with his repeated mis-pronunciations and grammatical solecisms and the character of Bob Harris is on hand to make sure that the Anglophone audience get the point through his ironic reframing and rephrasing. Thus, if English is the language globals speak, then fluent speakers of the language possess the dismissive hubris of the guardians of the imperial tongue. That mastering a language is often confused in the case of Anglophones with being masters as a result of speaking the language, is clear in episodes in restaurants, Sushi bars and a hospital reception where Harris, speaking no Japanese, is abrupt and con-descending in his exchanges with native Japanese. But there is another sense in which the joke is on Harris and his fellow Anglophones. The title of the film after all is *Lost in Translation*. What Harris, and to a lesser extent Charlotte, have to come to realize is that the spoken is constantly shadowed by the unspoken. A global language can only be global if speakers of other languages consent or are forced to translate themselves into that language, for whatever reason. Therefore, the fact of being able to communicate in that language is conditional on the relative success of the translation move. What Harris experiences in both the filming of the advertisement and the shooting of the stills is that there is no communication without translation and that the real loss in translation is a loss of communicative innocence. That is, the notion that speakers of a global lingua franca can somehow expect to be readily and instantly understood across the planet sets them up for a fall as they are consistently wrong-footed by conversational exchanges where they get things wrong, completely misunderstand what has been said or respond inappropriately.

It is the 'globals' who can appear clumsy and inept as their belief in a monophone world, without the banana skins of language difference and translation, is soon shown to be comically naïve as they grapple with the refractory reality of the local. A scene which further highlights this dimension to language domination is set in the hotel gym. The gym looks remarkably similar to the type of gym found in luxury hotels the world over. Bob Harris is working out on an elliptical exercise machine which starts accelerating uncontrollably. The machine issues instructions in a Japanese-accented English which Harris clearly cannot understand and the scene closes with him shouting 'Help!' The element of farce in the scene is groun-ded in the illusion of the global cocoon. Same high-class, modern hotel. Same well-equipped modern gym. Same language. But the joke is on the global as he funny-walks into panic. The sameness is illusory as even the familiar props of global elite travelers turn bewilderingly strange.

Johannes Fabian has used the term 'denial of coevalness' to describe the manner in which Western travelers have distanced themselves in time from the countries they visit (Fabian 1983: 35). The Western traveler represents the here and now, the trajectory of the modern while the country s/he visits is frozen in time. The response may either be to condemn this time-lag as further evidence of the feckless backwardness of the natives or to sentimentalize the glories of past greatness and adopt an elegiac salvage mode. Either way, the Western traveler is confirmed in his/her ready identification with modernity. This maneuver is not possible for the main characters in *Lost in Translation*. From the automatic opening of the hotel room curtains to the highly sophisticated amusement arcades to the repeated panning of the Tokyo skyline, the Japanese capital is clearly not situated at a remote point in time from the advanced modernity of the travelers. Although Charlotte does visit an ancient monastery in Kyoto and witnesses a traditional Japanese wedding, the emphasis in the film is firmly on the technological sophistication of modern city and country (even in Kyoto, Charlotte is shown arriving on the high-speed bullet train), which, if anything, makes the principal American characters feel somewhat overwhelmed. What the characters are presented with is an advanced modernity but one embedded in a different language and culture. This feature of modern Japan is more troubling than the consoling fictions of the denial of coevalness. The country may be distant in space for the American protagonists but it is not distant in time. Signs of advanced modernity are clearly everywhere. This should be a recognizably easy landscape for other moderns to navigate but it is not. Part of the difficulty, of course, is that modernity speaks many different languages. It is not because a Tokyo skyline bears a resemblance to the skyline of any large American city that the city will be any easier to understand or get round. The flashing Japanese characters in the neon advertisements are a constant reminder that there is nothing more unfamiliar than the seemingly familiar. Difference cannot be easily dismissed as inferiority, which makes difference more of a challenge for the protagonists. When Charlotte is taken to hospital to have her toe seen to, the doctor (Osamu Shigematu) patiently explains to her the meaning of the X-rays in Japanese. The hospital is clean, modern and efficient but the limits to translation are the limits to Charlotte's access to this other, non-Anglophone modernity. As we noted in Chapter 1, Shmuel Noah Eisenstadt has described the emergence of 'multiple modernities' in the modern world:

> Modernity has indeed spread to most of the world, but did not give rise to a single civilization or to one institutional pattern, but to the development of several modern civilizations, or at least civilizational patterns, i.e. of civilizations which share common characteristics, but which tend to develop different, even cognate ideological and institutional dynamics.
>
> (Eisenstadt 2000: 40)

Charlotte and Bob may find it difficult to make themselves understood in the hospital but they have no difficulty understanding that the hospital offers acceptable levels of healthcare.

The hospital as opposed to the hotel is where one is likely to find 'locals' rather than 'globals' and it offers a vision of modernity which is conducted in a language wholly other than the English of *ER* (1994), the widely distributed American serial medical drama based in the emergency room of the fictional County General Hospital in Cook County, Chicago. If Japan's multiple modernity challenges any facile denial of coevalness, it is the necessity of translation which is a precondition of the multiplicity. Differences in language and cultural norms are not situated in a period vignette or a primitivist tableau but in the urban and institutional décor of late modernity. The 'sets' then may be familiar but the language of course is not and this is where global mobility meets the limits of local understanding. In a scene shot in a sushi bar where Bob playacts with Charlotte's injured toe, he exploits the linguistic incomprehension of the kitchen staff saying 'they love black toe over in this country' and asks one of the staff for a sharp knife. He then comments that someone will eventually order 'black toe' (pronouncing the words with a fake Japanese accent) and rebukes the staff member behind the counter saying, 'What's with the straight face?'

The rebuke might equally be directed against Bob himself as the humor is predicated on a shared language and a stereotypical image of Funny Foreigners eating Funny Food. For the kitchen staff, the behavior of a foreigner speaking an incomprehensible language and playing with the leg of his dining partner is as odd as it is unpredictable. The straight face subverts any notion that humor might be universal by default or that actions stripped of their running commentary carry the same comic charge. Bob carries on the way he does in the full confidence that he will not be understood, but if he was understood he might not feel so confident about carrying on. In a sense, in the knowing absence of translation, one potential defensive strategy is to make the intercultural weakness a comic strength. Douglas Robinson taking his cue from Freud has noted with respect to projection how, 'what we most despise in ourselves we repress and then magically 'rediscover' in someone else' (Robinson 1997: 122). Kristiaan Aercke extends this insight to the realm of translation and travel writing where he observes that in the case of the late medieval traveler Konrad Grünemberg, the latter's reaction on attending a Greek religious service which he did not understand was to ridicule the body-language of the officiating clergy. Aercke adds, 'Grünemberg translates his unstated frustration at his inability to speak or understand into the allegedly childish and uncontrolled gesticulation of the bearded (and therefore adult) men' (Aercke 2006: 161). Projecting incomprehension on to the Japanese cooks is a way of compensating for Bob and Charlotte's own incomprehension, trying, so to speak, to cut the losses of translation by passing the debt on to someone else.

In a film crowded with the apparatuses of communication from fax machines to landlines to mobile phones, the proximity of similarity sharpens difference. Whether it is Charlotte talking to her friend in the United States or Bob being reminded of his daughter's ballet recital as he wanders through the streets of Tokyo holding his mobile phone, the implicit subtext is that 'home' is always a phone call or a fax message away. Talking to friends or loved ones is, in theory, a break from the incessant labor of translation in a foreign language or culture. Or more properly, it might be claimed, foreign languages and cultures, as Japanese is not the only language in the film aside from English. Bob Harris finds himself, for example, in a sauna with two German businessmen (Dietrich Bollmann and Georg O.P. Eschert) speaking away in their language which he cannot follow and he himself makes conversation in broken French with one of the young Japanese partygoers in the nightclub scene. In the scene from *La Dolce Vita* (1960) shown on the television watched by Charlotte and Bob in Bob's bedroom, the dialogue between Marcello (Marcello Mastroianni) and Sylvia (Anita Ekberg) is in a mixture of Italian and English with Japanese subtitles. So Tokyo, not untypically for a modern metropolis, is a site of multilingualism.

The networks of modern communication that figure so prominently on the screen ought to provide a monolingual haven in the crowded, polyglot space of the foreign city. Here there is ostensibly no need for translation as the language barrier is no longer an issue. The drama for the characters is that no such certainty exists. As Charlotte rings her close friend in some distress because of the sense that her relationship with her husband is not working out as she expected, the conversation founders as Charlotte cannot communicate her disarray to her friend. The friend assumes that Charlotte is simply lucky to be on holiday and away from the humdrum world of the everyday. Similarly, Bob's conversations with his wife Lydia (voice of Nancy Steiner) are largely failed exercises in communication. When he confesses at one point in a conversation with his spouse that 'I'm completely lost' it could be as much a comment on the failure of intralingual translation as a verdict on the difficulties of interlingual translation.

Globalized communication networks may bring people together virtually allowing them to inhabit the same virtual language space but that does not necessarily entail that the utopia of understanding is at hand. The physical 'translation' in space of Bob and Charlotte removes them from the everyday-life world of those close to them and this displacement brings with it a double burden of translation. Being away can lead to new experiences that re-frame the familiar as foreign (Charlotte no longer recognizes the man she married), and this new awareness needs to be translated into a language understood by those left behind. Equally, being away means that the context of utterances are now the foreign reality and not the domestic reality which again requires translation. Bob follows his 'lost' admission by the claim that he wants to look after his health and that he no longer wants 'to eat all that pasta.' He wants instead to 'start eating Japanese food.' His wife is unimpressed and notes acerbically, 'Well why don't you just stay there and you can have it every day.' Eating Japanese food in Japan is not especially exotic but consuming Japanese food in a US context, however explicitly multicultural, is not nearly as banal. The technology of proximity is no guarantee, therefore, against the translation costs of distance.

Control

If being away even temporarily brings the situated nature of other people's realities into sharp relief, then other more permanent forms of exile have their own translation stories to tell. Sydney Pollack's *The Interpreter* has as a tag line 'the truth … needs no translation' but an abiding concern of the film is what happens to truth in translation and what happens to language in a period of global tension and conflict. The action in the film switches between the imaginary African country of Matobo and New York City, the site of the headquarters of the United Nations Organization. New York is of course one of the leading cities of the world's primary superpower, the most spectacular target of the 9/11 attacks and also host to the organization established to promote peace, tolerance and understanding between the different nations on the planet. The city then lies on a faultline between the external politics of a superpower and the internal politics of a supra-national organization. The city can provide a backdrop for political violence linked to the domestic affairs of member states or be itself the object of violence linked to its iconic relationship to one particular member state, the United States. The multilingual city plays host to a multilingual organization and what emerges as a central concern in the film is what happens when language realities cannot be ignored and translation becomes not a peripheral but a central issue for those in control.

From a geopolitical perspective, the central problem of translation in general and interpreting in particular, is the problem of control. Bruce W. Anderson says of the interpreter that, 'his position in the middle has the advantage of power inherent in all positions which control scarce resources' (Anderson 1976: 218). Proximity is both desirable, the desire to manipulate – understanding what others are saying makes them easier to understand and control – and dreaded. The dread comes from the fear of being misled either by the native interpreter or by the non-native interpreter going native. The difficulty for the controlling agent is dealing with this monstrous doubleness, the potential duplicity of interpreters. William Jones in his *Grammar of the Persian Language* (1771) stated that for British officials, 'It was found highly dangerous to employ the natives as interpreters, upon whose fidelity they could not depend' (cited in Niranjana 1992: 16). These suspicions were in many instances justified. In a celebrated court case in Ireland in the eighteenth century, the Gaelic poet Seán Ó hUaithnín was put on trial for writing pro-Jacobite poems. He was acquitted because the court interpreter, Mícheál Coimín, another Gaelic poet and neighbor, deliberately mistranslated the poem to make it sound thoroughly inoffensive to the British Crown (Morley 1995: 76). This trade-off between information and control and the nervousness attendant on the potential duplicity of mediation makes the interpreter a highly symbolic figure in the context of post-Cold War politics and the 'war on terror.'

Silvia Broome (Nicole Kidman), an interpreter at the United Nations, allegedly overhears a plot to assassinate the leader of Maboto, Edmond Zuwanie (Earl Cameron). She reports what she has heard to the United Nations and becomes the subject of a US Secret Service Investigation. The investigation is led by Tobin Keller (Sean Penn) but when Keller is asked by his colleague Dot Woods (Catherine Keener) what he thought of her account, he states quite baldly, 'She's a liar.' He later has her undergo a lie test and when she wants to know when she will get the results, Keller retorts, 'Results? Right away. You know when you're lying, don't you?' After the terrorist attack on the regular commuter bus carrying a Mabotan leader Kuman Kuman (George Harris), Keller accuses Broome of repeatedly lying to him and not giving him a plausible explanation as to why she went to meet Kuman Kuman on the bus. Earlier in the film, she goes to great pains to explain to Keller that 'dead' and 'gone' do not mean the same thing and that if she interpreted dead as gone she would be 'out of a job' at the UN but the agent is unpersuaded, believing that ultimately she is only 'playing with words.'

At a certain level, Keller is right to be skeptical. Broome does lie about her revolutionary past, Zuwanie systematically lies to his people, Silvia's brother dies after mistakenly being led to believe that he will meet the rebel leader Ajene Xola (Curtiss Cook) at the football stadium. The American Ambassador to the UN, Ambassador Davis (Lynne Deragon), is more concerned with face saving than having Zuwanie tried before a court, the International Court of Justice, which the US refuses to recognize. The truth is infinitely malleable in the context of corrupt post-colonial regimes and cynical international *realpolitik* so that language immediately falls under suspicion. Who is telling the truth in a world where getting to the truth is bound up with the language of telling? When we first see Broome in her booth she is interpreting from Spanish. But what gets her into trouble is not her ability to interpret from a world language like Spanish but a minor language like Ku, which is described as 'a tribal dialect of Matoban' spoken in the 'South Central African Belt.' She is needed in order to establish the nature of the threat against the life of Zuwanie. She is the vital informant not because of her knowledge of Ku but because her 'position in the middle has the advantage of power inherent in all positions which control scarce resources,' she is both extremely influential (she triggers off a massive security operation) and extremely vulnerable (she is subject to intense surveillance by the US Secret Service and attempted assassination by Zuwanie's henchmen). Broome is expected to exercise fidelity as an interpreter but as an embodied agent, as a human who has suffered at the hands of Zuwanie's regime, she experiences the pull of another fidelity to the memory of her parents, sister, brother and to a lesser extent, to her former lover, Ajene Xola. Her difficulty is in attempting to reconcile two apparently conflicting forms of fidelity. But there is a sense in which there is another kind of fidelity Broome can practice which both honors the profession of translation and the memory of the victims of murder and injustice.

Minutes before the bomb goes off on the bus in New York, Kuman Kuman asks Silvia what she is doing in the city. She tells him that she is working as an interpreter in the UN and he dismisses her work claiming, 'so like the UN, layers of languages signifying nothing.' The declaration is a derisive echo to Keller's earlier claim that she was merely 'playing with words.' However, we learn in the film that playing with words was precisely what led to the death of Simon Broome (Hugo Speer). As a young boy, he and his sister made lists of things to pass the time and these included odd animal facts ('the leading cause of death among beavers is falling trees'), the number of times their mother used the F-word and odd or unusual words. The playing with words became a serious business when Simon used the copybooks to note down lists of the names of the victims of the Zuwanie regime. It is the words that undo the layers of lies which obscure the brutal reality of the dictatorship, soon to be abandoned by its erstwhile Western allies. So working with words is important and getting the meaning right is not simply a principle of effective pragmatic translation but a way of putting the record straight against the background of official lies and atrocity.

Broome articulates the position most clearly in the exchange with Zuwanie's Head of Security, Nils Lud (Jesper Christensen), who asks her where she stands politically. She argues that she is for 'peace and quiet,' 'quiet diplomacy' to which he replies sniffily, 'With respect, you only interpret.' She claims in her defense that, 'countries go to war because they have mis-interpreted each other.' Her defense of her work in the United Nations along with her more general commitment stated later in the film that 'words and compassion are the better way even if slower than a gun,' must be set in the context of the crisis at the UN over the refusal to sanction the invasion of Iraq. US Ambassador Harris in the film expresses obvious impatience with an obstreperous French delegation in a clear allusion to the refusal of the French government to support the initial invasion. When Broome is asked to do some consecutive interpretation for a meeting involving Ambassador Harris and Mabotan government representatives, the Mabotan officials are quick to condemn the opponents of Zuwanie as 'terrorists.' The theme is taken up by Zuwanie in his aborted speech at the UN where he offers the New York bus bombing carried out by his agents as incontrovertible evidence of the terrorist practices of his opponents. The cynical and indiscriminate use of the term 'terrorist' by the Mabotan leader suggests uneasy parallels with the use of 'the war on terror' as a means by which to discredit legitimate and lawful opposition to practices judged to be illegal or dangerous. This is why Broome must put the gun down at the end of the film when she threatens to kill Zuwanie. If she chooses the gun, then her words become null and void, they genuinely are lies. She becomes the 'terrorist' that will legitimize the state terrorism of the Zuwanie regime. In order for this not to happen, she has to do the one thing without which there can be no be interpretation, listen.

It is generally accepted in translation pedagogy that all good translation involves close reading (Kiraly 2000). Careless reading produces sloppy and inaccurate translation. The corollary for the oral form of translation is attentive listening. Poor listeners not only make for bad friends but for worse interpreters. *The Interpreter* reminds us that cinema is not only a visual but also an auditory medium, and throughout the film from Broome listening to the whispered conversation in the General Assembly room of the United Nations to Tobin Keller listening repeatedly to the recorded greeting of his dead wife on his telephone answering machine, paying attention to what is being said is as revealing as showing what has not previously been seen. When Broome is initially interviewed by Keller she says that she does not concentrate on faces but that she listens to voices, the voice is her medium, both heard and spoken. The sensitivity to voice takes on another dimension, however, when she confronts the African dictator at the end of the film. She asks him to read from his autobiography and the passage is telling:

> The gunfire around us is making it hard to hear but the human voice is different from other sounds. It can be heard over noises that bury everything else, even when it is not shouting, even if it is just a whisper. Even the lowest whisper can be heard over armies when it's telling the truth.

Implicit in Broome's admiration for these words of the youthful Zuwanie is what might be termed an ethics of listening. Part of the duty of the interpreter is to listen to what people are saying and to convey the import of their words, no matter how unpalatable the truth. They must listen to the 'lowest whisper' as well as the louder 'noises.' This is, in a sense, how the role of interpreter is interpreted in the film, as one who listens and one who ultimately is not afraid to speak. If Broome repeats her conviction that words must take precedence over bullets, she suggests an important caveat, that all the words must be listened to, all the 'layers of languages' that Kuman Kuman dismisses so contemptuously, and not just the words of diplomats and government officials for whom she is asked to interpret. It is because Broome, as Zuwanie's Head of Security reminds her, is a mere interpreter that she is paradoxically better placed than anyone else in the film to articulate the full complexity of politics in the post-Cold War period.

When Keller looks for background information on Broome, Police Chief Lee Wu (Clyde Kusatsu) tells him that Broome was born in the US, grew up in Africa, studied music in Johannesburg, linguistics in the Sorbonne and languages in various countries around Europe. She had a British mother and a white African father. His pithy conclusion to her brief biography is 'She is the UN.' Broome's composite identity makes her at one level a prototype of a new citizen of the world, a cosmopolitan agent functioning in a multilingual and a multicultural space. She embodies in her curriculum vitae a world of multiple belongings that would encapsulate the supra-national project of an international organization. This, of course, could imply a weightlessness, a kind of being from everywhere which means belonging nowhere. Indeed, Broome seems to almost suggest as much when she tells Keller early on in the film that 'You don't know me at all' and when she goes missing toward the end of the film one of Keller's fellow agents reports that despite checking all possible leads, 'no one knows her.' But the unknowability of Broome is not to do with the fact that there is an insubstantiality to a person who is so widely distributed in terms of cultural allegiances but that she knows too much.

Figure 6 Shot of Silvia Broome (Nicole Kidman) in her UN interpreters' booth.
The Interpreter (2005) Directed by Sydney Pollack, UK: Working Title Films

She not only hears the official version of what is going in Matobo through her work as consecutive interpreter in the meeting between the US Ambassador and the UN officials but she also has access through her knowledge of the language of the people and her lived experience of Matoban politics of what is being said in the lowest whispers. Broome offers Keller a word in Ku, 'kappela,' which she translates as standing on opposite sides of the river. She uses it to stress the fact that she and Keller are some-how apart, that they are divided. But it could, of course, be equally applied to the position of the translator who is standing not on one side but on both sides of a linguistic and cultural divide. Broome is the UN not so much because she is a transcendental, supra-national being but rather that she is a deeply divided being with conflicting loyalties who possesses particular insights. Being 'kappela' by virtue of her linguistic mediation she rejects the binary reductionism of the 'war on terror' or the 'fight for national libera-tion' and subverts monochrome readings of political complexities. Indeed, it is possible to argue that what Broome represents is an argument for a particular kind of being or belonging in a world beset by the social, economic and cultural pressures of globalization.

Denizens

One of the most common icons of the global age is not surprisingly the globe itself. From the shots of the blue planet suspended over abyssal darkness courtesy of the Apollo space missions to the sketchy outline of earth on notices encouraging hotel customers to re-use their towels, the images of the planet are increasingly common in the contemporary imaginary. Seeing things from a distance is as much a matter of subjection as observation. Occupying a superior vantage point from which one can look down on a subject people or a conquered land is a staple of colonial travel narratives (Pratt 1992: 216). There is a further dimension to the question of distance described by Tim Ingold where he draws a distinction between perceiving the environment as a 'sphere' or as a 'globe.' For centuries, the classic description of the heavens was of the earth as a sphere with lines running from the human observer to the cosmos above. As geocentric cosmology fell into discredit and heliocentric cosmology came into the ascendant, the image of the sphere gave way to that of the globe. If the sphere presupposed a world experienced and engaged with from within, the globe represented a world perceived from without. Thus, in Ingold's words, 'the movement from spherical to global imagery is also one in which 'the world', as we are taught it exists, is drawn ever further from the matrix of our lived experience' (Ingold 2000: 211).

In the movement toward the modern, a practical sensory engagement with the world underpinned by the spherical paradigm is supplanted by a regimen of detachment and control. As the images of the globe proliferate, often ironically to mobilize ecological awareness, the danger is that these images themselves distort our relationship to our physical and cultural environment by continually situating us at a distance, by abstracting and subtracting us from our local attachments and responsibilities. However, it is precisely such an ability which is often construed as a basic requirement for both national and, more latterly, global citizenship. It is the capacity to look beyond the immediate interests of the clan or village or ethnic grouping which creates the conditions for a broader definition of belonging at a national or indeed global level. Szersynski and Urry argue, for example, that 'banal globalism', the almost unnoticed symbols of globality that crowd our daily lives, might, 'be helping to create a sensibility conducive to the cosmopolitan rights and duties of being a 'global citizen', by generating a greater sense of both global diversity and global interconnectedness and belonging' (Szersynski and Urry 2006: 122).

The promise of such citizenship is an almost axiomatic contemporary defense of why anyone should bother with translation. When Pascale Casanova in her survey of the World Republic of Letters tries to synthesize those elements which have conditioned eligibility for citizenship of this Republic, translation is very much to the fore:

> Dans l'univers littéraire, si l'espace des langues peut, lui aussi, être représenté selon une figuration florale, c'est-à-dire un système où les langues de la périphérie sont reliées au centre par les polyglottes et les traducteurs, alors on pourra mesurer la littérarité (la puissance, le prestige, le volume de

capital linguistico-littéraire) d'une langue, non pas au nombre d'écrivains ou de lecteurs dans cette langue, mais au nombre de poly-glottes littéraires (ou protagonistes de l'espace littéraire, éditeurs, intermédiaires cosmopolites, découvreurs cultivés ...) qui la pratiquent et au nombre de traducteurs littéraires – tant à l'exportation qu'à l'im-portation – qui font circuler les textes depuis ou vers cette langue littéraire. [In the world of literature, if languages can also be represented using a 'floral figure,' that is to say a system where languages on the periphery are linked to the centre by polyglots and translators then it is possible to measure the literariness (the power, prestige, the volume of linguistico-literary capital) of a language, not by the number of writers and readers in a language, but by the number of literary polyglots (or main players in the literary arena, publishers, cosmopolitan inter-mediaries, well-educated talent spotters ...) who know it and by the number of literary translators – for export as well as for import – who cause texts to be translated into or out of this literary language.]

(Casanova 1999: 37)

The global standing of a literature depends on the efforts of those language learners and translators who can stand outside their own language and learn the other language for the purposes of reading and/or translation. But Szersynski and Urry ask the following questions, 'is this abstraction from the local and particular fully compatible with dwelling in a locality? Could it be that the development of a more cosmopolitan, citizenly perception of place is at the expense of other modes of appreciating and caring for local environments and contexts?' (Szersynski and Urry 2006: 123).

In opposition to the figure of the citizen we find the notion of the 'denizen,' which has been propagated notably by the non-governmental organization Common Ground, where a denizen is deemed to be a person who dwells in a particular place and who can move through and knowingly inhabit that place. Therefore, Common Ground dedicates itself to encouraging the pro-liferation of vernacular, ideographic and connotative descriptions of local places, which can take the form of place myths, stories, personal associations and celebrations of various kinds (www.commonground.org.uk). In other words, what denizenship posits is a knowledge from within and this knowledge if we consider the aims of Common Ground – place myths, stories, personal associations – is almost invariably though not exclusively expressed through language.

The relation of Silvia Broome to the matrix of her lived experience in Africa is represented visually to the spectator in the form of flashbacks and photographs but, of course, the experience itself has been lived through and expressed in more than one language. Broome has dwelled in a particular place and has knowingly inhabited and moved through that place, this is one of the reasons *inter alia* why she is such an effective interpreter from Ku. Although she works in a 'global' organization and would appear to have the ideal qualifications for global citizenship, she is in fact more beholden to a spherical than a global paradigm, to a world that is known and experienced from within rather than distanced and categorized from without. If the slogan of real estate agents is 'Location, Location, Location' there could hardly be a better definition at some level of what translators do. Part of the business of the translator is to understand what people actually say in a particular location and to bring this knowledge to another location, the target language. This is why the education and training of translators take years. It is not so much an abstraction from as an engagement in local attachments that is demanded by the translator's task, and this task takes time. Broome has spent years acquiring the languages at her command and the languages are bound up with experiences in the countries in which she has lived and studied. The interpreter's booth is not a glass cage. The interpreter has a body and a history and that embodied history allows her to do what she does.

One of those things that interpreters do is to bear witness. Because of the physical presence of the interpreter at events where they asked to perform, where the other participants would be not so much lost in as lost without translation, the interpreter is a metonymic reality. Interpreters are part of the events in which they participate. To this extent, they fulfill a testimonial function which in narrative terms is crucial (Cronin 2006: 75–119). That is to say, it is perfectly credible for the interpreter to be used as a vehicle with which to tell a story or offer an account of a particular event where their services were required because they actually had to be there for communication to take place. In this sense, the discreet presence to the side or in the background (Broome consecutively interpreting for Ambassador Davis) or isolated in the booth can watch history unfold. The peripheral figure in the exchange is a key character in terms of narrative plausibility and for this reason is inevitably compelling for the makers of fictions that are films. Being there is part of the story, and part of the story for translation scholars is what it means to be there, not only on screen but in the world.

Seeing and listening

The tag line for the film is 'If you want to be understood, listen.' The problem for the characters in Alejandro González Iñárritu's *Babel* is that even when they do listen they do not always understand. The version of the Babel story which is gravely intoned in the film's preview is explicit about the link between hubris and incomprehension:

> In the beginning all the Lord's people from all parts of the world spoke one language. Nothing they proposed was impossible for them. But fearing what the spirit of man did accomplish, the Lord said let us go down and confuse their language so that they may not understand one another's speech.

As the rifle shots ring out across the Moroccan desert, the implication is that to speak one language is to be all-powerful, to speak many is a manifesto for chaos. But, of course, it is the film itself ranging across three continents and seven different languages (English, French, Arabic, Berber, Spanish, Japanese and Japanese Sign Language) that recreates the Babelian project. From behind the lens of the camera it is possible to take in the multiplicity of the world in the single frame of the cinema screen. As the narrative rapidly shifts from Southern California to Morocco to Tokyo, the world unfolds before us as if the Tower of Babel was in fact an observation post, the cinema itself an observatory for a humanity brought together for our inspection. It is hardly surprising, then, when checklists are drawn up to establish the incontrovertible fact of a shrinking world that cinema and, in particular, the cinema output of Hollywood majors is regularly invoked as a shared element in an emerging global culture (Crane 2002). An inevitable consequence of globalization as visualization is the tyranny of the gaze. This has profound implications not only for the visual commodification of goods and services, the usual focus of discussions around the design-intensity of aestheticized goods such as branded clothing and rock music (de Zengotita 2005), but also for the very 'common ground' on which people rest.

One of the salient features of experience in the developed world is the emergence of a comparative cartographic gaze based on the twin imperatives of tourism and real estate. As the world opened up to travelers in the second half of the twentieth century and tourism rapidly became one of the most important items of trade on the planet, the range of potential destinations increased significantly (Urry 1990). The ending of the Cold War, for example, saw the emergence of many former Soviet bloc countries as prime destinations for tourists, as the economies of Central and Eastern Europe sought to accelerate infrastructural development and employment through tourism. It is no accident in this respect that many of the locations chosen for the shooting of the James Bond film *Casino Royale* (2006) are to be found in the Czech Republic or Montenegro. Destinations through brochures, television travel programs, magazine articles, Sunday supplements, can be visually compared across the globe and the planet from this cartographic perspective becomes a set of juxtaposed images on offer to the spectator who has the financial wherewithal to make choices. The correlative in real estate is the fate of property in a globalized world. As restrictions on the movement of funds and the acquisition of property were relaxed in many countries in the 1980s and 1990s, significant investment funds were directed toward real estate, which could now be purchased and evaluated on a worldwide basis. So now in Singapore, it is possible to buy 1000 feet of office space in London and vice versa (Sennett 2002: 46). When N.H. Seek, the president of the real estate firm GIC, designates the 'world winning cities' which represent optimal possibilities for property investment, the list includes Calgary, Austin, San José, Helsinki, Tallinn, Budapest, Barcelona, Cape Town, Santiago (Chile),

Porto Alegre, Delhi, Mumbai, Bangalore, Xian, Shenzhen, Shanghai, Beijing and Guangzhou (Seek 2006).

The popularity of programs in the United Kingdom such as the Channel 4 series *A Place in the Sun*, which helps 'buyers find their dream home in an exotic location,' further reinforce this powerful comparative cartographic gaze where the world is flattened into the collage of the holiday snapshot album, except that in the case of property buyers, the holidaymakers do not go away but stay behind. What is striking with this visual instrumentalism, whether it be in tourist discourse or real estate, is that, '[p]laces have turned into a collection of abstract characteristics, in a mobile world, ever easier to be visited, appreciated and compared, but not known from within' (Szersynski and Urry 2006: 127). *Babel* as a film which brings the spectator images of three different countries on three different continents could be said, then, to be complicit in the comparative cartographic gaze we have described. Is the one language spoken of in the Babel parable the language of image? Is seeing things on the screen a way of seeing them from a distance and is this form of seeing an instrument of subjection as well as a means of observation? Do certain forms of seeing confer a superior vantage point from which one can look down on a subject people or a conquered land that, as we mentioned earlier, has been a mainstay of colonial travel narratives?

To answer these questions, it is necessary to consider how the film treats ways of viewing the world and why translation almost invariably complicates worldviews. Richard (Brad Pitt) and Susan (Cate Blanchett) Jones are part of a group that is being taken on a guided tour of Morocco when Susan is accidentally shot by a young shepherd boy who is practicing shots with his father's newly acquired rifle. Before the shooting, we see the tourists in the bus looking out at the scenery, handling cameras and going through photographs that they have taken. After the incident, the bus is taken to the village of guide–interpreter Anwar (Mohammed Akhzam). As the tour bus arrives in his village, the tourists look out of with a mixture of wonder and apprehension at the sights of this remote village in South-West Morocco. The windows of the tour bus are the screens within the screen, framing the tourist gaze for the Jones' fellow travelers. On the other side of the ocean, the nanny Amelia (Adriana Barraza) decides to take the Jones' two young children, Debbie (Elle Fanning) and Mike (Nathan Gamble) to Mexico for her son's wedding as she cannot find anyone to look after the children. As the car crosses over the border into Mexico the children look out wide-eyed from the back of the car at the changing sights of Mexican streetscapes. The car window becomes an opening on to a world that is not familiar. What happens in both instances, however, is that once the travelling stops and the dwelling, however brief, begins, then there is a reversal of the gaze.

The American children are an object of curiosity for their Mexican peers at the wedding where the Mexicans not the Americans constitute the majority. As Susan lies stretched out on the floor of the house belonging to Anwar's grandmother (Sfia Ait Benboullah), she is watched by the children of the village, fascinated by this exotic presence. Similarly, Richard's desperate telephone calls are largely public affairs as the villagers crowd in to watch him seek help from different sources. Both the children and their parents on different continents are no longer looking from the outside in but are now looking from the inside out, and are looked at as outsiders by the insiders. The natives turn their gaze back on these objects of curiosity. That the power of the gaze cannot be gainsayed is emphasized in a scene in the film where the soundtrack consists of a Moroccan news broadcast in Arabic about the shooting incident. The broadcaster claims that the incident could have been a robbery, and then states that the American government was quick to suggest a 'terrorist link.' This is rejected by a Moroccan minister who is reported to have said that, 'terrorist cells have been eradicated in our country' and that 'an act of vulgar banditry followed by superficial evaluations the US places on it cannot ruin our image or our economy.'

The juxtaposition is illuminating. Images have substantial economic value. Ruining the image of a country abroad in terms of the comparative cartographic gaze is fatal for an industry, tourism, which is so heavily dependent on how a country is viewed from elsewhere. Thus, in Japan, many thousands of miles away, the story of the Jones' shooting appears on the television screen as Chieko (Rinko Kikuchi) flicks through the different channels, and toward the end of the film Susan Jones is shown leaving the hospital in Casablanca on a television screen in a busy Japanese bar. National images enjoy a global currency in both a literal and a metaphorical sense.

What *Babel* demonstrates, however, is what happens when images are used to get behind images and how translation reveals the limits to ways of subjugating the world to the commodification of the visual. Richard desperately seeks help for his wife after she has been shot and he runs out onto the road shouting the English word 'Help' to a Moroccan motorist who bewildered and, alarmed, eventually speeds off. The visual promise of the holiday is undercut by the linguistic reality of his surroundings. The inability to translate foregrounds a cultural blindness on the part of the traveler who finds he is not so much an empowered citizen of the world as the unwilling denizen of a place. In this sense, what the failure to translate does is to reinstate the importance of a particular kind of time in overly spatialized and visualized models of the global. The importance of instantaneous time is repeatedly emphasized by commentators on globalization who see the availability of cheap, ubiquitous computing as the portal to a flat world of instant, limitless connectedness (Friedman 2007). This standard time–space compression thesis lends itself effectively to panoptic ideals of global simultaneity, where the variousness of the world can be captured on a multiplicity of screens. However, this perception is in marked contradiction to the intensely local, place-bound existence of the majority of inhabitants on the planet. Geraldine Pratt and Susan Hanson, for example, argue that:

> Although the world is increasingly well connected, we must hold this in balance with the observation that most people live intensely local lives;

their homes, work places, recreation, shopping, friends, and often family are all located within a relatively small orbit. The simple and obvious fact that overcoming distance requires time and money means that the everyday events of daily life are well grounded within a circumscribed arena.

(Pratt and Hanson 1994: 10–11)

This is not to argue, of course, that place cannot be shaped by influences from elsewhere, even if people do not move. On the contrary, from the spread of Buddhism in China to the initiation of rural electrification projects worldwide, local lives can be dramatically transformed by developments which have their point of origin many thousands of kilometers away. What the prevalence of local lives does mean, however, is that local languages have a reality that resists the easy sweep of the comparative cartographic gaze.

Risk

A recurrent concern of modernity has been the category of risk. One of the key features of the modern age has been the disembedding of social relations from local contexts of action (Giddens 1991: 209). To disembed is to remove social relations from local involvements and to recombine them across larger stretches of time and space. As Urry and Lash point out, such disembedding implies trust: 'People need to have faith in institutions or processes of which they possess only a limited knowledge. Trust arises from the development of expert or professional knowledge, which gives people faith, including forms of transport which convey them through time–space' (Lash and Urry 1994: 254). Systems of mass travel and transport that developed in the nineteenth century saw the emergence of a whole new category of travel professionals, beginning with Thomas and John Cook, whose primary function was to minimize the risk, inconvenience and unpredictability involved in travel from one place to another. The increasing abstraction and complexity of modernity, with the extension in space and contraction in time implicit in globalization, leads to an increasing devolution of trust on to expert systems – trains, planes, itinerary planners, hotels – that will 'simplify' our journeys and eliminate attendant risks. For George Ritzer and Allan Liska, the result is the increasing 'McDisneyization' of the travel industry. In this view, society is seen as growing increasingly calculable, efficient, predictable and more and more controlled by non-human technologies. The putative rationality of modernity, however, generates its own irrationality. Not surprisingly, they find all these features present in the rationalized theme park of Disney World. Ritzer and Liska claim that because of the McDonaldized life world that has increasingly become the norm in the West, tourists want highly predictable (no smelly bathrooms), highly efficient (lots to do), highly calculable (no hidden expenses) and highly controlled (aerobics classes at two) holidays (Ritzer and Liska 1997: 99–100).

The characters in *Babel* are haunted by the specter of risk. When the tourists go to the town of Tazarine to seek help for Susan, it is not long before tensions arise in the group as their sense of vulnerability in an isolated local village means that the majority clamor for their departure. Tom (Peter Wright), the self-appointed spokesperson for the anxious tourists demands that the coach leave the village telling Richard, 'In Egypt in a town like this they slit the throats of thirty German tourists.' When Amelia, Santiago (Adriana Barraza) and the children cross into Mexico, Santiago exclaims, 'See how easy it is to get into paradise' to which Mike retorts, 'My mom told me Mexico is really dangerous.' Although Chieka is in her home city of Tokyo, once she strays outside familiar territory and starts experimenting with drink and drugs in a voyage through the city's night life, the element of risk begins to make its presence felt. What is apparent in all three locations is the close relationship between language and risk. In Morocco, the Western tourists can see but they increasingly realize they cannot understand and what they cannot understand makes them afraid. Mike and Debbie may have a limited understanding of Amelia's Spanish in the US but in the full-blown linguistic reality of Mexico they are at a loss to understand what is going on in the chicken-chasing game and its bloody sequel. Chieko finds herself among a group predominantly made up of non-sign language speakers and has difficulty understanding the intentions of her new-found friends and the contexts in which she finds herself. The seductiveness of the visual, underscored in Chieko's case in the nightclub where the soundtrack is regularly muted, gives way to an unease and anxiety about environments that are markedly constituted through language.

It is for this reason that it is frequently the interpreter who can find himself or herself the focus of intense hostility, as fear of dependency takes the form of active rejection. When the doctor (Hamou Aghrar), who is in fact the local vet, arrives to see what can be done for Susan, he tells Anwar if she stays in the village, 'she will bleed to death.' Richard notices the look of concern and asks Anwar what the doctor said and Anwar prevaricates, 'He says she will be fine.' Richard reacts violently crying, 'Don't you fucking lie to me! You tell me what he said! Tell me what he said!' Anwar as interpreter finds himself in the difficult in-between space of knowing too much (the prognosis for Susan) and not knowing enough (how to communicate this knowledge to an extremely anxious Richard). That he opts not to tell the truth is, of course, ethically problematic, but the scene highlights the emotional vulnerability not only of Richard but also of Anwar who is desperately trying to mediate different sets of knowledge and expectations in a highly charged situation. The extent of the pressure is clearly signaled in two scenes which are closely juxtaposed. In one scene, Richard and Anwar drink tea and chat about their wives and children. Anwar quietly and humorously puts Richard right about Western stereotypes of Muslim polygamy. The film then cuts to another scene with Richard kicking a door and shouting at a police officer (Youssef Boukioud). The police officer tells Richard through Anwar that an ambulance is not on its way and that another ambulance is not to be had. Richard shouts at the police officer saying, 'Fucking move!,' 'Fucking find me another ambulance!' and Anwar, undoubtedly conscious of the status of the officer within his own culture, interprets the peremptory order as a polite question, 'He wants to know how he will get his wife out of here?' The officer tells Anwar that the Americans stopped the ambulance and that they were going to send a helicopter but 'there are problems.'

The difficulty is that, what no one in the exchange fully realizes, as we are to learn later, Richard's wife is the subject of careful diplomatic negotiations between the Moroccans and the Americans over the 'terrorist' nature of the incident and the use of Moroccan airspace. Richard again shouting at the officer says, 'It's your fucked up country! It's your responsibility! Do something!' He finally leaves Anwar and the officer saying to both in turn, 'Fuck you!' The temporary truce of intimacy between Richard and Anwar is violated by the abrupt intrusion of international politics. Anwar, as much as the police officer, is helpless to determine the larger course of events, but they are both held to be metonymically responsible for what happened, united as they are in Richard's eyes by nationality and language. That this assumed unity is false is emphasized by the brutal treatment meted out by the Moroccan police to their fellow citizens whom they suspect of involvement in the shooting incident. However, the irony of Richard's outburst is that no one country bears responsibility for the imbroglio, and that all the parties are culpable for reasons to do with internal and external powerplay. Anwar as a figure of translation straddles an unhappy faultline between familiarity and exclusion. He is taken into Richard's confidence as a necessary ally in negotiating the linguistically and culturally foreign, but his status is always likely to alter as circumstances become more or less favorable. If Richard is

Figure 7 Richard Jones (Brad Pitt) in argument with tour guide/interpreter and police officer.

Babel (2006) Directed by Alejandro González Iñárritu, USA: Paramount Pictures dependent on Anwar, then Anwar, in turn, is dependent on a context over which he has limited control. Anwar is thus repeatedly challenged by Richard and occasionally excluded, but there is the repeated danger of exclusion in his own community if he does not carefully mediate exchanges with familiar figures of authority, whether it be his own grandmother, the veterinary doctor or the police officer. Anwar is a denizen and cannot afford the dismissive truculence of the sightseeing citizen of the world.

In the exchanges between Anwar and the other non-English-speakers as between Amelia and Spanish-speakers, the spectator in the film is provided with subtitles. As the title of the film suggests, there are a number of languages in the film and, therefore, a large number of subtitles. Subtitles are an aid to foreignization in that they maintain the linguistic alterity of what is on the screen, the soundtrack of language matching the identity of the image. What you see is what you hear. There is no attempt in effect to offer the domestic comforts of dubbing. It is worth considering, however, the function of subtitles beyond routine foreignization/domestication debates. Subtitles in a sense turn everyone into an interpreter. Spectators know before Richard and at the same time as the interpreter that his wife is bleeding to death. The subtitled exchanges between Santiago and Amelia mean that the English-speaking spectators knows before Amelia can tell the English-speaking children that things are going to go horribly wrong and that the wedding will not have a fairytale ending. Subtitles result in the spectator knowing more than the teenager in the fashionable Tokyo bar, who cannot understand what Chieko and her friend are saying and only gradually realizes they are deaf. In other words, though it is of course possible to analyze subtitles and judge to what extent they are accurate, what is equally worthy of attention is the message communicated by subtitles which goes beyond their informational content. The sense of cinema as panopticon, the camera sweeping across the globe, could arguably be replicated at another level by subtitles. What subtitles do is to make sense out of the Babelian confusion, all the languages of the world translated into the language of the subtitle. Reading the subtitles, the spectator vicariously translates the linguistic multiplicity of the planet into a familiar idiom. So what you hear is not what you read. But what you read confers a sort of omniscience, as if the all-seeing eye of the camera was paralleled by the all-understanding ear of the reader of subtitles. The spectator takes on the role of interpreter experiencing the joy of connectedness without the pain of connection, the time and effort necessary to master languages. However, the very availability of the subtitles themselves indicates the limits to any omniscience that might be assumed by their readers.

Spectators of a film cannot judge the quality of subtitles unless they speak the language and if the majority did, there would be no need for them. Their very existence assumes ignorance of non-native languages on the part of the spectator. Ironically, what the subtitles imply in *Babel* is that they are in a sense not to be wholly trusted, not because of any external demonstration of subtitlers' incompetence, impossible within the narrative frame of the film, but because of the internal pressures on the translation process itself. That is to say, the subtitles reveal the extent to which Amelia mediating linguistically between the young children and her nephew Santiago, or Anwar acting as intermediary between Richard and the authorities, are continually forced to change or modify their translation of what is being said in order to manage situations of tension or conflict. The subtitles then confer a form of reflexive awareness on spectators as they see how interpreters or language mediators have to negotiate exchanges between languages. Subtitles in *Babel* both release spectators from the burden of translation and simultaneously make them aware of the difficult, fraught process of translation itself. Subtitles provide a form of independence, which reveals other forms of dependence, or more properly inter-dependence, between languages and the processes of understanding that underpin the utopian project of translation.

It is misunderstanding rather than understanding that obsesses Chieko. When we first meet her, she is sent off at a volleyball match because she feels the referee has not understood what has happened in the course of play and she disagrees vehemently with his decision. Afterwards, in the car with her father (Kôji Yakusho), she says that unlike her late mother, 'You never pay attention to me.' She resents attitudes of the hearing community toward the deaf community and says to her friend, Mitsu (Yuko Murata), 'They look at us like we're monsters.' In one instance, Chieko accuses her father of not paying enough attention to her and in another, she resents too much attention being paid to her for the wrong reasons. When attention is paid to the powerless in *Babel*, it usually is for the wrong reasons. Villagers in remote areas only become a subject of interest when terrorist motives are attributed to a tragic accident. Amelia, after 16 years of domestic service as an illegal immigrant in the US, only becomes an object of attention when she is to be definitively deported. The FBI officer (R.D. Call) reprimands her for allegedly abandoning the children she had desperately tried to save. The problem with Babel, however, is not that the many languages make for many problems but rather that one language is an endless problem.

When the US government official tells Richard, 'It's all over the news. Everybody is paying attention,' he does not pause to consider if that is the kind of attention Richard or his wife need. In other words, global spectacle which does not engage with the complex realities of lived lives in a multilingual world is liable to lead to the wrong kind of attention being paid to all kinds of people. The failure of the Babelian project provides not reasons for despair but grounds for hope. What emerges in the film is that translation is the ultimate form of paying attention and that if Anwar refuses money from Richard at the end of the film it is not because he does not need the currency but because more importantly it is humanity itself which urgently needs Anwar's gift. The gift is not only of present concern, however, but also has implications for the future, and the final chapter will consider what happens to translation when it beats a path to the stars.

5 The empire talks back
Translation in *Star Wars*

Journeying to other planets is more often like return than departure. When fictional travelers head for other planets and galaxies, they do not so much leave problems of communication behind them as go back to old concerns in new forms, the inevitable return of the unexpressed (Mossop 1996: 1–27). In George Lucas' *Star Wars* trilogies, an ambitious space opera spanning more than a quarter of a century of film making from *Star Wars* (1977) to *Revenge of the Sith* (2005), communication in a multilingual galaxy is both a reality to be created and a problem to be solved. Translation is not a peripheral concern but a central issue for the different characters, entities and peoples who populate the imaginary worlds of films that grossed some of the highest box-office takings worldwide ever recorded for motion pictures. In this chapter, we will explore how translation is represented in the trilogies and what these representations can tell us about how translation is called upon to deal with issues of radical otherness.

The *Star Wars* trilogies in order of the chronological appearance of the films begin with *Star Wars* (1977), also called *A New Hope*. This film was followed by *The Empire Strikes Back* (1980) and *Return of the Jedi* (1983). When Lucas returned to making the second *Star Wars* trilogy in the 1990s, he decided to make a 'prequel,' in other words, the action in these films would in historical terms precede events in the first three films. The first film in the prequel trilogy was *The Phantom Menace* (1999). This film was followed by *Attack of the Clones* (2002) and *Revenge of the Sith* (2005). What is notable in most of the films of the trilogies is the prominence of a character who is robot rather than human, C-3PO. C-3PO is a 'protocol droid,' an intelligent, self-aware robot, whose primary tasks are diplomacy and translation. When in *The Return of the Jedi* he is asked the question that comes to haunt all translators, 'How many languages do you speak?,' his response is swift, 'I am fluent in over six million forms of communication.' So what function does C-3PO fulfill in the narrative and how does his role as a translator or more specifically interpreter influence the attitude of other characters toward him?

C-3PO and the task of translator

The first noticeable feature of C-3PO is that he is a particular kind of droid. His gait is ungainly, slightly comical and from the outset he shambles along in the company of another droid, R2-D2. He is not the menacing robot of science-fiction dystopias, all staccato speech and mindless firepower. His appearances indeed are almost invariably signaled by a change in the musical score, from threatening martial music to lighter, more playful melodies. His speech is notably different from most of the other characters, being identifiably British English and involving a vaguely parodic version of Received Pronunciation. The register of language that he uses is generally higher than that of the other characters, so in *Star Wars* he exclaims to Luke, 'Frankly, sir, I don't know what he's talking about,' while one of his first utterances in *The Empire Strikes Back* is 'Might I enquire what's going on?' There is a sense in which amidst the galactic swashbuckling of the Jedi Knights and the cowboy machismo of Han Solo (Harrison Ford), C-3PO is odd, not simply because of his droid status in the company of humans but in his somewhat effete manner and the marked difference of his language in terms of accent and register. This raises the question of the particular status of C-3PO, and, by extension, that of translation and the translator in the *Star Wars* trilogies.

   C-3PO offers a back-handed compliment to Luke Skywalker in *The Empire Strikes Back* when he observes to R2-D2 that Skywalker 'is quite clever, you know, for a human being.' When, later in the same film, he is introduced to Lando Calrissian (Billy Dee Williams), he announces his responsibility for 'human–cyborg' relations and appears miffed that Lando shows no interest in learning about or availing of his translation facilities. Thus, he possesses a range of skills that are far superior to those of the humans around him and he is not shy of reminding other characters of his superior multilingual skills. When asked by Luke's foster father in *Star Wars* if he speaks 'Bocce' (the jargon of intergalactic traders), there is a note of affronted dignity and condescension in his reply, 'Of course I can, sir, it is like a second language to me.' As we noted earlier R. Bruce W. Anderson has commented on the particular authority of the interpreter, 'his position in the middle has the advantage of power inherent in all positions which control scarce resources' (Anderson 1976: 218). In mastering six million forms of communication, the protocol droid has very explicit control over a scarce resource. It is his ability to communicate with the Ewoks that will eventually save the rebels in the culminating film of the original trilogy, *The Return of the Jedi*. When C-3PO starts to speak the 'primitive dialect' of the Ewoks, their initial hostility turns to veneration and he tells a baffled Han Solo that 'they seem to think I am some kind of God.' It is their belief in the droid's divinity that leads to their assistance being enlisted in the decisive struggle against the troops of the empire. It is C-3PO who is singled out for favorable treatment, whereas his companions, unable to communicate in a language other than Spoken Galactic Basic [identical, not surprisingly, to spoken English (Burrt 2001)], are initially to be served up at a celebration banquet in honor of C-3PO, a fact communicated to Han Solo by the newly deified translator. Therefore, though he is presented as a somewhat shambolic character, an innocent abroad in the galaxy, his specific set of skills and knowledge base as a translator (largely functioning in an oral mode) make the bumbling, otherworldly droid perform most effectively in other worlds.

As always, however, the position of the translator excites marked ambivalence. In *The Empire Strikes Back*, Han Solo can scarcely conceal his contempt when he tells C-3PO that the droid needs to talk to the Falcon (Han's spaceship) to find out what's wrong with the hyperdrive, and irritated with C-3PO's procrastination asks that somebody, 'Take the professor into the back and plug him into the hyperdrive.' He may be remarkably intelligent but he remains a tool, an object to be plugged into another machine to do the bidding of his human masters. The subservience is clearly marked in the films by C-3PO's continual recourse to submissive or formal forms of address, 'Master Luke,' 'Lieutenant Solo,' 'sir.' The subordinate position of the droid–translator is signaled in another setting, the meeting between Luke Skywalker and Jabba the Hutt, one of the most extended episodes of explicit translation in *The Return of the Jedi*. C-3PO becomes interpreter for Jabba the Hutt on foot of his predecessor's misfortune. When C-3PO informs one of Jabba's droids that he is fluent in many forms of communication, the response is unnerving, 'Splendid, we have been without an interpreter since our master got angry with the last protocol droid and disintegrated him.' At this point the camera switches to images of a protocol droid being 'disintegrated,' that is broken up or terminated. His first assignment is to interpret between Jabba and a bounty hunter who has captured Chewbacca, a hairy

Figure 8 C-3PO surrounded by adoring Ewoks who think he is a god.

Star Wars: Episode VI – Return of the Jedi (1983) Directed by Richard Marquand, USA: Lucasfilm

biped and constant companion to Han Solo. C-3PO as interpreter takes on the voice of his new master, 'The Illustrious Jabba bids you welcome and will gladly pay the ransom of 25,000.' Negotiations around the ransom to be paid are, however, tense. Jabba offers one sum but the bounty hunter wants twice as much. When C-3PO communicates the message to Jabba, the latter in a rage knocks the protocol droid over whose plaintive response is, 'What did I say?' C-3PO is acknowledged to be clever, learned, and he does play a crucial role in the unfolding narrative saving the rebels from certain destruction, but his power as translator is framed within a context of subordination. Even when C-3PO is elevated by the Ewoks to a god-like status, he protests vigorously claiming that it is against his programming to impersonate a deity. As C-3PO confesses to Luke in the first film of original trilogy, *Star Wars*, 'I'm not much more than an interpreter.' Part of the subordination relates to the nature of his task, which is principally oral translation in the case of sentient beings. With respect to oral communication, C-3PO must be physically present in the translation settings. Any utterance he makes must be sensitive to the context of the utterance. Therefore, whether it is Jabba expressing his unhappiness at the contents of a message or a trussed-up Han Solo demanding angrily to know what the Ewoks are saying, C-3PO is continually subject to the political, military or moral tensions prevailing in the relationships between the different individuals and groups. He becomes a vicarious object of abuse for difficulties the characters encounter in their contacts with each other. The message and the messenger become one and the consequences are rarely comforting. Translators in situations of conflict cannot, therefore, remain immune to the pressures of competing interests. If the narrative engine of the *Star Wars* trilogies is discord, the struggle between the rebels and the 'evil, galactic Empire,' then translators are by definition going to experience and have to deal with the necessary tensions.

There is, however, a dimension to C-3PO's role as interpreter which indicates why translators do feature in so many motion pictures. A consequence of necessary physical presence means that the interpreter has not only a communicative but also a testimonial function. In other words, because the interpreters must be there in order to ensure that individuals or groups may communicate with each other, they become witnesses to any number of dramatic or key events. If conflict is the fundamental driver of mainstream cinematographic narrative (no conflict, no story), it is reasonable to assume that in the space-opera genre in science fiction with its broad sweep across worlds, universes and galaxies, moments of tension or turning points are going to involve communicating across difference. As a result, the interpreter is ideally positioned to bear witness to important shifts in the development of the narrative. The attraction of the translator as interpreter (and in the *Star Wars* trilogies, the translation activity is overwhelmingly oral) is that the interpreter can function as a perfectly plausible narrative device not only to precipitate change but also to report on it. In a sense, what cinema offers is what is often denied the interpreter off screen, a visual confirmation of the functional duality of the interpreter as both communicator and witness. That is to say, the interpreter may be very effective at ensuring communication happens but in the case of diplomatic interpreting, in particular (C-3PO as a protocol droid is responsible for diplomacy and translation), it is rarely possible for reasons of confidentiality and secrecy to bear forthright, public witness to what has been said (Roland 1999). The camera, in a manner of speaking, makes explicit what the interpreter has to leave untold.

But it not just a question of seeing interpreters in action, it is also in the case of talking pictures about hearing them in action. In the *Return of the Jedi* there is a scene where C-3PO entertains the Ewoks with what appears to be an account of the exploits of Luke Skywalker, Han Solo and Princess Leia. It is possible to pick out the proper names, which provides some clue as to what might be the content of C-3PO's tale along with dramatic gestures and sound effects. However, the spectators are as bemused as Han Solo and Princess Leia who look on, mystified, if smiling indulgently. Spectators become aware of their relative helplessness in the absence of subtitles or interpreting which might elucidate the content of what is being said. The particular strength of the science-fiction genre is the ability to create languages which are in principle unintelligible to all humans. In other words, irrespective of a spectator's language abilities, there is a radical democratization of incomprehension when faced with languages that are wholly other. The presence of the necessity or the fact of translation becomes an inescapable reality for all. This is not to say, of course, that there are not science-fiction fans who will learn Huttese or Shyriiwook (the language of Wookies such as Chewbacca), but this is a learned response. Unlike natural languages, no one apart from their creators, has an innate command of these languages. So in the cantina scene in *Star Wars* where Han Solo finds himself assorting with various extra-terrestrial lowlifes, the strangeness of the place is not simply to do with the visual oddity of the creatures assembled there but with the incomprehensible babble of utterly foreign languages. Estrangement is as much a matter for the ear as for the eye.

It could be argued that scenes involving C-3PO in the *Star Wars* trilogies invite the spectator to experience not only the why of translation but also the how. The other prominent droid and loyal companion to C-3PO in the trilogies is R2-D2. He communicates in what to the human ear sounds like whirring and whistling sounds and is generally interpreted by C-3PO. However, in *The Empire Strikes Back* there is a long sequence where there is no C-3PO on hand to interpret for the audience. A common assumption, however, is that the frenetic bleeping and whistling would seem to indicate the imminence of danger, which does in fact, on occasion, materialize. Similarly, Chewbacca, the Wookiee, speaks a language which is understood by Han Solo and the translation is offered to the spectator in the form of consecutive paraphrase. However, when Jabba the Hutt decides to put Han Solo in a carbon freeze, Chewbacca loses not only his friend but also his interpreter. The spectator no longer has a translation available and has to guess at what the long series of animalistic roars and growls means, presumably distress at the loss of his beloved master. In both instances, the task of translation is thrust upon the audience so it is they rather than narrative surrogates who have to engage in the business of the translator. What is noteworthy is that in both instances it is emotions or feelings (of distress or alarm) that would appear to 'transcend' translation. The specificity of language and the need for mediation is dispensed within the limited situations of strong emotion. In a sense, what is happening in these scenes is the correlative of the common, human experience of travel where encounters with unknown, foreign languages mean that 'translation' of a kind has to be performed (Cronin 2000).

The act of translation is commonly understood to involve the knowledge of two languages and rendering of meaning in one language in another. However, there are many instances in travel where no such knowledge is available, the travelers do not know the language, but they must nonetheless attempt a 'translation' in order to make sense of a situation or place in which they find themselves. In these instances, the traveler–translator will try to correlate sounds, gestures, facial expressions with emotions that are familiar to him or her such as fear, joy, concern, menace or apathy. This dilemma is exemplified in the *Return of the Jedi* in Princess Leia's first encounter with an Ewok. She speaks to the diminutive furry creature in Spoken Galactic Basic, aka spoken English, but the Ewok does not respond in English. Leia then accompanies her words with gestures. An offer of food appears to be understood while the removal of her helmet is initially mistaken for an act of aggression. When Leia and the Ewok manage to escape the unwelcome attention of imperial troops, the Ewok gives directions by raising an arm and pointing the way. The communication then is primarily through gesture, as travelers gesticulating exaggeratedly in foreign countries are also wont to do, but the film makes the fatal and mistaken assumption that there is a universal grammar of gesture which somehow transcends specific language differences. Irrespective of the validity of the procedure or the assumptions, however, what the scene presents the audience with is again the inescapability of the translation fact. The spectators are as lost as Princess Leia in attempting to interpret the untranslated presence of the Ewok.

C-3PO in his moments of linguistic braggadocio does not count his languages in millions but his 'forms of communication.' In addition, he repeatedly points out that he is responsible for 'human–cyborg relations.' So there is an explicit sense in which C-3PO straddles the divide between the human and the non-human, the sentient and the inanimate, the cultural and the material. If C-3PO is envisaged as an in-between figure, a translator who must translate in a way between these different realms, how does this affect the representation of translation and translators in the films themselves? C-3PO is R2-D2's main conduit to human speech, the protocol droid who changes mechanical sounds into intelligible words. In *A New Hope* it is pointed out

early in the film that C-3PO speaks the 'binary language of moisture eva-
porators.' As we saw earlier, it is C-3PO who is plugged into the hyperdrive
on Han Solo's Falcon to investigate a malfunction. The droid treats the
communication system on the ship as if it were akin to a human language
noting, 'I don't know where your ship learned to communicate but it has the
most unusual dialect.' When R2-D2 later in *The Empire Strikes Back* uses
an incorrect code and admits to having got it from the City Central
Computer, C-3PO berates the droid saying, 'You know better than to trust a
strange computer.'

The forms of communication and the carriers of the forms become in a
sense anthromorphized in C-3PO's descriptions. It could be argued, however,
that the very interchangeability of machine and human forms of communication in C-3PO's worldview means that what he comes to represent is a
vision of translation which is reductive and misleading. That is to say, the
entrusting of the task of translation to a robot, albeit formidably intelligent,
conveys the message that translation is fundamentally a mindless task of
semantic transfer which could be performed by a competent machine.
Language itself, rather than being the epitome of subjective creativity and
expressiveness, becomes a code like any other. The language of the hyperdrive is no more or less to be wondered at than the utterances of the Ewoks.
In this view, an efficient and suitably submissive protocol droid nourishes
monoglot complacency and technocratic hubris by suggesting that translation
problems and language differences are nothing that cannot be solved by the
right algorithms from an Anglophone engineer.

The behavior of C-3PO, however, contradicts this reductionist view of the
task of the translator. One of C-3PO's earliest complaints in *A New Hope* is
that being 'made to suffer' is part of his lot in life. Part of this suffering stems
from his awareness of the import of his translation. He is not simply imper-
sonally transmitting transmitted material but he is represented as being
acutely sensitive to the implications of his translation for his target audience.
This metacommunicative awareness is signaled to the audience by his per-
sonalized interpretation of the messages he must interpret. In *Return of the
Jedi*, for example, C-3PO is caught between the cantankerous despot Jabba
the Hutt and the avaricious bounty hunter holding a thermonuclear device
which he is ready to explode if he is not satisfied with the ransom sum
offered for Chewbacca. Interpreting between the bounty hunter and Jabba
the Hutt, C-3PO communicates Jabba's final offer with a note of supplication
and warning, 'Jabba offers the sum of 35[000] and I do suggest you take it.'
Conscious of the destructive potential of a thermonuclear device and the
irascibility of his new master, C-3PO does not adhere to a putative notion of
absolute fidelity to the original message but intervenes to inflect the reception
of the words he has to interpret. Later, when Luke Skywalker and Han Solo
are brought before Jabba, C-3PO indicates his distress at the news he has to
translate into Spoken Galactic Basic when he declares, 'Oh Dear! His
Exalted Highness Jabba the Hutt has decreed you are to be terminated

immediately.' On the other hand, when Han Solo instructs C-3PO to tell that 'slimey, worm-ridden piece of filth,' Jabba, that he will not beg for mercy, C-3PO judiciously refuses to interpret. Thus, what is apparent in the case of the protocol droid is that translation cannot be a straightforward instance of linguistic transcoding with the elimination of the translation subject. C-3PO may be programmed to deal effectively with six million forms of communication but there is nothing programmatic about his translation practice. On the contrary, in the instances where he is called upon to translate, his attitude to what he translates and how he frames his translation is determined by his relationships to the participants in the exchange.

The protocol droid could be seen at one level as a 'machine translator,' he is after all a robot, but it is his dual attributes, translation *and* diplomacy, which bring the machine to life. The droid is anthropomorphized as much through what he has to do as by the manner in which he is built. In other words, it is not only the shambling gait and broadly human form that marks C-3PO out as a machine which excites empathy on the part of the audience, but his very activity as an interpreter shows that he too is capable of exercising that empathy, in his careful imagination of the consequences for those around him of the words he has to interpret. When he objects to being called a 'mindless philosopher' by R2-D2 at the beginning of *A New Hope*, his objection is an oblique rebuke to a view that would consider translation as a merely mechanical task, that translation could in any proper sense of the term be 'mindless.' It is a robot who paradoxically reminds us most forcefully of what it means to be human when engaged in the act of translation.

Subtitles

Translation on the screen is also inevitably bound up with screen translation. In other words, the science-fiction genre when it allows explicitly for language difference, has potential recourse to the techniques of translation which are commonly used for audio-visual media. One of these techniques is subtitling and the *Star Wars* trilogies make noticeable use of subtitles throughout the different films. The first instance of subtitles being used is when Han Solo is cornered by Greedo in the cantina. Han Solo can understand his language, Huttese, but the audience cannot and as this is a key moment in the narrative, it is important to understand the substance of Greedo's threats. The use of subtitles is an effective device for plot clarification but it is possible to argue that in the context of science-fiction cinema and translation they have a further important function. Subtitles are, in effect, a form of recognition. The placing of subtitles on the screen gives a substantive reality to the existence of difference. Subtitles signal otherness in a direct and immediate way, not to be masked by the familiarizing intimacy of dubbing. This is not to say that subtitles cannot be domesticating, wholly adapted to the language system and values of the target audience, but rather to point to the ability of subtitles to leave the auditory distinctness of other speech forms intact. A corollary of difference is mediation. Although Spoken Galactic Basic is, not surprisingly, identical to spoken English, subtitles do signal the break with the monoglot fiction that Out There Is like In Here. The translation moment is the moment when that fiction is no longer tenable. What we read is not what we hear and we have to read because hearing is no longer enough. The galaxy is no longer a star-studded projection of the unilingual pieties of home. When Jabba the Hutt speaks without an interpreter and the translation of his words duly appear in the subtitles, the audience are no longer in a state of complacent autonomy (the galaxy populated with beings speaking Middle American) but are literally made aware of an acute translation dependency. For an Anglophone audience, the subtitles mark a minoritizing moment where from having galactic realities offered in the familiar accents of the English-speaking world, words suddenly become opaque and meaning must be mediated through an explicit translation presence. Language difference is at one level, of course, a necessary part of the project of verisimilitude. If attention is lavished on the construction of Klingon in the *Star Trek* series or on the Elvish languages in J.R.R. Tolkien's *Lord of the Rings*, it is to make the unbelievable believable. Not only seeing difference but hearing difference makes all the difference.

At another level, the language difference must be contained if it is not to become so radically other as to be indecipherable and, by implication, uncontrollable. Translation is that moment of containment where the other becomes capable of being understood and equally importantly, becomes susceptible to influence. It is for this reason that moments of narrative tension, whether it be the failure of the hyperdrive to function effectively or the initial encounter with the Ewoks, revolve around potential *translation failure*. In other words, if a language cannot be understood, then the protagonists are no longer in control of the situation. If there is no translator or means of translation to hand, the characters no longer have a way of interpreting and influencing events. Humankind cannot bear too much untranslated reality. To cope with this reality, therefore, science-fiction cinema can have recourse to intra-diegetic or extra-diegetic translation techniques (Gennette 1988). Intra-diegetic translation techniques are forms of translation contained within the narrative structure of the film. These would include, for example, the translation activities of C-3PO and the consecutive interpreting practice of Han Solo. Extra-diegetic techniques, on the other hand, are those which are extraneous to the narrative but are necessary if the audience is to understand what is going on. Subtitles are an example of an extra-diegetic translation technique. What these techniques have in common is that they are ultimately bound up with forms of control. If the rebels are seeking to escape the control of the Empire and take charge of their own destiny, they must be able to influence their circumstances and, in a multilingual galaxy, translation is the key to survival. Without translation, they are controlled by the uncontrollable.

Language variety

The activity of translation is not always signaled by radical otherness in form but can be more discreetly suggested by syntactic manipulation. Yoda is a character who appears for the first time in *The Empire Strikes Back* when Luke Skywalker crash lands on the planet Dagobah. He emerges as a key figure as it is he who completes Luke's training as a Jedi Knight. His diminutive size and prominent ears are not the only striking features of this unlikely mentor and trainer. He also speaks in a way that is decidedly original. When he first meets Luke, he says, 'Away put your weapon, I mean you no harm' and continues, 'Help you I can, yes.' Further on, Yoda tells Luke, 'Father, powerful Jedi was he' and when he despairs of his charge exclaims, 'The Boy, I cannot teach him.' The syntactic structure of modern English – Subject, Verb, Object (SVO) – is inverted and we get English spoken with a predominantly Object, Subject, Verb (OSV) order. Yoda's language has been described as a 'dialect' of Spoken Galactic Basic and the inventor of the language, Frank Oz, claimed that Yoda's way of speaking demonstrates his ability to foresee the future (Burtt 2001). Leaving aside the strong form of linguistic relativism implicit in Oz's comments, what is significant from the point of view of translation is that both the characters and the audience who engage with Yoda are continually obliged to engage in intralingual translation. That is to say, what Yoda represents is a translation challenge which is implicit rather than explicit. In the original English-language version of *The Empire Strikes Back*, there are no extra-diegetic or intra-diegetic techniques used when Yoda is on screen. There are no interpreters close by to render his speech in standard English nor are there subtitles offered to ease comprehension for the spectators. Like Luke, the audience must do their own intralingual translation work.

The importance of Yoda's speech form is to capture translational complexity within one language. In other words, the appellation 'dialect' or the presence of a different word order almost invariably points to the presence of another language subtending or ghosting the main language. Using a different order of words in a language is as much about capturing a past as foreseeing the future. The fact of having to translate or be translated from another language means that part of the history of language encounter or transfer gets embedded in the new language. The translation effort of the translated is in a minor, but significant, way now transferred to the core speakers of the main language who have to translate what the translated are saying into standard speech. Luke's training is essentially a lesson in feeling. He must sense the Force around him and develop a stoic indifference to strong, negative emotions. But it could also be argued that his apprenticeship with Yoda is an exercise in language humility, an acknowledgement that Basic is not so simple. In dealing with Yoda's variety of Spoken Galactic Basic, Luke learns that part of the Force is language and that communication is as much a matter of translation as feeling and that the Dark Side is as much to do with monoglot hubris as with unresolved anger at Oedipal wrongs.

When Qui-Gon Jinn (Liam Neeson) arrives on the planet Naboo in *The Phantom Menace*, the first film of the prequel trilogy, one of his first encounters is with a horse-like creature, the Gungan, Jar Jar Binks. As with Yoda, Binks speech is not subtitled nor is anyone performing an obvious translation task. This is, in part, due to the fact that the phrases and expressions used by the character have a sufficient similarity to English to make for a reasonable level of intelligibility. *Oie boie!* (Oh Boy!), *Oyiee, mooie, mooie* (Oh, my, my), *Wesa goin' underwater* (We are going under-water), *Yousa in big dudu this time* (You're in big trouble this time). Variations in the form of affixes attached to recognizable English words, irregular syntactic constructions and the use of an accent which resembles an exaggerated form of a Caribbean accent in English, make the Gungan language different but familiar to speakers of Basic. When words are unknown ('dudu') their meaning can generally be intuited from their immediate context. Jar Jar Binks and his fellow Gungans feature prominently in *The Phantom Menace*. It is striking that both they and the Neimoidians, who are prominently involved in the Trade Federation, are distinguished by heavily accented forms of English, heavily accented that is with respect to the standard American and British accents used by the assorted humans in the film. In the case of the Neimoidians, their accent was based on a version of Thai-speakers using English (Burrt 2001: 162). In the *Star Wars Galactic Phrase Book and Travel Guide* we are given a 'history' of the Neimoidian language:

> Historically, as the Neimoidians ranged out from their home planet and developed the extensive commerce network that dominates the central system, they found that Pak Pak [Neimoidian native language] just couldn't be reproduced or understood by other races. They came to the realization that, in order to hold sway over the myriad of business franchises and trade contracts they controlled, they would have to adapt. Therefore, they forced their rigid vocal cords to mimic Basic which resulted in the dialect that is still most commonly heard today. (105–6)

In the pseudo-history of the invented language, it is trade and business which compel the Neimoidians to abandon their native language and opt for the lingua franca of Basic. And it is a dispute around trade and taxation that sets in train the events that lead to the blockade and invasion of Naboo. So if the original *Star Wars* trilogy has virtuous Republicans fighting the designs of an evil Empire, a post-Cold War trilogy revolves around interests that are economic as much as political. The radical expansion of market penetration that is commonly associated with the notion of 'globalization' in the last two decades of the twentieth century finds a recognizable parallel in the galactic imbroglio of *The Phantom Menace*.

A feature commonly associated with the growth of economic liberalism has been the spread of English as the language of the global market (Crystal 1997; Nic Craith 2005). As a global language engages more and more speakers, it can, as in the case of Yoda that we saw earlier, carry with it lexically or syntactically the translation remainder or residue of languages it has displaced. Another equally powerful, and indeed arguably more common, trace of translation is accent. The Neimoidians force their 'rigid vocal cords' to speak Basic but it is this very effort that signals the prior presence of Pak Pak. Like the Gungans, they make themselves understood but it is not so much that they dispense with translation as they internalize it. It is they who in this new galactic economy become their own translators. Their accent reveals translation as much as it conceals it. But the afterlife of language in the marked difference of non-standard accent is not simply a result of changing circumstances. It also becomes the site of a set of associations that add a further dimension to the influence of translation on perception.

In the *Star Wars Galactic Phrase Book and Travel Guide* the reader is informed that 'many common Gungan expressions will sound familiar to most travelers.' As a result, 'Most speakers of Basic, with a little practice, can comprehend what is said to them in Gunganese, save for the occasional purely Old Gungan word' (Burtt 2001: 99). What characterizes the first speaker of Gunganese that we encounter in the film, Jar Jar Binks, is his physical clumsiness and childlike naivety. It is clear that he is to play the role of comic fall guy in the film and his physical awkwardness is in a sense magnified by his linguistic 'awkwardness,' his non-standard speech marking him out as something of an oddity. Indeed, C-3PO makes this clear at one point in an aside to R2-D2 when he remarks, 'You know I find that Jar-Jar creature to be a little odd.' A stock feature of theatre and cinema in many traditions has been the playing of comic roles by characters with non-standard regional or class accents (Moore 2007: 18–29). Accent as the ineradicable sign of origin becomes the humorous marker of failed translation. The characters speak the dominant language of the culture but they do not speak with the accent of the dominant class. They have moved, as implied in that spatial sense of translation (e.g. rural characters moving to the city), but they have not moved far enough. So this partially successful translation leads to a ready equation of accent with a form of arrested development.

The point is made rather baldly if tellingly by Qui-Gon Jinn when he says to Jar Jar, 'The ability to speak does not make you intelligent.' Jar Jar Binks' wide-eyed clowning leads to repeated paternal advice from Qui-Gon Jinn and he is generally treated in *The Phantom Menace* as if he were a mildly obstreperous but endearing child. So what we find with respect to accent is the dual valency of translation in a multilingual galaxy, which is increasingly subject to the linguistic tensions and cultural pressures of economic expansion and political ambition. In the case of the Neimoidians, difference in accent signals a sinister dimension to their character and dealings. Like textbook villains, when they open their mouth they are not to be trusted. The translation remainder invites suspicion. On the other hand, Jar Jar Binks is presented not as threatening but as comic. His clumsiness gives rise to solicitude rather than distrust. The translation remainder is a cue for laughs. So accent as a trace of translation within Basic, the dominant language, can be represented negatively or positively, though even the 'positive' representations carry within them a strong undercurrent of condescension and the infantilization of the other, a standard figure of colonial writing (Fabian 1986).

In this context, it is striking that when key characters in the *Star Wars* trilogies speak other languages, they do not abandon their original accents. When C-3PO addresses the Ewoks in *Return of the Jedi* and regales them with stories in Ewokese, his accent is perfectly audible and it is the one he normally uses speaking Basic, a variety of Received Pronunciation (RP) in British English. In *The Phantom Menace*, Anakin Skywalker communicates in Huttese with his employer Watto and when Jar Jar Binks finds himself involved in a brawl with Sebulba, Anakin extricates the Gungan from a difficult situation through some timely linguistic mediation in Huttese. Apart from the early association of Skywalker with language and mediation, the scene is noteworthy for the fact that again the accent of a major character (a variety of standard US English when he is speaking Basic) is clearly discernible in the foreign language. It is a common aim of language learners to want to pass themselves off as native speakers of the language they are learning, and to help them achieve this aim phonetic exercises of various kinds (implicit or explicit) are an integral part of language teaching methods. However, accents are rarely neutral and around them cluster anxieties about self and identity. If C-3PO was to speak with a perfect Ewokese accent or if Anakin was to enunciate his fluent Ewokese without a trace of his original US accent, would that in some way diminish their sense of recognizable identity? Are the limits to translation to be found not so much in the words that they use but how they say them? That is to say, the real threat to a secure sense of identity on the part of the characters in situations of language contact may be less language knowledge than language use.

The accent of their language of origin or the dominant language of their formative period remains obdurately present as if to ward off the dissolution of primary identity in assimilation to another language. Characters will translate into and be translated into other languages, but accent signals the untranslatable, the residual sense of a source language and culture. Furthermore, on the screen, if the language transition was to be wholly achieved with characters speaking in the accents of their target languages, would this create problems of narrative identification for an audience? The characters might look the same, but if they sound different, are they the same people? It is interesting, in effect, to consider why, for example, Anakin and C-3PO, the protocol droid who was in fact built by Anakin, should keep their accents. Although, Anakin is a slave on Tatooine, he is quick to remind Queen Amidala's handmaiden, Padmé, that he is a 'person' and that he is different from all those around him. He may speak their language but he is not one of them. C-3PO is deified by the Ewoks and though he protests that deification is not in his program and he is suitably submissive to his human masters, he nonetheless repeatedly makes play of his language skills and superior intelligence. They both consider themselves to be special and this sense of difference is affirmed through a refusal to let go of (accentual) difference in situations of (language) difference.

The sense of fidelity to a language or culture of origin is not necessarily admirable. It may, indeed, constitute the grounds of resistance in the face of linguistic or cultural oppression but equally, of course, it can signal an unrepentant sense of ethnic or social superiority. The cultural capital of a particular accent can be used to alert listeners to the fact that even though translation may be taking place, communication is being established through speaking the foreign language, there is to be no thought of going native. The audible foreignness of the accent in the foreign language marks the limits of assimilation. The master may use your words but you can still hear him speaking as master. Thus, how accent is performed on screen and who is doing the performing provides crucial insights into questions of power, positionality and the limits to translation.

Translation effects and mobility

One of the rare instances of written translation, or more properly, written to oral translation, that occurs in the *Star Wars* trilogies is to be found in *The Phantom Menace*. Anakin Skywalker is flying a starfighter in the Battle of Naboo and a message comes up on his console in Aurebesh. Aurebesh is the alphabet used to represent the Galactic Basic (or English) language in the *Star Wars* trilogies. The message from R2-D2 can be rendered as 'Anakin turn the ship around and go back home straight away.' Anakin responds instantly to the command from R2-D2 by replying, 'Go back? Qui-Gon told me to stay in this cockpit, so that's what I'm going to do.' Aurebesh is formed from the first two letters of the alphabet, Aurek and Besh, on the model of the English word, alphabet, derived from the first two letters of the Greek alphabet, alpha and beta. The scene in *The Phantom Menace* is one of the only moments in the trilogies where the written language actually means something. Generally, when Aurebesh characters appear they simply represent consonants and have no identifiable meaning. What Aurebesh represents in essence is a form of transliteration, the literal rendition of English words into a non-Latin alphabet. No translation is provided for what appears on Anakin's console and, without formal study of the frames, the spectator has to intuit from Anakin's dialogue what the message was on the screen. The significance of Aurebesh goes beyond, however, its random or non-systematic use in the trilogies and relates to what might be termed a *translation effect*. We mean by this that the appearance of a non-Latin alphabet which is readily understood by characters speaking what we hear to be English, complicates the transparency of the language for those who understand the language. Galactic Basic both is and is not English. The visual evidence of Aurebesh sets up a hiatus between spoken words that can be understood and written words that cannot. The audience are suddenly rendered illiterate. Translation is necessary at two levels. Not only must the spoken language be made comprehensible to spectators but also Aurebesh introduces the written dimension. Literate languages are seen to exist in two translation realms, written and oral, and mastery of one does not necessarily imply mastery of the other, a point deftly emphasized by the presence of the foreignizing Aurebesh alphabet. The translation effect is the consequence of the use of Aurebesh. An alphabet that does not correspond to any known existing alphabet estranges the spectator from a sense of uncomplicated familiarity with language, and signals that, even for those who speak English, translation is an inevitable feature of Galactic Basic.

Faraway in space is invariably far away in time but the direction of the distance itself varies. Each film in the trilogy begins with the storybook phrase, 'A long time ago, in a galaxy, far, far away.' The phrase itself expresses a paradox that is frequently associated with the science-fiction genre, namely that the distant future can often look strangely like the remote past. The technology on display in the films is extremely remote from the current technical capacities of human beings, notably in the area of space travel, yet the meta-narrative framing the trials and tribulations of the Republic speaks of events taking place '[a] long time ago.' The modes of dress, the lightsaber duels, the mixing of feudal aristocracy with institutions reminiscent of Republican and Imperial Rome, and the architectural quotations from the Old Library in Trinity College Dublin (model for the Jedi archives) to the Cathedral of the Sagrada Familia in Barcelona (model for the droid factory) situate the futuristic space opera in identifiable human pasts.

The bi-directionality of a journey into the past which becomes an expedition into the future, is explicitly echoed at the level of language and translation strategy. As we noted earlier in *Return of the Jedi*, C-3PO uses a highly formal and distinctively archaic register when interpreting for Jabba the Hutt, 'The illustrious Jabba bids you welcome.' This register is used later in the same film by Darth Vader when he addresses the Emperor, 'What is thy bidding, my Master?' In *The Phantom Menace*, Watto offers an opinion on Obi-Wan's incredulity which is subtitled, 'Your friend is a foolish one, methinks' and when C-3PO is reunited with his maker, Anakin Skywalker, and Padmé, in *Attack of the Clones* his comment is a quaint, 'Bless my circuits, I am so pleased to see you both.' The use of words, phrases or expressions from earlier periods in the development and use of the English language serves at one level the obvious function of signaling distinctness. The characters who use different kinds of language are different in benign (C-3PO) or malign (Darth Vader) ways. There is another level at which archaism functions and this is as an unmasking of the translation process involved in any usage of language over time. This process was notably described by George Steiner in *After Babel*, where he argued that any attempt to read a text from an earlier historical period in a language involved, of necessity, a close translation. Older syntactic forms, differences in illocutionary force, shifting semantic fields, changed historical circumstances, implicit webs of intertextual reference, all conspire to make the rendering of a text from a previous era, an arduous exercise in translation (Steiner 1975). The past is not so much a different country as, in a sense, a different language.

If space travel is about travel to different planets and different solar systems, then not only is difference signaled intralingually as we have seen with respect to language, but there is also the factor of historical time. What the archaisms imply is that the spectator will have to translate earlier usages of the language into a modern idiom to make the meaning apparent. Though the translation task is not particularly complex for the spectator of the *Star Wars* trilogies where archaisms are used sparingly, it is nonetheless evidence of a mechanism that subtends the history of any language, namely, the replacement of forms of usage, which, as they slip out of currency, can only be retrieved by a process of intralingual translation. An implicit association is further established between particular historical forms of the language and suggested political norms in the culture. In other words, when archaic language forms are used it is usually in the context of subservience where submissiveness is connoted by older and, to modern ears, more obsequious forms of address. If translation is inevitably about movement from one form of language to another, it must inevitably imply a process of comparison. If the forms are not compared, there is no way of knowing what, if anything, needs to be changed. It is this process of comparison that invites a cultural relativism, which is arguably at work each time the translator translates both within and between languages. By noting a form of language as dating from an earlier period, it is not simply a question of identifying words that are different but a whole way of relating to others through language that has changed. Part of the process of intralingual translation is identifying the nature of the cultural and political changes made manifest in language itself. The task is made easier for the spectator of the *Star Wars* trilogies in that hierarchical relations are clearly delineated in all six films. A long time ago may not be so far, far away, in terms of the contemporary relevance of how democracy comes to be defined and who connives at its destruction.

Clones

If democracy is about a establishing a community of equals, then cloning in the trilogies is about creating a community of equals who are not equal. In *Attack of the Clones* when Obi-Wan arrives on the planet of Kamino, he is brought to see the new clone army by Lama Su, the prime minister of the planet. She argues that clones are 'immensely superior to droids' because they can 'think creatively.' However, Lama Su then informs Obi-Wan that, 'they are totally obedient, taking any order without question.' Their genetic make-up is modified so that the clones 'are less independent than the original host.' The clones are equal in every respect of their physical appearance but they are genetically 'programmed' to accept their subordinate position, their basic lack of equality. There is a less sinister and more parodic version of cloning in an encounter between Obi-Wan and a depressed habitué of a club on the planet Coruscant. The young man offers Obi-Wan some 'death sticks' and then proceeds to repeat exactly everything that Obi-Wan says, only changing the subject pronoun. When Obi-Wan counsels him, 'You want to go home and rethink your life,' the young man responds, 'I want to go home and rethink my life.' Like a verbal clone, he mirrors every word that Obi-Wan proffers. What cloning most effectively brings to the fore are questions that are central to the practice and perception of translation, namely, questions of identity and difference.

Adam Phillips, discussing the notion of sameness, draws attention to the choice of animal for the first successful cloning experiment:

> It seems somehow appropriate – whatever the scientific equivalent of poetic justice may be – that the first animal to be successfully cloned was a sheep. Sheep, after all, are not famous for their idiosyncrasy, for the uniqueness of their characters. We had assumed that sheep were virtually clones of each other, and now we have also been reminded that they are inevitably – all but two of them – genetically different.
>
> (Phillips 2000: 334)

Dolly the clone was, in effect, different from all the other sheep except one by virtue of being identical. Phillips goes on to note that one of the persistent longings of the modern age has been to create a sense of community but that we get uncomfortable if people want to be too like or identical to their image of themselves, 'From our experience of small-scale cults and large-scale fascism we have become fearful when too many people seem to agree with each other – seem to be of the same mind about something – or claim to know who they really are' (334). Democracies need a minimum of consensus to survive but too much can spell its doom. So being the same can make a difference but not always for the better. Where does this leave translation which, in one version, is all about sameness, trying to reproduce the same message in another tongue? In *The Phantom Menace*, the sports commentator at the pod race on Tatooine, has two heads, one head speaking in English and the other in Huttese. Is there something monstrous then about this bicephalous bilingual, saying the same thing in both languages? Is there something unnerving or 'unnatural' about the practice of translation, where like the young depressive in the club in Coruscant, translators are condemned to repeat the words of their masters of the moment, a kind of clone army of language?

One way of answering these questions is to look at what happens to a being who is classed as inferior to a clone by Lama Su, a droid. Whatever Lama Su's claims about the creativity of clones, they share one crucial trait with droids, namely that they are programmed to serve. As we saw earlier with respect to the protocol droid, C-3PO, he constantly reminds his inter-locutors that he is at their service. In *The Phantom Menace*, we see the young Anakin Skywalker assembling the future protocol droid. The idea is that the droid will help his mother with translation tasks on Tatooine. As Anakin grows into manhood in *The Attack of the Clones*, a subtext to the creation of C-3PO becomes more immediately apparent. In a key scene where the distraught Skywalker confesses to having slaughtered the Tusken raiders who had kidnapped his mother and tortured her to death, he speaks of his skill at fixing things and exclaims, 'I will even learn to stop people from dying.' This wish is an almost exact parallel to the ambition of Dr Victor Frankenstein in Mary Shelley's eponymous novel to vanquish death. Traumatized by the death of his mother, Frankenstein vows to discover the secret of life and end the spectacle of human mortality. The trauma is amplified in *The Revenge of the Sith* where foreseeing his wife's death in childbirth leads Anakin to ally himself with the Sith and conspire against the Republic in the hope of learning to master and overcome death. Like Anakin, he assembles his 'Creature' and just as C-3PO complains about the incomplete nature of his maker's work (his inner parts are showing) the Creature put together by Victor Frankenstein turns out to be more botched than beautiful.

If the Old Testament God was to make man in his likeness, Victor Frankenstein usurping the divine prerogative wants to make a man who would be like him in his humanity but unlike him in his perfection. The tragedy for Frankenstein is that the Creature is all too human and, denied affection, turns against his maker with terrible consequences. Anakin Skywalker created C-3PO specifically to help his mother but his creation can do nothing to prevent her death, just as Skywalker reincarnated as Darth Vader is powerless to prevent the death of Padmé. What does happen, however, is that the Creature that Anakin Skywalker brings into being, like his nineteenth-century predecessor, ultimately turns against his maker. Anakin Skywalker will finally turn to the 'dark side of the force' and emerge as Darth Vader. As we have already remarked, it is the translation skills of C-3PO that will ultimately frustrate the efforts of the emperor and Darth Vader to destroy the rebels and the ideal of the Republic. The translator for all his protestations of obedience and humility turns against his master and maker. In a sense, Victor Frankenstein and Anakin Skywalker, do realize their ambitions. They produce creatures who are capable of an autonomous existence. It is this very autonomy that constitutes their life force. Only death immobilizes. But it is precisely because they do engage with the world that both C-3PO and Frankenstein's creature become subject to the formative pressures of cir-cumstance as opposed to the rigid prescriptions of design. The internal con-flict is most vividly illustrated in the scene we discussed earlier where C-3PO in *Return of the Jedi*, partly as a result of his language skills, is hailed as a god by the Ewoks. C-3PO protests that impersonating a deity is contrary to his programming. However, the situation is such that C-3PO eventually decides to go along with the fiction and his mediation skills allow Han, Luke and Princess Leia to be admitted as members of the Ewok community.

C-3PO routinely complains about the vagaries of human behavior but unpredictability and changing circumstances are, of course, the stuff of life itself. This is why the fantasy of translation as droid-speak or as a form of verbal cloning runs aground on the shifting realities of context. Lama Su's lyrical phantasm of clones genetically modified to be totally submissive is a variation on Frankensteinian desire to give birth to creatures who will do the bidding of their masters and be shaped in their perfect image. But in the life world, beings are not simply static programs that produce responses independently of context. We both shape and are shaped by the situations in which we find ourselves. People carry with them beliefs, values and historical memories, which come with being raised in a particular culture, but part of the business of engaging with other languages and cultures is that the cultural 'programs' are no longer adequate, they are only one element in a multidimensional exchange which involves not only other languages and cultures but also changing contexts. In other words, the determinist ideal of coercive making, whether at the level of bodies, genes or machines, is constantly subverted by the fact of being in the world, whether here on Earth or in a galaxy, far, far away. The translator who becomes a site for these fantasies of servitude by design shows indeed that even when translators appear to be repeating literally what has been said, they elicit very different responses. The English speakers and the speakers of Huttese do not react with the same degrees of enthusiasm to the bilingual commentary of the bicephalous commentator at the pod race in *The Phantom Menace*. Translation in this respect becomes synonymous with the nemesis of determinism rather than with its final flowering. The target audience of a translation are ultimately free to respond to a message in a manner determined by context rather than design.

The retreat from translation

A constant preoccupation throughout both trilogies but more marked in the prequel trilogy is the fragility of democracy. What *The Phantom Menace*, *Attack of the Clones* and *Revenge of the Sith* chart is the irresistible ascension of the Empire and the weakening of democratic institutions. Chancellor Palpatine dreams of concentrating all executive powers into the person of the chancellor and revoking the powers of the senate. The emergency powers that are vested in him for the duration of military conflict start to take on a more permanent character as wars do not so much end as start anew. It is the handmaiden turned senator who, not surprisingly, is the most articulate and steadfast defender of the democratic ideals of the Republic. In *Revenge of the Sith*, she confesses to Anakin that she fears the 'democracy we are serving no longer exists.' As for the war against the 'separatists,' she favors diplomacy over military action and claims, 'This war represents a failure to listen.' The choice of verb is crucial. What listening involves is not only attention but also comprehension. Adversaries are unlikely to be listened to if they are not understood. In a multilingual galaxy, understanding speaks many tongues. It is only possible to listen if the translators are there to make this possible. In this respect, there is a striking parallel between the rise of autocracy in the prequel trilogy and the retreat from translation.

In *Attack of the Clones* when Jango the bounty hunter speaks to his son in his own language on Kamino, there is no translation offered. Later, when Anakin goes to Tatooine to find out what has happened to his mother, there is an extended passage of conversation in Huttese with Watto. Unlike the earlier films, no translation is offered by way of subtitles and it is only when Watto recognizes the adult Anakin that he switches to English. In the War Room scenes when creatures speak other languages, no translation is offered, either intra or extra-diegetically. The one exception is the leader of the Techno-Union army, a self-translator, who begins in English then shifts to his own droid-like language before literally switching (he fumbles with buttons on his chest) back to English. In *Revenge of the Sith* when Yoda lands on Kashyyyk there is no Han Solo on hand to translate Shyriiwook or Wookie-speak. Similarly, when Obi-Wan Kenobi arrives on Utapau he is met by the Port Administrator Tion Medon (Bruce Spence) who speaks both in English and a local language which is left untranslated. C-3PO does a limited amount of translation for R2-D2 in *Attack of the Clones*, but for the most part in the final two prequel films the droids R2-D2 and R4 are left without translation. Neither *Attack of the Clones* nor *Revenge of the Sith* carry any subtitles in their original English-language versions. What is noteworthy, on the other hand, is the increasing prominence in the final film of the prequel trilogy of on-screen characters who speak the language of Empire, English or Basic. General Grievous, between coughing fits, expresses his thoughts and gives his commands in English. The battle droids speak English. The clones speak English.

As the Empire emerges and gathers force under the manipulative influence of Chancellor Palpatine doubling up as Darth Sidious, the language of the Empire comes more and more to the fore. The plurality of languages and voices in the galaxy are increasingly marginalized. Intra-diegetic and extra-diegetic translation becomes a scarce resource. C-3PO is largely redundant and his most important role in *Revenge of the Sith* is as a pilot rather than as a translator. What are the implications of the peripheral status of explicit on-screen translation? One consequence is that as the Empire seeks to impose its will through force, coercion takes precedence over dialogue. If the separatist leaders are rarely translated, it is in part because Lord Dooku is not particularly interested in what they have to say as they will be sacrificed anyway on the altar of imperial ambition. Similarly, the clone army and their leaders are not overly concerned with the opinions of their Wookie allies as they will ultimately betray and slaughter them. If the practice of diplomacy has long been associated with the practice of translation (Roland 1999), when diplomacy breaks down translation is in trouble. The crisis of translation is indeed evident in the scene in *Attack of the Clones* where C-3PO finds himself unwillingly recruited to the droid army (his head was attached to a battle-droid body in the droid factory). In the Arena on Geonosis, C-3PO is horrified to find that he is in the middle of a battle exclaiming, 'I'm programmed for etiquette not destruction.' Etiquette may have acquired the quaint associations of crooked fingers and bone china teacups, but for the protocol droid it is about talking not fighting and involves listening to not destroying others. It is significant that in the scene in the same film when Anakin Skywalker massacres a group of Tusken raiders, killing all irrespective of guilt, gender or age, the spectators never get to hear them speak. The absence of language or language that is intelligible through translation makes it easier to dehumanize others. Where there is no translation, the people perish. If language is an attribute of intelligent beings, then to deny a person or group language is to place them outside or beyond the pale of acceptability. Thus, when Anakin confesses his crime to Padmé he declares, 'They're [the Tusken raiders] like animals and I slaughtered them like animals.' Incapable of communicating with them it is easier for Anakin to exile the Tusken raiders from a community of rights-bearing citizens. In this way, they can be treated as subhuman and therefore not entitled to the normal protections of the rule of law.

If seeing others as animals is to deny them fundamental rights, it also implies dichotomous forms of thinking. They are absolutely not like Us. It is precisely this form of thinking that Obi-Wan Kenobi finds so disturbing in a changed Anakin. The latter warns his former master that, 'If you're not with me, then you're my enemy.' Obi-Wan reminds his treacherous apprentice that, 'Only a Sith deals in absolutes.' One kind of absolutism is linguistic. The refusal to either acknowledge or engage with the multilingual diversity of one's environment, local, planetary or galactic, means that 'a failure to listen' is endemic rather than accidental and that wars are the not surprising outcome of the decay of dialogue. Anakin who starts life preoccupied by language issues, interpreting between Huttese and Basic and inventing the protocol droid, C-3PO, ends up immobilized in a binary trap of mutual exclusiveness. If his work as a translator involved movement between peoples and forms of communication, where Anakin primarily functioned in his own words, as a 'fixer,' or mediator, his role as the vanguard of imperial ambition is the fixing not the dismantling of boundaries, the reinstatement not the weakening of absolutes.

It is possible to see translation as a form of triangulation which prevents the clash or the violent and dogmatic synthesis of binary opposites. Whether it is the rhetorical maneuvers of the Cold War or the paranoid scapegoating of the War on Terror, absolutes are all the easier to maintain if there is no attempt at listening to what the other might have to say, if translators are not allowed, in other words, to do their work in the space inbetween languages and cultures. A variation on 'If you're not with me, then you're my enemy' is 'If you do not speak my language, then you're my enemy.' For empire to emerge, there must be a certain communicative cohesion and this is best ensured by getting subject peoples to speak the language of empire (Ostler 2005). In 1596, as we saw, the Elizabethan poet, Edmund Spenser, advocating the suppression of the Irish language gave a familiar justification, 'the speech being Irish, the heart must needs be Irish for out of the abundance of the heart the tongue speaketh' (Spenser 1970: 68). When all have been translated into the language of empire, there is no further need for translation.

In *Revenge of the Sith*, Padmé notes the surrender of freedom by the Republican Senate to autocratic absolutism saying, 'This is how liberty dies ... with thunderous applause.' As translation as an explicit intervention recedes from the last two films of prequel, the liberty that Padmé speaks of is not only political but also linguistic and cultural. As fewer and fewer languages are accorded the courtesy and status of translation and the screen is increasingly dominated by the reduced language of battle droids and clones speaking Basic, then separatists or rebels of any hue, political, linguistic or cultural, will not enjoy tolerance for much longer. In *Revenge of the Sith*, C-3PO exclaims at one point as the overall situation deteriorates, 'I feel so, so helpless.' His confession is eloquent of the distress experienced in situations where mediation has broken down, where the skills of the translator become redundant, an unwelcome reminder of a polyvocal Republic that might have been rather than the univocal Empire that has come to be.

Alien languages

Establishing the polyvocality of the *Star Wars* world involved particular kinds of transformation and it is useful to reflect on what the genesis of languages in the film trilogies can tell us about the nature and dilemmas of language contact and translation. The languages spoken in the films include Bocce, Droidspeak, Ewokese, Gunganese, Huttese, Jawaese, Neimoidian, Shyriiwook (Wookiespeak), Sullustan, Ubese and Tusken. The languages were created largely by the sound designer Ben Burtt with occasional assistance from the director George Lucas. Burtt acknowledged that generating new languages was the most challenging problem he faced in working on sound during a quarter-century of involvement with the *Star Wars* films:

> Overall, the creation of alien languages has been the hardest task. A language, or more accurately, the *sensation* of language, has to satisfy the audience's most critical faculties. We are all experts at identifying the nuances of intonation. Whether we understand a given language or not, we certainly process the sound fully and attribute meaning – perhaps inaccurate – to the emotional and informational content of speech. Our minds are trained to recognize and process dialogue. The task, therefore, of creating a language is all the more difficult because of the strength of the audience's perception.
>
> (Burtt 2001: 122)

Burtt's new languages fell into three categories; languages composed of animal sounds, languages derived from human-produced sound and languages synthesized from acoustical and electronic sounds. Part of Burtt's research was to identify foreign languages that could be used as a viable basis for alien languages. His choice of using natural language was that 'it possesses built-in credibility. A real language has all the style, consistency and unique character that only centuries of cultural evolution can bring.' Choosing a foreign language was also necessary for credibility but in a sense not just any foreign language,

> I found that if I relied on my familiarity with English, my imagined 'alien' language would just be a reworking of the all too familiar phonemes of everyday, general American speech. I had to break those boundaries, to search for language sounds that were uncommon and even unpronounceable by most of the general audience.
>
> (Burtt 2001: 133)

To this end, Burtt listened to language sample tapes from university linguistics departments, trawled through recorded language lessons and listened to shortwave broadcasts from around the world. The distortions of speech in the shortwave broadcasts were particularly interesting as they provided ideas for electronic processing.

Listening to recordings of foreign languages, Burtt 'found inspiration among many that were entertaining and exotic to my ears' (132). So Quechua became the basis for Huttese, pseudo-Tibetan and Kalmuck (a Mongolian language) the basis for Ewokese, Hyah (a Kenyan language) was used to originate Sullustan and the Zulu language was employed in the creation of Jawaese. It is significant that describing his work in language sourcing, Burtt couples together the adjectives 'entertaining' and 'exotic.' The incomprehensible can either be a source of wonder or a target of ridicule. If one understanding of comedy is that we do not feel implicated in the consequences of actions the way we do in tragedy (Aristotle 1965: 29–76), then the same observation can be extended to language. If the words spoken are ones that can be readily understood and their implications apparent, then the listener is bound to feel engaged by the meaning of what has been said. If, on the other hand, the meaning is opaque, it is possible to feel wholly distanced from the import of the words that have been spoken and this distance in itself becomes a basis for potential comedy. So the Funny Foreigners go on with their Funny Talk. This is not say, for example, that comedy is not possible within a language, an absurd idea clearly contradicted by the history of comedy in cinema, but to argue that the 'exotic' and the 'entertaining' are often linked by the alibi of distance.

What emerges in the trilogies is nonetheless a challenge to the untranslatable as a cue for laughter. With the possible exception of the Ewoks and the Gunganese, there is nothing especially comic about the speakers of other alien languages, as they go about their business in the different films of the trilogies. Indeed, it could be argued that translation itself, expressed intra-diagetically and extra-diagetically, has the effect of reducing the distance between the spectators and the characters. The spectators become implicated in meaning in a way that would not be possible if the words were to remain wholly and irreducibly foreign. Of course, the notion as to what is 'foreign' contains a set of assumptions as to who the 'general audience' is. If the 'general audience' were constituted exclusively of speakers of Quechua, Zulu and Hyah then the idea of the 'foreign' and the 'alien' would have to be redefined and (in sound terms) redesigned. By using certain natural, human languages as the basis for 'alien' languages, the very process of generating new languages makes a clear statement about both the limits of translatability and the language geopolitics of film audiences.

For the notion of an alien language to be acceptable, not only must it pass the credibility test described above, the possibility for language users to experience the '*sensation* of language' but the language must also not be familiar. If the 'general audience' can translate it without intermediaries then it is no longer 'alien.' It is recognizable human language albeit in the mouths of aliens but no longer credible in its absolute difference. The definition of an alien language in effect is a language that most of the audience cannot translate. Implicit in the thesis of untranslatability is that the films will be largely viewed by speakers of some languages rather than others. When *Return of the Jedi* was shown in Kenya, certain spectators correctly identified the language spoken by Lando Calrissian's co-pilot, Nien Nunb (Richard Bonehill) but outside of Kenya this would be a minority experience. This then is the core paradox of the alien languages in *Star Wars*, they must be familiar as language but not known as specific language. They must be familiar and yet unfamiliar. They must be capable of being translated, this makes these languages similar human languages, but it is precisely because we have to translate them that they are alien.

What of languages that are spoken not by living organisms but by machines? Burtt (2001) observed that few film makers prior to Lucas had taken seriously the consistent creation of a language to be spoken by a robot or the form of robot known as the droid:

> There was little or no precedent in cinema history for droid languages. Most robots had spoken English or were mute menaces. Some, like Bobby in the classic *Forbidden Planet*, had a normal voice intercut with various mechanical noises and electronic tones, but no film maker had tackled the idea of strictly electronic communication.
>
> The real difficulty in bringing R2-D2 to life was creating a sense of character, feeling and intelligence, using only non-verbal sounds. (140)

As Burtt notes further in connection with the use of voice distortion in English for the battle droids, 'Machines are not as interesting and involving as something that projects an illusion of will and intelligence' (158). If a machine is going to communicate using non-verbal sounds, on what basis is the spectator to construct a sense of character so as to remain interested in the actions or fate of astromech droids such as R2-D2 or R4? The solution that Burtt finally arrived at was to mix the electronic and the organic. Astromech droidspeak was, in effect, an interactive blend of synthesized tones and fake baby babble.

As we noted earlier, there is clear connection between passages of droidspeak and Wookiespeak and feelings of strong emotion. Burtt declares that '[a]ll sounds bring them an association with something emotional,' a fact that is confirmed by emotional effect of the non-verbal medium of music. Young infants similarly communicate emotion in the pre-verbal phase of their development. So what the astromech droids are inviting spectators to engage in is a dual form of translation. On the one hand, they are asked to translate droidspeak into a specific human language, Basic, a task performed variously by Han Solo and C-3PO and, on the other, to translate the droidspeak into a language of the emotions, where certain sounds are associated with puzzlement, distress, alarm. In the latter case, perceived emotion is what allows meaning to be conferred on what are in part pre-verbal rather than non-verbal sounds. As the trilogies unfold, it is increasingly the latter form of translation that is preferred in dealing with droidspeak as on-screen translation is gradually marginalized. When it comes to communication and translation the astromech droids are finally in a very real sense of the word left to their own devices.

It is not only the machine forms of communication that come within the translation purview of the *Star Wars* trilogies. There is also the realm of non-human, animal communication. The subject emerges in an oblique manner in the genesis of Shyriiwook or Wookiespeak. A young cinnamon bear called Pooh was prevailed upon to produce a series of sounds by being made to wait for his food and having various animals included lions paraded outside his cage. The vocalizations he produced were then classified as angry or happy or inquisitive. By varying the pitch and speed of the sounds and then combining them in various ways, Burtt was able to create the impression of real speech. Other animal sounds that were used to extend the range of Chewbacca's speech were the sound of walruses stranded at the bottom of a pool which had been drained for routine cleaning. When it was necessary to get more Wookie sounds for a *Star Wars Holiday Special*, Burtt went to the Olympic Game Farm in Sequim, Washington to get more bear vocalizations, although the most useful sound was that of a lion devouring a cow's head. If, as we saw earlier, denying language the status of human language can have murderous consequences, it does not follow that language which closely resembles non-human, animal sounds is invariably considered to be dangerous or menacing. On the contrary, the relentless human desire to anthropomorphize the animal world means that animal sounds can be annexed to a human lexicon of emotion and variously interpreted as angry, happy or inquisitive.

The Wookies are depicted in wholly positive terms in the *Star Wars* trilogies and their appearance as large, furry animals further strengthens the benign association of the creatures with creatures from the child's nursery rather than with menacing others from a non-human otherworld. They may revert to King Kong cameos for the battle against the droid army in *Revenge of the Sith* but the principal Wookie character, Chewbacca, is more akin to a faithful family retainer than a howling monster from out of the unknown. Part of the 'domestication' of Chewbacca in the original trilogy lies in the translation relationship with Han Solo. Solo by consecutively interpreting what Chewbacca has to say confers will and intention upon his companion. Identification is made easier because communication has been established. The animalistic roars and growls, which might in a non-translated medium come across as intimidating or threatening, are through the good offices of translation heard as simply part of a yet another alien language in a galaxy replete with language difference. Han, the reluctant rebel, cannot go Solo. He needs the assistance of Chewbacca, C-3PO, Luke Skywalker to survive and they like him find themselves straddling languages and cultures in a period of intense crisis and conflict. If the Dark Side of the Force in Anakin's own words is heartless egotism, then the Dark Side can only thrive when Force and Language become synonymous, when translation gives way to terror and the middle ground becomes a graveyard. Tracing the multiple presences of translation in mainstream film consumption is a step toward undoing the dark side of intolerance and investing in a forward-looking engagement in language and culture with renewed and enduring force. Seeing could again become a form of believing.

Bibliography

Aercke, K. (2006) 'The Pilgrimage of Konrad Grünemberg to the Holy Land in 1486', 159–73, in Carmine G. Di Biase (ed.) *Travel and Translation in the Early Modern Period*, Amsterdam and New York: Rodopi.

Aijmer, G. (1992) 'Comment on article by P. Steven Sangren', *Current Anthropology* 33 296–97.

Ambler, C. (2004) 'Popular Films and Colonial Audiences in Central Africa', 133–57, in Stokes, M. and Maltby, R. (eds.) *Hollywood Abroad: Audiences and Cultural Exchange*, London: British Film Institute.

Anderson, R.B.W. (1976) 'Perspectives on the Role of Interpreter', 208–28, in Brislin, R.W. (ed.) *Translation: Applications and Research*, New York: Gardner Press.

Ang, I. (1985) *Watching 'Dallas': Soap Opera and the Melodramatic Imagination*, London: Methuen.

Antoine, F. and Wood, M. (1999) *Humour, Culture, Traduction(s)*, Villeneuve d'Ascq: Maison de la recherché, Université Charles de Gaulle – Lille III.

Aristotle, Longinus, Horace (1965) *Classical Literary Criticism*, trans. T.S. Dorsch, Harmondsworth: Penguin.

Barnouw, E. and Krishnaswamy, S. (1981) *Indian Film*, 2nd edn., Oxford: Oxford University Press.

Bauman, Z. (1998) *Globalisation: The Human Consequences*, Cambridge: Polity Press.

Bayly, C.A. (2004) *The Birth of the Modern World 1780–1914*, Oxford: Blackwell.

Beer, G. (1996) *Open Fields: Science in Cultural Encounter*, Oxford: Clarendon Press.

Bose, M. (2006) *Bollywood: a History*, Stroud: Tempus.

Bowen, M., Bowen, D., Kaufmann, F. and Kurz, I. (1995) 'Interpreters and the Making of History', 245–77, in Delisle, J. and Woodsworth, J. (eds.), *Translators in History*, Amsterdam: John Benjamins/Unesco.

Braidotti, R. (1994) *Nomadic Subjects: Embodiment and Sexual Difference in Contemporary Feminist Theory*, New York: Columbia University Press.

Branchadell, A. and Lovell West, M. (2005) (eds.) *Less Translated Languages*, Amsterdam: John Benjamins.

Brewster, B. (1998) *Stage Pictorialism and the Early Feature Film*, Oxford: Oxford University Press.

Brownlow, K. and Kloft, M. (2002) *The Tramp and the Dictator*, London: British Broadcasting Corporation.

Bryson, B. (1994) *Made in America: An Informal History of the English Language in the United States*, New York: Avon Books.

Burtt, B. (2001) *Star Wars: Galactic Phrase Book & Travel Guide*, New York: Del Rey.

Casanova, P. (1999) *La République mondiale des lettres*, Paris: Seuil.

Castells, M. (1996) *The Rise of the Network Society*, Oxford: Blackwell.

Central Board of Film Certification (2008) 'An Overview of Films Certified from 1.1.2003 to 12.12.2003'. Available online: http://www.cbfcindia.tn.nic.in/statistics/statistics-page-2003-11.htm (accessed 25 February 2008).

Chanan, M. (1990) 'Economic Conditions of Early Cinema', 174–88, in Elsaesser, T. (ed.) *Early Cinema: Space – Frame – Narrative*, London: British Film Institute.

Coppola, S. and Murray, B. (2003) 'A Conversation with Bill Murray and Sofia Coppola', *Lost in Translation*, Momentum Pictures: DVD.

Costigliola, F. (1984) *Awkward Dominion: American Political, Economic and Cultural Relations with Europe, 1919–1933*, Ithaca, NY: Cornell University Press.

Cowie, P. (2004) *John Ford and the American West*, Abrams, New York.

Crane, D. (2002) *Global Culture*, London and New York: Routledge.

Crosby, A.W. (1989) *Ecological Imperialism: The Biological Expansion of Europe 900–1900*, Cambridge: Cambridge University Press.

Cronin, M. (1996) *Translating Ireland*, Cork: Cork University Press.

—— (2000) *Across the Lines: Travel, Language, Translation*, Cork: Cork University Press.

—— (2006) *Translation and Identity*, London: Routledge.

Crystal, D. (1997) *English as a Global Language*, Cambridge: Cambridge University Press.

Darwin, C. (1986) *Journal of Researches into the Geology and Natural History of the Various Countries visited by the H.M.S. 'Beagle'*, Part I in Paul Barrett and R.B. Freeman (eds.) *The Works of Charles Darwin*. London. Vol 2.

de Beauregard Costa, R. and Stokes, M. (2004) 'The Reception of American Films in France c.1910–20', 21–34, in Stokes, M. and Maltby, R. (eds.) *Hollywood Abroad: Audiences and Cultural Exchange*, London: British Film Institute.

Debo, A. (1976) *Geronimo: The Man, His Time, His Place*, Norman: University of Oklahoma Press.

Debray, R. (2000) *Introduction à la médiologie*, Paris: Presses Universitaires de France.

Delabastita, D. (1993) *There's a Double Tongue: An Investigation into the Translation of Shakespeare's Wordplay, with Special Reference to Hamlet*, Amsterdam: Rodopi.

Delabastita, D. and Grutman, R. (2005) 'Introduction: fictional representations of multilingualism and translation', 11–34, in Delabastita, D. and Grutman, R. (eds.) '*Fictionalising Translation and Multilingualism*', special issue of *Linguistica Antverpiansia*, NS4.

de Landa, M. (2000) *A Thousand Years of Nonlinear History*, New York: Swerve.

de Linde, Z. and Kay, N. (1999) *The Semiotics of Subtitling*, Manchester: St Jerome.

de Montaigne, M. (1978) *Essays*, Harmondsworth, Penguin.

—— (1988) *Les essais*. 3 vols. Paris: Quadrige/PUF. Vol. 1.

Descartes, R. (1637) *Discours de la méthode*, Paris: Colin, 1959.

de Zengotita, T. (2005). *Mediated: How the Media Shape Your World*, London: Bloomsbury.

Dolan, T. (1998) *A Dictionary of Hiberno-English*, Dublin: Gill and Macmillan.

Dumenco, S. (2001) 'Stopping spin Laden', *New York Magazine*, 12 November. Available online: www.nymag.com/nymetro/news/media/features/5379/index2.html (accessed 12 December 2007).

Eckert, C. (1978) 'The Carole Lombard in Macy's Window', *Quarterly Review of Film Studies*, 3, 3–12.

Egoyan, A. and Balfour, I. (2004) (eds.) *Subtitles: On the Foreignness of Film*, Cambridge, Mass.: MIT Press.

Eisenstadt, S.N. (2000) *Multiple Modernities in an Age of Globalization*, Jerusalem: Truman Institute Reprints.

Elsaesser, T. (1990) 'Introduction', 11–30, in Elsaesser, T. (ed.) *Early Cinema: Space – Frame – Narrative*, London: British Film Institute.

Erdogan, N. (2004) 'The Making of Our America: Hollywood in a Turkish Context', 121–32, in Stokes, M. and Maltby, R. (eds.) *Hollywood Abroad: Audiences and Cultural Exchange*, London: British Film Institute.

European Audiovisual Observatory (2005) *Yearbook 2005: Economy of the Radio and Television Industry in Europe*, Strasbourg: European Audiovisual Observatory.

Fabian, J. (1983) *Time and the Other: How Anthropology Makes its Object*, New York, Columbia University Press.

—— (1986) *Language and Colonial Power*, Cambridge: Cambridge University Press.

Fiebig-von Hase, R. and Lehmkuhl, U. (1997) *Enemy Images in American History*, Oxford: Berghahn.

Forsdick, C. (2005) *Travel in Twentieth-Century French and Francophone Cultures: the Persistence of Diversity*, Oxford: Oxford University Press.

Frederick, C. (1929) *Selling Mrs Consumer*, New York: The Business Bourse.

Friedman, T. (2007) *The World is Flat: A Brief History of the Twenty-First Century*, 2nd edn., London: Picador.

Gambier, Y. (2003) 'Screen Transadaptation: Perception and Reception', *The Translator*, 9, 2, 171–89.

Gaudreault, A. (1985) 'Bruitages, musique et commentaires aux débuts du cinéma', *Protée*, 13, 2, 25–29.

—— (1990) 'Showing and Telling: Image and Word in Early Cinema', 274–81, in Elsaesser, T. (ed.) *Early Cinema: Space – Frame – Narrative*, London: British Film Institute.

Geduld, H.M. (1971) (ed.) *Focus on D.W. Griffith*, Englewood Cliffs, NJ: Prentice Hall.

Gennette, G. (1988) *Narrative Discourse Revisited*, trans. J.E. Lewin, Ithaca, NY: Cornell University Press.

Gentzler, E. (2001) *Contemporary Translation Theories*, Clevedon: Multilingual Matters.

—— (2007) *Translation and Identity in the Americas: New Directions in Translation Theory*, London and New York: Routledge

Giddens, A. (1990) *The Consequences of Modernity*, Stanford, Calif.: Stanford University Press.

—— (1991) *Modernity and Self-Identity*, Cambridge: Polity.

Gish, L. (1973) *Dorothy and Lillian Gish*, New York: Scribners.

Golden, N.D. (1928) 'American Motion Pictures Abroad', *Transactions of the Society of Motion Picture Engineers*, 12, 33, 41–57.

Gomery, D. (1982) 'Movie Audiences, Urban Geography, and the History of American Film', *The Velvet Light Trap*, 19, 23–29.

—— (1986) 'What is Being Done for Motion Pictures', 7–10, in Gomery, D. (ed.) *The Will Hays Papers*, Frederick MD: University Publications of America.

Hansen, M. (1990) 'Early Cinema: Whose Public Sphere?', 228–46, in Elsaesser, T. (ed.) *Early Cinema: space – frame – narrative*, London: British Film Institute.

—— (1991) *Babel and Babylon: Spectatorship in American Silent Film*, Cambridge, Mass.: Harvard University Press.

Gunning, T. (1990a) *D.W. Griffith and the Origins of American Narrative Film*, Champaign: University of Illinois Press.

—— (1990b) 'Non-Continuity, Continuity, Discontinuity: A Theory of Genres in Early Films', 86–94, in Elsaesser, T. (ed.) *Early Cinema: Space – Frame – Narrative*, London: British Film Institute.

Hagège, C. (1986) *L'Homme de paroles*, Paris: Fayard.

Heidegger, M. (1977) *The Question concerning Technology and Other Essays*. New York: Harper.

Hermans, T. (1985) 'Images of Translation: Metaphor and Imagery in the Renaissance Discourse on Translation', 95–108, in Hermans, T. (ed.) *The Manipulation of Literature: Studies in Literary Translation*, London: Croom Helm.

Higson, A. and Maltby, R. (1999) *'Film Europe' and 'Film America': Cinema, Commerce and Cultural Exchange, 1920–1939*, Exeter: Exeter University Press.

Hoffman, E. (1989) *Lost in Translation*, London, Minerva.

Ingold, T. (2000) *The Perception of the Environment: Essays in Livelihood, Dwelling and Skill*, London and New York: Routledge.

Indian Cinematograph Committee (1928) *Indian Cinematograph Committee: Evidence Volume 1*, Calcutta: Government of India Central Publications Branch.

Jackson, D. (1973) 'The Irish Language and Tudor Government', *Éire-Ireland*, 8.1, 21–28.

Jaikumar, P. (2004) 'Hollywood and the Multiple Constituencies of Colonial India', 78–98, in Stokes, M. and Maltby, R. (eds.) *Hollywood Abroad: Audiences and Cultural Exchange*, London: British Film Institute.

Jarvie, I. (1992) *Hollywood's Overseas Campaign: The North Atlantic Film Trade, 1920–1950*, Cambridge: Cambridge University Press.

Kiberd, D. (1995) *Inventing Ireland*, London: Jonathan Cape.

Kiraly, D. (2000) *A Social Constructivist Approach to Translator Education: Empowerment from Theory to Practice*, Manchester: St. Jerome.

Kitamura, H. (2004) '"Home of American Movies": The Marunouchi Subaruza and the Making of Hollywood's Audiences in Occupied Tokyo, 1946–49', 99–120, in Stokes, M. and Maltby, R. (eds.) *Hollywood Abroad: Audiences and Cultural Exchange*, London: British Film Institute.

Lash, S. and Urry, J. (1994) *Economies of Signs and Space*, London: Sage.

Lea, R. (2007) 'Lost: Translation', *The Guardian*, November 16.

Maltby, R. (2004) 'Introduction: "The Americanisation of the World"', 1–20, in Stokes, M. and Maltby, R. (eds.) *Hollywood Abroad: Audiences and Cultural Exchange*, London: British Film Institute.

Mayne, J. (1982) 'Immigrants and spectators', *Wide Angle*, 5, 2, 32–41.

McCole, N. (2007) 'The Magic Lantern in Provincial Ireland', *Early Visual Culture*, 5, 3, 247–62,

Meers, P. (2004) '"It's the Language of Film!": Young Film Audiences on Hollywood and Europe', 158–75, in Stokes, M. and Maltby, R. (eds.) *Hollywood Abroad: Audiences and Cultural Exchange*, London: British Film Institute.

Merritt, R. (1976) 'Nickelodeon Theatres 1905–14: Building an Audience for the Movies', 59–70, in Balio, T. (ed.) *The American Film Industry*, Madison: University of Wisconsin Press.

Mirandé, A. and Enríquez, E. (1979) *La Chicana. The Mexican-American Woman*, Chicago: University of Chicago Press.

Mithun, M. (1999) *The Languages of Native North America*, Cambridge: Cambridge University Press.

Moore, R. (2007) 'Images of Irish English in the formation of Irish publics, 1600-present', *Irish Journal of Anthropology*, 10, 1, 18–29.

Morley, V. (1995) *An Crann ós Coill: Aodh Buí Mac Cruitín c.1680–1755*, Dublin: Coiscéim, .

Mossop, B. (1996) 'The Image of Translation in Science Fiction and Astronomy', *The Translator*, 2, 1, 1–26.

Müller, M. (1871) *Lectures on the Science of Language*, 2 vols., London: Longmans, Green and Co.

Musser, C. (1990a) *The Emergence of Cinema: The American Screen to 1907*, New York: Scribner, Macmillan.

—— (1990b) 'The Travel Genre in 1903–4: Moving Towards Fictional Narrative', 123–32, in Elsaesser, T. (ed.) *Early Cinema: Space – Frame – Narrative*, London: British Film Institute.

Naficy, H. (2003) 'Theorizing "Third World" film spectatorship: the case of Iran and Iranian cinema', 183–201, in Guneratne, A.R. and Dissanayake, W. (eds.) *Rethinking Third Cinema*, London: Routledge.

Nash Smith, H. (1950) *Virgin Land: The American West as Symbol and Myth*, Cambridge, Mass.: Harvard University Press.

Newman, K. (1990) *Wild West Movies*, London: Bloomsbury.

Nic Craith, M. (2005) *Europe and the Politics of Language: Citizens, Migrants and Outsiders*, London: Palgrave.

Niranjana, T. (1992) *Siting Translation: Translation, Post-Structuralism and the Colonial Context*, Berkeley, Calif.: University of California Press.

Nornes, A.M. (2007) *Cinema Babel: Translating Global Cinema*, Minneapolis: University of Minnesota Press.

O'Brien, K. (1962) *My Ireland*, London: Batsford.

O'Connell, E. (2003) *Minority Language Dubbing for Children: Screen Translation from German to Irish*, Oxford: Peter Lang.

Ong, W.J. (1989) *Orality and Literacy*, London and New York: Routledge.

Ostler, N. (2005) *Empires of the Word: A Language History of the World*, London: HarperCollins.

Parker, P. (1991) 'Note', *A Tosser's Glossary*, Press Pack for *The Commitments*.

Phillips, A. (2000) *Promises, Promises*, London: Faber and Faber.

Powdermaker, H. (1962) *Copper Town – Changing Africa: The Human Situation on the Rhodesian Copperbelt*, New York: Harper and Row.

Pratt, G. and Hanson, S. (1994) 'Geography and the Construction of Difference', *Gender, Place, Culture*, 1, 1, 5–29.

Pratt, M.-L. (1992) *Imperial Eyes: Travel Writing and Transculturation*, London: Routledge.

Rajadhyaksha, A. and Willemen, P. (1999) *Encyclopedia of Indian Cinema*, rev. edn., Chicago: Fitzroy Dearborn.

Ritzer, G. and Liska, A. (1997) '"McDisneyization" and "Post-Tourism"', 96–109, in Rojek, C. and Urry, J. (eds.) *Touring Cultures: Transformations of Travel and Theory*, London, Routledge, 1997.

Robinson, D. (1997) *Translation and Empire*, Manchester: St. Jerome Press.

Roland, R. (1999) *Interpreters as Diplomats*, Ottawa, University of Ottawa Press.

Rorty, R. (1980) *Philosophy and the Mirror of Nature*, Oxford: Blackwell.

Scognamillo, G. (1991) *Cadde-I Kebir'de Sinema*, Istanbul: Metis.

Seek, N.H. (2006) 'International Property Investment Trends'. Available online: http://www.prres.net/Papers/Seek_International_Property_Investment_Trends.pdf. (accessed 5 December 2006).

Sennett, R. (2002) 'Cosmopolitanism and the Social Experience of Cities', 42–47, in Vertovec, S. and Cohen, R. (eds.), *Conceiving Cosmopolitism: Theory, Context, Practice*. Oxford: Oxford University Press.

Shivelbusch, W. (1980) *The Railway Journey: Trains and Travel in the 19th Century*, New York: Urizen Books.

Slater, Eamonn (1998) 'Becoming an Irish *Flâneur*', Eamonn Slater and Michel Peillon (eds.), *Encounters with Modern Ireland*, Dublin: Institute of Public Administration.

Smith, A.D. (1990) 'Towards a Global Culture?', 165–82, in Featherstone, M. (ed.) *Global Culture: Nationalism, Globalization and Modernity*, London: Sage.

Spenser, E. (1970) *A View of the Present State of Ireland*, ed. W.L. Renwick, Oxford: Clarendon.

Steiner, G. (1975) *After Babel*, Oxford: Oxford University Press.

—— (2008) *My Unwritten Books*, London: Weidenfeld and Nicolson.

Stephanson, A. (1995) *Manifest Destiny: American Expansionism and the Empire of Right*, New York: Hill and Wang.

Szersynski, Bronislaw and Urry, John (2006) 'Visuality, mobility and the cosmopolitan: inhabiting the world from afar', *The British Journal of Sociology*, 57, 1, 113–31.

Taylor, C. (2007) *A Secular Age*, Cambridge, Mass.: Belknap Press of Harvard University Press.

Taylor, T. (1998) 'Living in a Postcolonial World: Class and Soul in *The Commitments*', *Irish Studies Review*, 6, 3, 291–302.

Trumpbour, J. (2002) *Selling Hollywood to the World: US and European Struggles for Mastery of the Global Film Industry*, Cambridge: Cambridge University Press.

Tylor, E. (1871) *Primitive Culture: Researches into the Development of Mythology, Philosophy, Religion, Language, Art and Custom*. London.

Tymoczko, M. (1999) *Translation in a Postcolonial Context*, Manchester: St. Jerome.

Ulff-Møller, J. (2001) *Hollywood's Film Wars with France: Film Trade Diplomacy and the Emergence of the French Film Quota Policy*, Rochester NY: University of Rochester Press.

Urry, J. (1990) *The Tourist Gaze: Leisure and Travel in Contemporary Societies*, London: Sage.

Valenti, J. (2001) 'Copyright and Creativity – The Jewel in America's Trade Crown'. Available online: http://www.mpaa.org/jack/ (accessed 30 December 2007).

Venuti, L. (2008) *The Translator's Invisibility: A History of Translation*, revised edn., London: Routledge.

Wadensjö, C. (1998) *Interpreting as Interaction*, London: Longman.

Wood, M.P. (2007) *Contemporary European Cinema*, London: Hodder Arnold.

Zinn, H. (2005) *A People's History of the United States. 1492 – present*, HarperCollins: New York.

Index

Translation in Global News

Esperança Bielsa and Susan Bassnett

'Innovative and interdisciplinary, this book adds a valuable new dimension to the study of global news.'
Professor Daya Thussu, *University of Westminster*

'In our media-saturated and conflict-driven world I cannot think of a more urgent and timely book than *Translation in Global News*. Bassnett and Bielsa show how translation lies at the very heart of the circulation of news information in the modern world and how our right to know is crucially affected by our freedom to translate. The book is essential reading for students of globalization, media studies, sociology and translation studies and indeed for anyone who is concerned about the fate of knowledge and information in our globalized world.'
Michael Cronin, *Dublin City University*

Translation in Global News examines how news agencies, arguably the most powerful organisations in the field of global news, have developed historically and how they conceive of and employ translation in a global setting.

Incorporating the results of extensive fieldwork in major global news organisations such as Reuters, Agence France Presse and Inter Press Service, this book addresses the new pressures facing translation as the need for a flow of accurate information which must transfer successfully across geographic, linguistic and cultural boundaries becomes increasingly more important.

Bringing together the common concerns of globalization studies, media studies, sociology and translation studies, *Translation in Global News* is the first text of its kind to deal extensively with the issue of translation in the context of global news and will be key reading for students of translation studies, media studies and journalism, as well as anyone with an interest in how news is transferred around the world.

Esperança Bielsa is Lecturer at the Department of Sociology at the University of Leicester.
Susan Bassnett is Professor in the Centre for Translation and Comparative Cultural Studies at the University of Warwick.

ISBN13: 978-0-415-40973-5 (hbk)
ISBN13: 978-0-415-40972-8 (pbk)

Related titles from Routledge

Translation and Identity
Michael Cronin

Identity is one of the most important political and cultural issues of our time. *Translation and Identity* looks at how translation has played a crucial role in shaping debates around identity, language and cultural survival in the past and in the present.

The volume explores how everything, from the impact of migration to the curricula for national literature courses and to the way in which nations wage war in the modern era, is bound up with urgent questions of translation and identity. The book examines translation practices and experiences across continents to show how translation is an integral part of how cultures are evolving, offering new perspectives on how translation can be a powerful tool both to enhance difference and to promote intercultural dialogue.

Drawing on a wide range of materials from official government reports to Shakespearean drama to Hollywood films, *Translation and Identity* demonstrates that translation is central to any proper understanding of the emergence of cultural identity in human history, and the book offers an innovative and positive vision of the way in which translation can be used to deal with one of the most salient issues in an increasingly borderless world.

ISBN13: 978-0-415-36464-5 (hbk)
ISBN13: 978-0-415-36465-2 (pbk)

Available at all good bookshops
For ordering and further information please visit:
www.routledge.com

Introducing Translation Studies
Theories and Applications
Second Edition
Jeremy Munday

'Jeremy Munday's book presents a snapshot of a rapidly developing discipline in a clear, concise and graphic way. This is a book which raises strong awareness of current issues in the field and will be of interest to translation trainers and trainees alike'

Basil Hatim, *Heriot-Watt University, UK*

This introductory textbook provides an accessible overview of the key contributions to translation theory.

Munday explores each theory chapter-by-chapter, and tests the different approaches by applying them to texts. The texts discussed are taken from a broad range of languages- English, French, German, Spanish, Italian, Punjabi and Portuguese, and English translations are provided. A wide variety of text types are analyzed, including a tourist brochure, a children's cookery book, a Harry Potter novel, the Bible, literary reviews and translators' prefaces, film translation, a technical text and a European Parliament speech. Each chapter includes the following features:

- a table introducing key concepts
- an introduction outlining the translation theory or theories illustrative texts with translations
- a chapter summary
- discussion points and exercises.

Including a general introduction, an extensive bibliography and websites for further information, this is a practical, user-friendly textbook that gives a balanced and comprehensive insight into translation studies.

ISBN13: 978-0-415-39694-3 (hbk)
ISBN13: 978-0-415-39693-6 (pbk)

Available at all good bookshops
For ordering and further information please visit:
http://www.routledge.com/textbooks/its.html

eBooks – at www.eBookstore.tandf.co.uk

A library at your fingertips!

eBooks are electronic versions of printed books. You can store them on your PC/laptop or browse them online.

They have advantages for anyone needing rapid access to a wide variety of published, copyright information.

eBooks can help your research by enabling you to bookmark chapters, annotate text and use instant searches to find specific words or phrases. Several eBook files would fit on even a small laptop or PDA.

NEW: Save money by eSubscribing: cheap, online access to any eBook for as long as you need it.

Annual subscription packages

We now offer special low-cost bulk subscriptions to packages of eBooks in certain subject areas. These are available to libraries or to individuals.

For more information please contact webmaster.ebooks@tandf.co.uk

We're continually developing the eBook concept, so keep up to date by visiting the website.

www.eBookstore.tandf.co.uk